D1047347

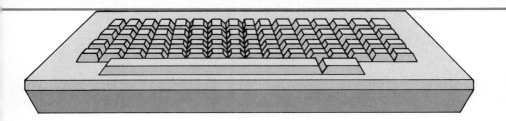

# PROGRAMMING
# IN
# BASIC

**Jerry Cummins, Gene Kuechmann**

**Charles E. Merrill Publishing Co.**
A Bell & Howell Company
Columbus, Ohio
Toronto • London • Sydney

ISBN 0-675-05650-0

Published by
**Charles E. Merrill Publishing Co.**
A Bell & Howell Company
Columbus, Ohio 43216

Copyright © 1983 by Bell & Howell. All rights reserved.
No part of this book may be reproduced in any form, electronic or mechanical, including photocopy, recording, or any information storage or retrieval system, without permission in writing from the publisher.

Printed in the United States of America

# AUTHORS

**Jerry Cummins** is head of the Mathematics Department at Proviso West High School, Hillside, Illinois. It was here that he developed a course in computer programming and implemented a course that used computer-assisted instruction to aid students with below average mathematical abilities. Mr. Cummins has been involved with computer instruction for 15 years during which time his school has been a model and a pioneer for the IBM Corporation. Mr. Cummins earned his B.S. in mathematics education and his M.S. in educational administration and supervision from Southern Illinois University. He also holds an M.S. in mathematics education from the University of Oregon. Mr. Cummins has conducted research in the instruction of computer programming and is co-author of *Merrill Geometry.*

**Gene Kuechmann** is a technical editor for Argonne National Laboratory, Argonne, Illinois. She has taught mathematics at the high school level and was a mathematics editor for an educational publishing company for 13 years. Ms. Kuechmann earned her B.S. in mathematics at Tulsa University and her M.A. in mathematics at U.C.L.A. She has been involved in using computers and writing computer materials for many years, and helped launch a software corporation.

# CONSULTANT

**John Detrick**
Chairman of Mathematics Department
Columbus Academy
Gahanna, Ohio

# REVIEWERS

**Wilson L. Bryant, Jr.**
Head, Mathematics Department
Highland High School
Albuquerque, New Mexico

**Dr. Ellen L. Hocking**
Coordinator of Secondary
   Mathematics
Montgomery County Public Schools
Rockville, Maryland

**Horace N. Butler**
Instructor: Mathematics and
   Computer Science
Mauldin High School
Mauldin, South Carolina

**Dr. Alexander Tobin**
Director of Mathematics Education
School District of Philadelphia
Philadelphia, Pennsylvania

# EDITORIAL STAFF

Project Editors: Cynthia Lindsay, Carolyn Kaiser
Assistant Editor: Michael H. Thorne
Book Designer: Paul Helenthal
Artist: Glenn Wasserman
Photo Editor: Russ Lappa

# PHOTO CREDITS

**2,** Sperry Univac; **5,** Doug Martin; **29,** IBM; **30,** Tim Courlas; **72,** Lightforce; **104,** Doug Martin; **105,** Courtesy of F.A.A.; **106,** File Photo; **142,** File Photo; **144,** Burroughs Corp.; **170,** Honeywell Inc.; **172,** Tim Courlas; **212,** Lightforce; **213,** File Photo; **214,** NASA; **250,** Tim Courlas; **252,** File Photo

# PREFACE

*Programming in BASIC* introduces students to computer programming in the BASIC language. The text can be used with any microcomputer or time-sharing system, and is designed to provide hands-on experience with that system. Requiring only a first-year algebra background, the text emphasizes the use of computers in data processing rather than scientific situations.

**Laboratory Activities**  These activities provide hands-on experience including the use of a computer and programming activities. Also included are exercises to be used without a computer.

**Real-life Applications**  Applications provide a practical approach to computer programming in BASIC. Such applications include simple interest, budgets, stock inventory, and gas mileage.

**Easy-to-Read Presentation**  The open format facilitates reading and comprehension. Blocks of color emphasize major concepts and definitions of BASIC functions. Examples of programs are clearly delineated and explanations are enhanced by student annotations.

**Organization**  *Programming in BASIC* is organized into seven chapters and an appendix with numbered sections for easy reference and understanding. The text offers a variety of special features to aid the student in learning BASIC.

| | |
|---|---|
| **Selected Answers** | Allow students to check their answers as they work. These answers are provided at the back of the text. |
| **Chapter End Material** | Vocabulary, chapter summary, and chapter test provide students with a list of major concepts and problems for checking their progress. |
| **Computer Literacy** | Is stressed with a special feature at the end of every chapter. Topics in computer history, computer careers, and artificial intelligence are discussed. |
| **Pascal** | Introduces students to the programming language Pascal. This feature is found in every chapter. |

**Appendix**   Introduces computer generated graphics. The appendix contains exercises and laboratory activities.

**Glossary**   Provides students with definitions of important words, concepts, and BASIC keywords and functions.

*Programming in BASIC* provides a relevant, practical approach for learning to program in BASIC and for learning how to use the capabilities of a computer.

# CONTENTS

The first electronic computer was called ENIAC (**E**lectronic **N**umerical **I**ntegrator **A**nd **C**alculator). It went into operation in 1946. ENIAC weighed about 30 tons and occupied about 140 square meters (about 1,500 square feet) of floor space, which is a little smaller than a singles tennis court. ENIAC could perform 5,000 additions or 300 multiplications per second. Compared to the computer you will be using, ENIAC was very large and slow.

# INTRODUCTION TO COMPUTERS

Before you learn how to give instructions to, or program, your computer, you need to learn what a computer is and how it works. This chapter deals with these subjects and introduces many important terms and ideas which will be used throughout the rest of the book.

## 1.1  WHAT IS A COMPUTER?

One dictionary defines **computer** as follows:

a programmable electronic device that can store, retrieve, and process data.

Of course, the words in this definition have definitions of their own. Here is an explanation of what the words mean as they are used in the definition of computer.

A **programmable device** is able to receive, store, and carry out a set of instructions called a **program.**

An **electronic device** (a radio, for example) is operated by electricity and does its work using electricity. However, it may have some mechanical parts, such as switches. In contrast, a *mechanical device* (a pencil sharpener, for example) may be operated by electricity, but it does its work by means of moving parts. An electronic device works much faster than does a mechanical device, and usually wears out much more slowly.

To **store** means to put somewhere for safekeeping or later use. When done by a computer, storing is also called *writing*.

To **retrieve** means to get and bring back. When done by a computer, retrieving is also called *reading*.

To **process** means to calculate, compare, arrange, or otherwise act upon.

**Data** (plural of datum) are facts or information.

Some computers operate using smooth, continuous changes in electrical signals. These are called **analog computers;** they have important but often quite special uses. Most general-purpose computers are **digital computers;** they use electrical signals that switch on and off, like light bulbs, as the computer operates. The word computer is usually used to mean digital computer or digital computer system.

Before you start writing computer programs, the **software,** you need to learn something about the computer itself, the **hardware.**

The figure below shows the main parts of a computer. The arrows show the directions data may travel between the parts.

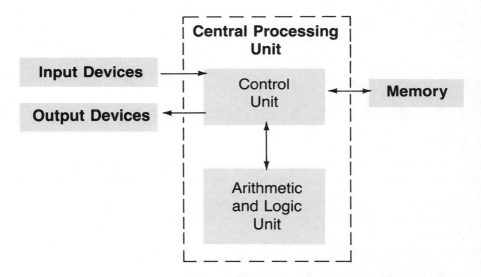

The heart of a computer is the **central processing unit (CPU).** The CPU contains an arithmetic and logic unit and a control unit.

The **arithmetic and logic unit** performs such operations as addition and subtraction and comparing numbers. The **control unit** is a master set of programs which interprets the user's program, and then supervises the overall operation of the computer.

The CPU cannot handle much information at one time, so programs and data are stored in computer **memory** and are called for by the CPU as they are needed. Some of the programs and data in memory may be stored there when the computer is manufactured. The rest come from external storage or from input devices. When data are processed, the results are data that are also stored in memory.

The most common input device, and the one we assume you are using, is a keyboard. The keyboard may be in the same case as the computer, or it may be separate, in a terminal. A **keyboard** is used to enter programs and data, or **input,** into a computer. Other input devices you might use are light pens, joysticks or game paddles, and graphics tablets.

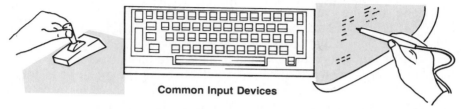

**Common Input Devices**

The two most common output devices are the cathode-ray tube (CRT) and the printer.

**Cathode-ray tubes (CRTs)** are used in television sets. The wide end of the cathode-ray tube is the television screen. The same type of tube may be used with a computer. The tube, along with its controls, is called a **monitor.** In fact, it is possible to use a television set as a computer monitor. The monitor displays both the input to the computer and the **output** from the computer (the results of processing data).

A printer may be used instead of a CRT or along with it. A **printer** produces a *printout* or *hard copy* of computer output.

Input devices and output devices are often referred to together as **I/O devices.**

A **microcomputer** or **personal computer** is a small computer with a CPU and I/O devices all in one case or in several closely attached cases. A microcomputer may be ready to use as soon as it is switched on, or it may require a few simple procedures to get it ready.

The CPU and memory of a large computer may be connected to I/O devices that are in another room, another building, or hundreds of miles away. The connection is often made using the regular telephone line. You dial the number just as you would if you were calling another person. The connection from the computer to the telephone line is made through a device called a modulator-demodulator, or modem. The terminal is connected to the telephone line the same way. A *modem* changes the signals from the computer or terminal so they can be sent over the telephone line. It also changes the signals that come over the telephone line back into signals the computer or terminal can use. Some modems are connected directly to the telephone wire, but others communicate through the telephone hand set.

Computers operate so quickly that they can often be used by more than one person at a time, in a **time-sharing system.** (A microcomputer is sometimes used in a time-sharing arrangement, with the I/O devices not far from the computer.) Each person using a time-sharing system has a separate terminal that is connected to the computer directly or by telephone. The computer keeps track of each person's program and data. If many people use the system at once, output may be returned a little more slowly than usual. Otherwise, time sharing is not very different from using a separate computer.

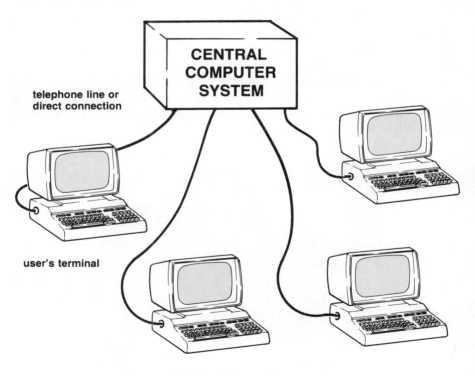

Time-sharing system

# Exercises

1. What is a program?
2. What does it mean to say a computer is programmable?
3. Using the explanations given for "programmable" and "program," explain what "to program" and "programmer" mean. (Use a dictionary also, if you wish.)
4. What is an electronic device? Name three ways in which it differs from a mechanical device.
5. What are data?
6. What are some of the ways computers process data?
7. How do the electrical signals in an analog computer differ from those in a digital computer?
8. What are the four basic parts of a computer system?
9. What part of a computer actually does the arithmetic operations?
10. What is the purpose of computer memory?
11. What does the computer do with the results of processing data?
12. What is the purpose of an input device?
13. What is the purpose of an output device?
14. Name two input devices and two output devices.
15. What is a CRT? a computer monitor?
16. What is a time-sharing system?
17. What is a modem used for?

# Laboratory Activities

1. Is the computer you will be using a microcomputer (personal computer) or a time-sharing computer?
2. What I/O devices will you be using?
3. Draw a diagram like the one in this section, naming the specific I/O devices in the system you will be using. If you are using a time-sharing computer, show in your diagram how the modems are related to the terminal and the computer.
4. Find out the rules for computer users at your school. If the rules are in printed form, read them carefully and ask about any you do not understand. (The reasons for these rules will become clear as you read the rest of this chapter.)

**List each step of each of the following as applied to the system you are using. Then, if possible, practice each step.**

5. Switch on the computer or terminal, or check to see if it is ready for use. If you are using a microcomputer, find out if there are any special procedures that must be followed before the keyboard can be used.
6. Switch on the I/O devices, or check to see if they are ready for use.
7. Establish the connection between the terminal and the (time-sharing) computer, using a modem if necessary.
8. Switch off the system or leave it in the correct mode, according to your teacher's instructions. (If you are using a time-sharing system, disconnect the terminal from the time-sharing computer and leave the terminal in the correct mode.)

# 1.2 KEYBOARDS AND CRTs

A computer or terminal keyboard looks a lot like a typewriter keyboard. Both keyboards have keys marked with characters such as letters and numbers, punctuation marks, and mathematical symbols. These keys are used to print the characters marked on them. The character keys are usually in the same order on both keyboards. Some computers also have a separate set of number keys. Both the typewriter and the computer keyboards have a space bar or key in front that is used to print spaces, such as those between words.

Both keyboards also have at least one key labeled SHIFT. Holding this key down is called *shifting*. Shifting may cause a key to print a (shifted) character that is different from the usual (unshifted) character it prints. For any key with two characters on it, the shifted character is shown above the unshifted character. For any key with one character on it, if the unshifted letters are lower case, or "small" letters, the shifted letters are capital letters. However, many computers print only capital letters and shifting usually has no effect on keys labeled with only one character.

When a computer is ready to accept input from a keyboard, an indicator called a **cursor** is usually displayed on the monitor to show where the next input will be printed.

Besides character and shift keys, a computer keyboard has some special keys. Not all computers use the same special keys, but every system has keys that do the following.

**BREAK or RESET** Pressing this key stops whatever the computer is doing. However, it may have other effects which you can find described in the user's manual. You should always use this key with great caution.

**ENTER or RETURN** Pressing this key, sometimes called CARRIAGE RETURN, or CR, results in all characters typed after it was last pressed being entered into the computer as input. If the characters represent a command to the computer, the computer carries out the command immediately. Otherwise, the computer stores the input, and the cursor is sent to the beginning of the next line.

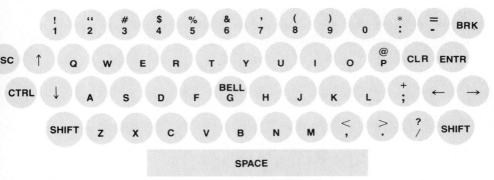

**A typical computer keyboard**

Most computers also have the following special keys. Their effects can be quite different from computer to computer. If your computer has either key, you will explore its effects in the Laboratory Activities for this section.

**CONTROL** When this key is held down, it changes what happens when some of the other keys are pressed. For example, on many keyboards, control-G (holding down the CONTROL key while pressing the G key) causes an internal speaker to emit a beep.

**ESCAPE** When this key is pressed first, it may change what happens when some of the other keys are pressed. This key must be used with great caution.

You will be asked in the Laboratory Activities to find out which keys or combinations of keys you should avoid or use with caution. It is hard to damage a computer by pressing any of the terminal keys in any combination. However, you can damage programs and data that it has taken someone— maybe you—time and effort to create. Be especially careful when you are using a time-sharing system.

*Note:* We assume the output from your computer is displayed on a CRT (though many of the things we say also apply to printers).

When programs or data are typed on a terminal keyboard to be entered into the computer as input, the characters appear on the monitor screen as they are typed. It is not necessary to be an expert typist to use a computer. Characters and words can be moved, changed, or erased after they are typed. This process is called **editing.**

Each character position across the screen is in a *column* that extends from the top of the screen to the bottom. Different computers display different numbers of columns—usually between 32 and 80. Each character position down the screen is in a *line* that extends across the screen from side to side. The number of lines displayed also varies, but is usually between 16 and 30. On many computers, the cursor shows in which column and line the next input character typed on the keyboard will appear.

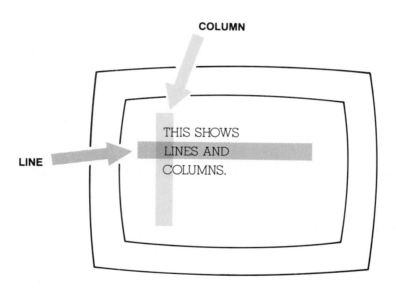

There is probably some way, using one or more keys, to do the following things from the terminal you are using.

**Move the cursor**    Move the cursor right, left, up, and down; home the cursor (return it to the upper left corner).

**Edit input**    Delete (remove) a character; delete a line; insert a character; insert a line; copy a character; repeat a character.

**Erase**  Clear the entire screen or just the part of a line to the right of the cursor. This does not erase input that has already been entered.

After all the lines on the screen are used, each additional line typed is added at the bottom of the screen, and a line at the top of the screen scrolls up and out of view. In some systems, there is no easy way to look at the lines that have scrolled off the top of the screen. However, if they are part of a program, they are still in memory and there are ways to display them. Some systems allow the screen to scroll in either direction under keyboard control, so earlier lines are easily brought back to the display.

# Exercises

1. Which kinds of keys on a computer keyboard are like those found on a typewriter?
2. What is the main use of character keys?
3. What effect does shifting have on a key with two characters shown on it?
4. What effect does shifting have on letter keys if they usually print lower case letters?
5. If the unshifted letters are not lower case letters, what effect does shifting usually have on keys labeled with only one character?
6. What is a cursor?
7. What does the BREAK or RESET key do?
8. What does the ENTER or RETURN key do?
9. If input is a command to the computer, what happens when it is entered?
10. If input is not a command, what happens when it is entered?
11. Why do you need to know which keys to avoid or use with caution?
12. Can input be edited from the keyboard?
13. What does the process called editing do?
14. Are characters in the same column one above the other? Side-by-side?
15. Are characters on the same line one above the other? Side-by-side?
16. When a line is added at the bottom of a full screen, what happens to the line at the top of the screen?

# Laboratory Activities

1. Make a diagram of the keyboard you will be using. (This can be done by marking off squares or rectangles on a sheet of notebook paper or graph paper.) Keep this diagram with you when you use the computer, at least until you are very sure you know the effect of each key.
2. Label each "key" on your keyboard diagram just as it is labeled on the keyboard.
3. Mark in red (for "stop") each key you are instructed not to press.
4. Mark in lighter red each key that must be used with caution, such as the BREAK or RESET key. Check with your manual or teacher to find out if there are other keys that you must use with caution.
5. Make a Key Table with these labels down the left side: cursor right, cursor left, cursor up, cursor down, cursor home, character copy, character delete, character repeat, clear to end of line, clear to end of screen, line feed (move cursor to the same column in the next line down), cancel line (don't enter the line as input when RETURN is pressed), and enter or return. Label the next column KEY. (You will complete this table as you do the activities below.)

*Caution:* The following activities involve only the keyboard and the CRT. Time-sharing users should NOT connect the terminal and computer.

6. Press each character key (unshifted) and note the result. Record any unexpected results on your keyboard diagram.
7. How many columns can be displayed by your computer? (Type characters until a line is full; then count the number of characters on the line.)
8. Hold down the shift key and press each character key; note the result. Record any unexpected results on your keyboard diagram.

**If any of the activities below clear the screen, type more characters before continuing.**

9. Test various special keys (such as the ones marked with the left and right arrows) to see which keys, if any, do each of the things listed down the left side of your Key Table. Record the results in your Key Table in the column labeled KEY.
10. If your keyboard has a control key, add a column labeled CONTROL to the right of the column labeled KEY. Test the effect of holding down the control key while you type each character key. Record the results in your Key Table in the column labeled CONTROL. (Some effects of the key can't be detected this way.)

11. If your computer has an escape key, add a column labeled ESCAPE. For each letter and number key, test the effect of pressing the escape key before pressing the character key. Record the results in your Key Table in the column labeled ESCAPE.

12. If your computer has neither a control key nor an escape key, find out from your teacher or the manual how to do those things in the left-hand column of your Key Table for which you have no entry in the KEY column.

13. Check with your teacher or the manual to be sure you have your Key Table complete and correct. Add any useful keys not already in the table. (For example, some keyboards have TAB keys.)

14. Find out how many lines can be shown on your monitor display. You should be able to do this by experimenting with the keyboard. For example, see how many "line feeds" it takes to move the cursor to the bottom of the screen.

15. If you will be using a printer to obtain a hard copy of the computer output, find out whether the printer can be controlled from the keyboard. For example, some printers can be controlled by pressing a character key after first pressing the control or the escape key. If the printer can be controlled from the keyboard, record the method in your Key Table.

# 1.3 MEMORY

What happens to the information in a computer's memory when the electricity goes off?

In a microcomputer, many instructions, such as those that tell the computer how to add and subtract and otherwise process data, are stored in the computer's memory when the computer is manufactured. The computer can read (retrieve) the instructions, but it cannot write (store) anything more in this part of its memory, which is called **read-only memory,** or **fixed memory.** Read-only memory is not affected when the power goes off.

In all computers, data and programs that come from an input device or external storage go into a part of memory where the computer can read them. But the computer can also write in this part of its memory, so this is called **read-write memory.** Everything in read-write memory is lost when the power goes off. This is true whether the power is shut off on purpose or accidentally, for instance during an electrical storm.

It would be difficult and time-consuming to retype programs and data every time you want to use them. So if there are programs and data in read-write memory that are worth saving, they should be stored somewhere else before the computer is turned off. Programs and data are usually stored on tapes—the same kind used to record music—or on disks that look somewhat like phonograph records without grooves. The *tapes* and *tape recorders* and the *disks* and *disk drives* (devices that hold disks and record programs and data on them), are **external storage,** or **mass storage,** devices.

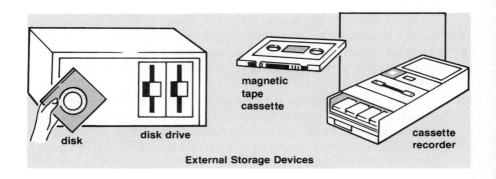

magnetic
tape
cassette

disk          disk drive

cassette
recorder

**External Storage Devices**

Tapes and disks store information in electromagnetic form. This is the same form in which music is stored on tape. Electricity magnetizes the tape or disk in a pattern. This pattern can be read to reveal the information that formed it. A time-sharing user does not usually handle the mass storage devices, but all computer users need to know how to protect stored data and programs and the terminal and its electronic parts. Here are some of the dangers you must protect them from.

*Heat* Do not block the vents on the terminal; the trapped heat can shorten the life of the parts inside. Do not set disks in the sun or on a warm surface; heat warps disks and makes them unusable.

*Static electricity* Static electricity is a problem, especially in winter. One spark can destroy the usefulness of a disk or a tape, and it can also ruin parts inside a terminal. Always ground yourself to get rid of static electricity before working with a computer. You can do this by touching the monitor case or a water pipe.

*Magnetic fields* A magnetic field can destroy information stored electromagnetically. Keep disks and tapes away from magnets, transformers, and all other sources of magnetic fields, such as television sets. If you use a television set as a monitor, do not put tapes or disks any closer to it than necessary.

*Liquids* A computer uses electricity and is "live" when switched on. Spilled liquids could cause a short circuit that would damage the computer and give you a shock. Keep liquids at a distance.

*Handling and dirt* Electrical contacts and the surfaces of tapes and disks are damaged by skin oils—do not touch them. Disks are also damaged by bending and by dirt. Even though a disk has a permanent plastic cover over most of its surface, keep it in its protective envelope when it is not in use. Handle disks carefully and only at the label corners. Keep tapes in their boxes when they are not in use. Avoid dropping tapes and disks.

Recall that the electrical signals in a digital computer switch on and off. Each signal, called a **bit,** can be thought of as a 1 (when it is on) or a 0 (when it is off). The pattern formed by a group of bits stands for a number, and that number itself may stand for a character or even a whole word. Usually, eight bits make up one **byte.** Computer size is often stated in bytes of read-write memory or in total bytes of read-write and read-only memory.

In mathematics and business 1k = 1,000; in a computer, 1k = 1,024. A small personal computer may have only 4k bytes of read-write memory, but most have from 16k to 64k bytes. A time-sharing computer may have 20 times as much.

One of the important things a time-sharing computer has in memory is a list of the people who may use it. The first thing to do after establishing a connection between a terminal and a computer is to tell the computer who you are. If your name or identifying number is on its list, then you may use the computer. This identification procedure is called *logging on.* When you are finished with the computer, you tell it so by *logging off.* A time-sharing computer usually keeps a record of how long each person uses it. It may also compute the cost for whoever is paying the bill.

# Exercises

1. What does it mean to say a computer can read memory?
2. What does it mean to say a computer can write in memory?
3. In what part of memory is the computer unable to write?
4. In what type of memory is input from external storage stored?
5. What happens to programs and data in read-only memory when the computer is switched off? What happens to programs and data in read-write memory?

6. Where can programs and data be stored for later use?
7. Explain why each of the following is bad for tapes and disks: heat, static electricity, magnetic fields, liquids, and handling.
8. How can a bit that is on be represented? A bit that is off?
9. What is a byte?
10. If you had $1k, how much money would you have? If a computer has 1k bytes of memory, how much memory does it have?

# Laboratory Activities

1. How big is the computer you use? That is, how much memory does it have?
2. Examine, as far as possible, a disk and a computer tape. Identify the parts that can safely be touched and the parts that should not be touched.

**If you will be responsible for handling tapes or disks, do the following activities.**

3. Find out where tapes or disks are stored in your laboratory. Find out how they are labeled and identified.
4. Find out what rules have been set up for the use and handling of the tapes or disks you will be using. If the rules are printed, study them.
5. Practice inserting tapes into the tape recorder or disks into the disk drive. Also practice removing and storing them properly.

**If you will be using tapes for external storage, do the following activities.**

6. Play a computer tape as you would a music tape, but keep the volume low. Notice that you hear several different types of sounds, indicating different parts of the information storage process.
7. Find out how to enter programs or data from tape into the computer.
8. Find out from your teacher or the manual whether the tape can be controlled from the keyboard. If it can, add this information to your Key Table.

**If you will be using disks for external storage, do the following activity.**

9. Find out from your teacher or the manual how to control the disk drive from the keyboard. Add this information to your Key Table.

**If you are using a time-sharing system, do the following activities.**

**10.** Find out from your teacher or the manual what kinds of external storage the computer uses. (If you can, arrange to see the computer and the external storage devices in use.)

**11.** List the steps required to log on and the steps required to log off. Be sure you understand each step. If possible, practice logging on and logging off.

**12.** Make a separate Key Table showing how to use special, control, and escape keys to control the input from the terminal to the computer and the output from the computer. (Do NOT log on and use these keys without permission.)

# 1.4 COMPUTER LANGUAGES

A computer can do complicated calculations. It can sort through data to find a single piece or a particular kind of datum. It can arrange long lists of words in alphabetical order to make an index like the one for this book. It can control a factory, or it can keep track of the time and switch on the coffee pot in time for breakfast. But it can only do these things if someone programs it (tells it how and when) to do them.

Some computers can be programmed in machine language. **Machine language programs** tell the computer, using numbers, exactly which bits are to be switched on and which are to be switched off. Early computers were programmed in machine language because other languages did not exist. Besides, languages are stored in memory, and in the early days of electronic computers memory was very expensive. However, machine language is still useful today. Machine language programs take less memory than programs in other languages, and they are faster. However, machine language is quite difficult for people to read and write.

```
05 15 00 00    READ X
05 16 00 00    READ Y
01 15 16 17    CALCULATE X+Y=Z
06 17 00 00    WRITE Z
09 00 00 00    HALT
```

A simple machine-language program, with comments to the right of each line

It is no longer necessary to program computers in machine language. Special machine language programs have been written so that programs can be written in languages that are easier to read and write. The special program turns the input into machine language so the computer can follow the instructions and process the data.

| Line 3 5 6 | Label | Operation 15 16  20 21  25  30  35  40 | OPERAND 45 |
|---|---|---|---|
| 01 |  | MCW  @TOTAL@.245 |  |
| 02 |  | MLCWAEDIT.I..28.I |  |
| 03 |  | MCE  ACTTOT.28.I |  |
| 04 |  | W |  |
| 05 |  | CS |  |
| 06 |  | CS |  |
| 07 |  | B  WRTHDR |  |
| 08 |  | MCW  @FINAL TOTAL DEBITS@.258 |  |
| 09 |  | MLCWAEDIT..28.I |  |
| 10 |  | MCE  DRTOT.28.I |  |
| 11 |  | MCW  @*#@.283 |  |
| 12 |  | W |  |
| 13 |  | CS |  |
| 14 |  | CS |  |
| 15 |  | CC  J |  |
|  |  | MCW  @FINAL TOTAL CREDITS@.259 |  |

**Part of a program written
in an assembly language**

*Assembler programs* were the first special programs developed to make programming easier. However, though assembly languages are easier for humans to learn than machine languages, they are still not easy to learn. It seems that the ideal language for most English-speaking computer users should be the language they already know—ordinary English. But this is a poor choice for a computer. It would take so much memory to enable a computer to"understand"English that there would not be any memory left for other programs or data. Many computer languages now in use are somewhat like English, but they use only a few words. Each word has just one, well-defined meaning. Each type of statement that can be made in the language has a pattern, or **syntax,** that must be followed exactly. Also, the use of punctuation marks in a computer language is very different from their use in English.

---

**EXAMPLE 1**

$$\text{IF } X = 2 \text{ THEN } X + 2 = 4 \qquad X + 2 = 4 \text{ IF } X = 2$$

In English, these two statements (properly punctuated) mean the same thing, and either pattern can be used for this type of statement. In a computer language, only the statement on the left has meaning. All statements of this type follow the same pattern.

---

**BASIC** (**B**eginner's **A**ll-Purpose **S**ymbolic **I**nstruction **C**ode) is one of the most widely-used languages for microcomputers and time-sharing systems. In fact, many people continue to use BASIC long after they are no longer beginning programmers. BASIC is the language in which you will learn to program computers.

```
10 REM THIS BASIC PROGRAM CALCULATES AND
20 REM PRINTS THE SUM OF THE INTEGERS
30 REM FROM 1 TO X, INCLUDING 1 AND X
40 LET N = 0
50 PRINT "ENTER A POSITIVE INTEGER"
60 INPUT X
70 IF X>0 THEN 100
80 PRINT "A POSITIVE INTEGER, PLEASE!"
90 GOTO 60
100 FOR I = 1 TO X
110     LET N = N + I
120 NEXT I
130 PRINT N
140 PRINT "DO YOU WANT TO TRY AGAIN?"
150 PRINT "ANSWER BY ENTERING YES OR NO"
160 INPUT A$
170 IF A$ = "YES" THEN 40
180 END
```

**BASIC program**

Machine language is called a *low-level language.* BASIC is an example of a *high-level language.* Some other high-level languages are *COBOL* (for business use), *FORTRAN* (for scientific use), and *PL/1* and *APL* (for general use). **Pascal** is a language that somewhat resembles BASIC, and its use is growing rapidly. You will find sections throughout this book that show how *Pascal* is used.

There are many versions of BASIC. Where there are important differences in popular versions of BASIC, we will tell you how to test your system to see what variation it uses. Whenever possible, we use general forms that work in most versions of BASIC.

While BASIC is a programming language, there are certain BASIC words that can be used to give a computer instructions, or *commands,* that it will carry out at once. When a computer is used this way, it is said to be in calculator mode. In *calculator mode,* a command is entered by typing it on the keyboard and then pressing the ENTER or RETURN key. The monitor shows the command as it is typed. When ENTER is pressed, the output is printed on the line below the command.

## EXAMPLE 2

| | | THE COMPUTER PRINTS: |
|---|---|---|
| a. PRINT 2 <br> 2 | b. PRINT 1 + 1 <br> 2 | a. Numbers as entered. <br> b. Results of calculations. |
| c. PRINT "ABC" <br> ABC | d. PRINT A <br> Ø | c. Letters within quotation marks. <br> d. Numbers for letters not within quotation marks. |
| e. PRINT "F" <br> F | f. PRINT "∧∧G" <br> G | e. and f. Spaces only if they are in quotation marks. (In this text, ∧ indicates a space. Two spaces are printed before the G.) |

If PRINT is misspelled or left out, most computers give an error message of some sort.

Several different types of programs turn BASIC input into the zeros and ones for the computer. You do not need to know which type your computer uses. You do need to know, however, whether the computer already has this program in its read-only memory, or whether the program must be entered *(loaded)* into read-write memory from tape or disk.

# Exercises

1. What do we call the language that tells the computer exactly which bits are to be switched on and which are to be switched off?
2. Are there special programs to make it possible for a user to enter input in ordinary English? Why or why not?
3. What are two differences between ordinary English and the high-level computer languages now in use?
4. Name at least two high-level computer languages.
5. What is *Pascal?*
6. Is there more than one version of BASIC?
7. Can a computer have BASIC in read-only memory? In read-write memory?
8. What happens to the output when a computer is used in calculator mode?

**Suppose you entered the given command in calculator mode. What would be displayed on the monitor?**

9. PRINT 3 + 1

10. PRINT "QR∧S"

# Laboratory Activities ▬▬▬▬▬▬

1. Is BASIC in the read-only memory of your computer, or must it be loaded from external storage?

2. If you are responsible for loading BASIC from tape or disk when you use the computer, find out at this time how to load the tape or disk. Practice loading it several times.

3. Even with BASIC in memory, some computers require certain other procedures before BASIC can be used. If your computer is one of these, find out how to "get into" BASIC, and practice the procedure.

**Use the computer in calculator mode to do the following activities.**

4. Enter the commands in Example 2 and compare your results with those given in the example.

5. Enter the first command in Example 2, but misspell PRINT. Did your computer give an error message? What was it?

6. Enter a number without the word PRINT. What is the result?

7. Enter just the command PRINT. What is the result?

8. Enter this command and record the result.

   PRINT 3 + 4 − 2 + 7 − 10 − 1

9. Have the computer print your full name starting at the left side of the screen.

10. Have the computer print your full name starting 10 spaces from the left side of the screen.

11. Add 10 to the number of columns your screen displays. Have the computer print the letter Z this many times. *(Hint:* Does your keyboard have a repeat key?) What happened when the input reached the right edge of the screen? What happened when the output reached the right edge of the screen? (This is called *wrap-around.)*

12. Enter this command and note the output. (Most computers will give 0.)

    PRINT P

13. Now enter this command. (If the output in Activity **12** was 5, use a different value here.)    LET P = 5

14. Repeat the command in Activity **12**. The output now should be 5 (or whatever value you used in Activity **13**). The command LET P = 5 instructs the computer to store 5 in memory and label it P. The PRINT command directs the computer to go to memory and read the number labeled P.

# PASCAL                    VARIABLES

BASIC is a high-level programming language. Another high-level language is *Pascal*. It was developed in the late 1960's by Professor Niklaus Wirth of Switzerland. The language was named in honor of a famous mathematician, Blaise Pascal.

As a computer language, *Pascal* is growing in popularity at a remarkable rate. Many microcomputers can be used with either *Pascal* or BASIC.

Certain aspects of *Pascal* are similar to BASIC. Problems that are long and complex in BASIC can be much shorter and simpler in *Pascal*. However, many people feel *Pascal* is a good language to learn after mastering BASIC. Compared to other high-level languages, *Pascal* is one step closer to English.

Variable names in *Pascal* can be as long as you wish. However, only the first eight characters are read by the computer. Therefore, COMPUTER-LOVER and COMPUTERHATER are considered to be the same name in *Pascal*. Only COMPUTER is read as the variable name. Since there is almost no limit on their length, *Pascal* allows you to choose variable names that describe a purpose.

Just as in BASIC, a keyword, such as PRINT, cannot be part of a variable name. Some of the other rules for variable names in *Pascal* are also similar to those in BASIC.

| RULE | VALID NAME | INVALID NAME |
|------|-----------|-------------|
| 1. The first character must be a letter. | PANTHER7 | 7PANTHER |
| 2. No special characters are allowed. | PACKRAT | PACKRAT! |
| 3. No embedded blanks are allowed. | GOTEAMGO | GO TEAM GO |

## Exercises

Tell whether each variable name is valid or invalid in *Pascal*. If invalid, tell why.

1. SUPER MAN
2. R2–D2
3. SIMPLEINTEREST
4. WHYNOT?
5. CELSIUS100
6. FAHRENHEIT212
7. C3PO
8. "QUOTATION"
9. A
10. #1
11. XXXXXXXXX
12. WONDERWOMAN
13. X↑8
14. SOONER/LATER
15. IGOOFEDONCE

# Vocabulary

computer (3)

programmable device (3)

program (3)

electronic device (3)

store (3)

retrieve (3)

process (4)

data (4)

analog computer (4)

digital computer (4)

software (4)

hardware (4)

central processing unit (4)

arithmetic and logic unit (4)

control unit (4)

memory (4)

keyboard (5)

input (5)

cathode-ray tube (5)

monitor (5)

output (5)

printer (5)

I/O devices (5)

microcomputer (5)

personal computer (5)

time-sharing system (6)

cursor (8)

BREAK (9)

RESET (9)

ENTER (9)

RETURN (9)

CONTROL (9)

ESCAPE (9)

edit (10)

erase (11)

read-only memory (13)

fixed memory (13)

read-write memory (13)

external storage (14)

mass storage (14)

bit (15)

byte (15)

machine language (17)

syntax (18)

BASIC (19)

*Pascal* (19)

# Chapter Summary

1. A computer is a programmable electronic device that can store, retrieve, and process data.
2. A computer has a central processing unit (a control unit and an arithmetic and logic unit), input devices, output devices, and memory.
3. The most common input device is a keyboard. The most common output devices are the cathode-ray tube (in a monitor) and the printer.
4. A microcomputer, or personal computer, is a small, compact computer system.
5. A large computer may be connected to I/O devices directly or by telephone lines through modems.
6. Computers operate so rapidly that they are often used by more than one person, in a time-sharing system.

7. A computer keyboard looks and functions much like a typewriter keyboard. However, it has some special keys that vary from computer to computer.

8. Editing involves moving, changing, or erasing characters and words that have been typed.

9. Each character position across the screen is in a column that extends from the top of the monitor screen to the bottom. Each character position down the screen is in a line that extends across the monitor screen from side to side.

10. Each line typed after all the lines on the monitor screen are used is added at the bottom of the screen, and a line at the top of the screen scrolls up and out of view.

11. A computer has two types of internal memory, read-only memory and read-write memory.

12. Read-only memory contains many of the operating instructions for the computer. Read-only memory is not affected when the power to the computer is switched off.

13. Data and programs that come from input devices or external storage are entered in read-write memory. When the power to the computer is switched off, all information in read-write memory is lost.

14. Information may be transferred from read-write memory to external storage devices such as tapes and disks, which must be protected from such hazards as heat and magnetic fields.

15. Information in a computer is in the form of electrical signals called bits. A bit is denoted by a 1 when it is off or a 0 when it is on. Eight bits usually make up one byte.

16. Computer size is often stated in bytes of read-write memory or in total bytes of read-write and read-only memory.

17. Time-sharing computer users must identify themselves to the computer by logging on and logging off.

18. A computer may be programmed in machine language, in an assembly language, or in a high-level language such as BASIC.

19. BASIC (Beginner's All-Purpose Symbolic Instruction Code) is one widely-used language for microcomputers and time-sharing systems.

20. High-level computer languages are somewhat like English, but they only use a few words. Each word is clearly defined. Computer languages have strict rules of syntax.

21. Most computers can either be programmed or operated in calculator mode. In calculator mode, a computer carries out commands as soon as they are entered.

22. One BASIC command consists of the word PRINT, followed by a character, a mathematical expression, or characters in quotation marks.

# Chapter Test

1. What is a computer?
2. What is a programmable device?
3. What is an electronic device?
4. Name two ways in which a computer may process data.
5. Is the word computer usually used to mean analog computer or digital computer?
6. Draw and label a diagram to show the main parts of a computer. Use arrows to show the directions in which data may flow. If some parts of the system you are using are connected by telephone, show the modems in your diagram.
7. What unit performs such operations as addition and subtraction and comparing numbers?
8. What is the control unit?
9. Name two input devices.
10. Name two output devices.
11. What are I/O devices?
12. If a key on your computer keyboard has two characters on it, what should you do to cause the character on top to be printed?
13. Which of the following special keys does your computer keyboard have?
    a. CONTROL
    b. BREAK (or RESET)
    c. ESCAPE
    d. ENTER (or RETURN)
14. What keys must be used with caution in the system you are using?

**Describe the purpose of each of the following keys.**
15. SHIFT
16. space bar
17. BREAK or RESET
18. ENTER or RETURN

19. What does the process called editing do?
20. After all lines on the screen are used, what happens when the next line is typed?
21. If the power to a computer is switched off, what happens to the information in read-write memory? What happens to the information in read-only memory?
22. In what form is information stored on tapes and disks?
23. What are disk drives?
24. List three sources of damage to tapes and disks.
25. What number indicates a bit is off? What number indicates a bit is on?
26. How is the size of computer memory often stated?

**27.** Name one advantage and one disadvantage of machine language.

**28.** Why is it no longer necessary to program computers in machine language?

**29.** What were the first special programs developed to make programming easier?

**30.** Give two differences between English and the high-level computer languages now in use.

**31.** What do the letters in the word BASIC represent?

**32.** Name one low-level programming language.

**33.** Name two high-level programming languages.

**34.** What happens when the ENTER or RETURN key is pressed after a command has been typed?

**Suppose you entered the given command in calculator mode. What would the output be?**

**35.** PRINT 9

**36.** PRINT 9 + 8

**37.** PRINT "HELLO"

**38.** PRINT H

**39.** PRINT "Q"

**40.** PRINT "⋀⋀GO"

**41.** Name one BASIC command.

**42.** Is BASIC in read-only memory in the computer you are using, or must it be loaded into memory from external storage?

**Choose the best lettered item that completes the sentence to make a true statement.**

| | |
|---|---|
| **a.** hardware | **b.** software |
| **c.** read-write memory | **d.** read-only memory |
| **e.** a digital computer | **f.** an analog computer |
| **g.** calculator mode | **h.** a time-sharing system |

**43.** _____ operates using smooth, continuous changes in electrical signals.

**44.** Instructions that tell the computer how to add and subtract and otherwise process data are stored in _____ when the computer is manufactured.

**45.** A computer, monitor, and disk drive are all called _____.

**46.** A computer that may be used by more than one person at a time is in _____.

**47.** _____ uses electrical signals that switch on and off.

**48.** A computer stores data and programs in _____.

**49.** Computer programs are called _____.

**50.** When instructions are to be carried out at once, a computer is used in _____.

**Match each numbered item with the best lettered choice.**

**51.** syntax

**52.** cursor

**53.** bit

**54.** CPU

**55.** 16k in a computer

**56.** column

**57.** computer program

**58.** *Pascal*

**59.** monitor

**60.** read

**61.** data

**62.** load

**63.** edit

**64.** disk

**65.** input

**66.** keyboard

**67.** printer

**68.** CRT

**69.** byte

**70.** microcomputer

**71.** line

**72.** write

**73.** characters

**74.** log on/log off

**75.** command

**76.** process

**77.** output

**78.** modem

**a.** extends from top of the screen to the bottom

**b.** facts or information

**c.** calculate, compare, arrange, or otherwise act on

**d.** change input or program

**e.** computer language that somewhat resembles BASIC

**f.** pattern of a statement

**g.** small computer

**h.** produces hard copy of output

**i.** stores programs and data externally

**j.** CRT with controls

**k.** electrical signal

**l.** 16,384

**m.** letters and numbers

**n.** extends across the screen from side to side

**o.** store

**p.** identify user

**q.** usually eight bits

**r.** central processing unit

**s.** result of processing data

**t.** cathode-ray tube

**u.** used to enter input

**v.** instruction to a computer to be carried out at once

**w.** indicates where next input will be shown on screen

**x.** set of instructions to be carried out later

**y.** changes signals so they can be sent over a telephone line

**z.** retrieve

**aa.** enter

**bb.** programs and data

# COMPUTER LITERACY

It is impossible to determine what the first computing device was. Perhaps it was a pile of stones that represented the number of people in a tribe. It may have been a stick used to scratch tally marks in the sand. In any event, it marked the first time that a person had the idea of using a physical object to record and process data.

Prehistoric computing devices were fine for dealing with small numbers. But as civilization developed, the need arose for a more useful computing device. The abacus, created over 2,000 years ago, met this need. The abacus uses several rows of beads to represent numbers. By taking advantage of a place-value system, the abacus can be used to record and compute with large numbers. Each row stands for a place-value position, and the arrangement of beads in a row stands for a digit.

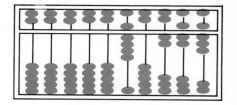

A Chinese abacus. The beads are arranged to represent 90,278.

The abacus is a manual device; in order to perform a computation, the beads are moved by hand. A great deal of experience is required to compute quickly with the abacus.

In 1642, Blaise Pascal was 19 years old and working in his father's tax collection office. He spent his days performing a large number of tedious calculations. To help him with his work, Pascal designed a calculating machine.

The machine used a series of gears. Like the rows of beads in the abacus, the gears were arranged in a place-value system and the gear teeth represented digits. To perform a calculation, all Pascal had to do was enter the numbers, indicate whether they were to be added or subtracted, and pull a lever. The machine did the rest.

The interlocking gear system developed by Pascal was used in almost every mechanical calculator built during the next 300 years. The calculator enabled people to perform calculations quickly, without requiring them to have a great deal of experience using the device.

In 1833, a mathematician named Charles Babbage adopted the idea of interlocking gears to design an analytical engine.

# HISTORY

By design, the analytical engine was something more than a calculator. In fact, it had all the elements of a modern digital computer: input, output, control and arithmetic units, and a storage unit that could hold 50,000 digits.

The idea behind this device was a series of punched cards used to operate a complex arrangement of gears. Some of the cards would instruct the engine to take certain data, store them, process them, or display them. The rest of the cards would give the engine the data. Unfortunately, the engine could not be built, since the parts required a greater precision than was possible at the time.

About the time of Babbage's death (1871), a great deal of research was being done with electricity. People were learning how to use electrical energy to operate machinery and were inventing new devices such as the radio and light bulb. And of course people turned their attention to creating a computer that operated electrically.

Between 1887 and 1944, a number of electromechanical computers were built. These devices used electrical energy to control a series of relay switches, with the positions of the switches representing numbers. Then, in the mid-1940's, relay switches were replaced with vacuum tubes to create the first electronic digital computers. Since then, the development of computers has gone hand-in-hand with rapid developments in electronics. As a result, computers have steadily become smaller, more powerful, and less costly.

**A model of Charles Babbage's
analytical engine.**

A computer can be used in many ways. For example, in the picture above Yvonne Rhodes is using a microcomputer to compute her federal income tax. However, before Yvonne began using the computer, she had to tell it how to compute her tax. Telling a computer what to do and how to do it is a very important part of working with a computer.

# INTRODUCTION TO BASIC

To use a computer, you must communicate with it in a language it is programmed to accept. Many computers accept BASIC. Because BASIC is similar to English it is easy to learn, but there are several versions, and their rules vary somewhat. In this chapter, we begin to develop a standard version that works on most computers that accept BASIC.

## 2.1 OPERATIONS IN BASIC

Listed below are some operational symbols as they appear in arithmetic and in BASIC.

| Operation | Arithmetic | BASIC |
|---|:---:|:---:|
| Addition | + | + |
| Subtraction | − | − |
| Multiplication | × or · | * |
| Division | ÷ | / |

In arithmetic, exponents are denoted by a raised numeral, such as the 2 in $3^2$. In BASIC, exponents are denoted by the symbol ↑, ∧, or **, depending on the computer. For example, the arithmetic expression $3^2$ would be written in BASIC as 3 ↑ 2, 3∧2, or 3**2. We will use the symbol ↑.

To see how these symbols are used in BASIC, compare each arithmetic expression below with the corresponding BASIC expression.

| Arithmetic | BASIC |
|:---:|:---:|
| $4 + 5 - 3$ | 4+5−3 |
| $6 \times 9$ | 6*9 |
| $24 \div 8$ | 24/8 |
| $2^3$ | 2↑3 |

To change an arithmetic expression to a BASIC expression, replace the arithmetic symbols with BASIC symbols.

<table>
<tr><th style="text-align:center">Arithmetic</th><th style="text-align:center">BASIC</th></tr>
<tr><td style="text-align:center">$3^2 + 7 \times 5 - 4 \div 2$</td><td style="text-align:center">3↑2+7*5−4/2</td></tr>
<tr><td style="text-align:center">$8 \div 2^3 - 5 \times 4$</td><td style="text-align:center">8/2↑3−5*4</td></tr>
</table>

There is a rule in arithmetic stated *"multiply and divide before adding and subtracting."* The following example shows step by step how to evaluate an expression using this rule.

---

**EXAMPLE 1**

$$8 \div 4 + 23 - 5 \times 4 = \quad \text{Start at the left.}$$
$$2 + 23 - 20 = \quad \text{Divide 8 by 4 and multiply 5 by 4.}$$
$$5 \quad \text{Add 2 and 23, then subtract 20.}$$

---

BASIC uses the same rules as arithmetic to govern the *order of operations.* These rules are given below.

All operations in parentheses are performed first, from the innermost parentheses outward, using the three steps below. If no parentheses appear in an expression, use the three steps in order.

**First:** Evaluate powers.

**Second:** Do multiplications and divisions from left to right.

**Third:** Do additions and subtractions from left to right.

A computer evaluates a BASIC expression according to the order of operations given above.

---

**EXAMPLE 2**

$$6*4+(2+3)↑2/1-7 = 6*4+(5)↑2/1-7 \quad \text{Do operations within parentheses.}$$
$$= 6*4+25/1-7 \quad \text{Evaluate powers.}$$
$$= 24+25-7 \quad \text{Multiply and divide.}$$
$$= 42 \quad \text{Add and subtract.}$$

---

Parentheses can be used to show the order in which operat
performed.

---

**EXAMPLE 3**

4*3−1+2↑3/4
4*3−1+(2↑3)/4                    Group numbers with exponents first.
(4*3)−1+((2↑3)/4)                Group multiplication and division next.

The number of left-hand parentheses, (, must be the same as the number of right-hand parentheses,). In this example, there are 3 left-hand parentheses and 3 right-hand parentheses.

---

When there are several operations inside parentheses, the computer performs the operations according to the order of operations. For example, in the expression (6+3*4)/2, the computer performs the multiplication before the addition.

The examples below show how the value of an expression depends on parentheses.

| | | |
|---|---|---|
| (6+3*4)/2 = | ((6+3)*4)/2 = | 6+3*(4/2) = |
| (6+12)/2 = | (9*4)/2 = | 6+3*2 = |
| 18/2 = | 36/2 = | 6+6 = |
| 9 | 18 | 12 |

A computer can be used in calculator mode (shown in Chapter 1) to evaluate expressions.

PRINT 6*4/3+((5+3)/4)
10 ⟶                    The value of the expression is 10.

A **PRINT command** tells the computer to evaluate the expression and then print the result.

The value of $\frac{10+8}{4+5}$ is 2. Someone experimenting with a computer might try to type the expression as follows.

PRINT 10+8/4+5

However, this expression gives an output of 17 since the division is performed before the addition. On the other hand, the following expression gives the desired output of 2.

PRINT (10+8)/(4+5)

The operations in parentheses are performed first.

...on for each of the following.

**2.** $6 \times 4$

**4.** $3^2$

**6.** $6 \cdot 5 \cdot 7 - 4$

**8.** $3 \times 4^2 - 5 \times 2$

**10.** $7^{(3 + 1)}$

**9.** 3 (...

**11.** $(5 + 10 + 15) \div 5$

**12.** $\dfrac{3(6 + 5)}{2(3 + 4)}$

**13.** $3 + \dfrac{6 \times 7 - 2}{3 + 8 \times 6}$

**14.** $9(2^3 + 5 \times 4 + 8)$

**15.** $4(3 + 5) \div 2 \times 7^3 - 8$

**16.** $10^5 \times 4 \div (-4 - 3)$

**17.** $(12(3 - 1)) \div (2^2(5 + 6))$

**18.** $4 \div 3 \times 2 \times 4 \div 6 - 1 + (-2)^3$

**Write an arithmetic expression for each of the following.**

**19.** $10-3+5$

**20.** $3*2+1$

**21.** $7-2*3$

**22.** $28/8$

**23.** $36/9+2$

**24.** $5 \uparrow 2*4+5$

**25.** $2*((4+8)/2) \uparrow 5$

**26.** $(8-5)*3 \uparrow 2/4-7$

**27.** $2 \uparrow 5-6*(8/4)$

**28.** $(3+2*6)/4*5 \uparrow 2$

**29.** $3*(2 \uparrow 3-6)/(4*7+2)*4 \uparrow 2$

**30.** $((8/4+1)*(7 \uparrow 2-2)/3)*5 \uparrow 2$

**Put parentheses in each expression to show the order of operations.**

**31.** $2*3+1$

**32.** $2-5/4$

**33.** $4+2*3/6-1$

**34.** $5 \uparrow 2/3*6+2$

**35.** $-2-12 \uparrow 2-4*6/3$

**36.** $3*5-2 \uparrow 2/3*6-1$

**37.** $3 \uparrow 2-5*6/3-2$

**38.** $3 \uparrow 3-10+6*8/4$

**39.** $2 \uparrow 4-5+6*3 \uparrow 2/12$

**40.** $-4*3*-2/-4*-3*-2 \uparrow 5+32$

**Evaluate each BASIC expression. Show a step-by-step solution.**

**41.** $2*6+3*6/3$

**42.** $7+3/3*6$

**43.** $3+4+2 \uparrow 2-7$

**44.** $12-2*3 \uparrow 2/3$

**45.** $12/2 \uparrow 2+5-4$

**46.** $4 \uparrow 3/4*3-12$

**47.** $2+3 \uparrow 2-6/3+4$

**48.** $7*3-2 \uparrow 2/2$

**49.** $16/2*8+4-4$

**50.** $6*(2+4*4)$

**51.** $7*3/3-1+3*(2+5)$

**52.** $3 \uparrow 2+2*2/2 \uparrow 2$

# Laboratory Activities

1. Use the computer in calculator mode to evaluate the expressions in Exercises **19-30**.
2. Use the computer in calculator mode to evaluate the expressions in Exercises **41-52**.
3. Use the computer in calculator mode to evaluate the expressions (without parentheses) in Exercises **31-40**.
4. Use the computer in calculator mode to evaluate the expressions (with parentheses) in Exercises **31-40**. Compare the results with those in Activity **3**.

**Use the computer in calculator mode to evaluate each expression.**

5. 25*60+37*(56/20)
6. (25*60+37*56)/20
7. 156+95/50*125
8. (156+95)/(50*125)
9. 367+40*3.7 ↑ 3−758
10. (367+40)*3 ↑ 3−158
11. 128−18*3 ↑ 4/100
12. (8*3) ↑ 4/100−128
13. 56.2/2 ↑ 3+568.4−1256.7
14. (56/2) ↑ 3+568.4−1256.7
15. (71.2−36.1)*10.2/6 ↑ 2−1.5
16. (71−36/10)*(36−1.5)

**Write a BASIC expression for each of the following. Then evaluate each expression using the computer in calculator mode.**

17. $4^2 \times 586 \times 3 - 15486$
18. $52 \div 26 \times 18.6 - 58.7 - 0.0003 + (0.01)^2$
19. $15.8^2 \div 10^3 - 0.65$
20. $3^3 \div 10^2 \times 5.6 - 38595.6$
21. $-15.6 \times (-12.3) - 8.4 \div 4.2 - 2^5 + 4.8$
22. $12^3 - 6 \times 24 \div 3^2 - 4.9 \times 30.8$

# 2.2 NUMBER NOTATION

Numbers are expressed somewhat differently in BASIC than they are in arithmetic. For example, commas are used in arithmetic to help make numerals easier to read. In BASIC, numerals are written without commas.

| Arithmetic | BASIC |
|:---:|:---:|
| 14,820 | 14820 |
| 6,134,528 | 6134528 |
| 1,795.58 | 1795.58 |

In arithmetic, a zero is often used at the beginning or end of a numeral. In BASIC, these zeros are omitted.

| Arithmetic | BASIC |
|:---:|:---:|
| −12.30 | −12.3 |
| 0.56 | .56 |
| −0.280 | −.28 |

Computers can accept and express numbers in three different forms.

1. Integer form
2. Decimal form
3. Exponential form

Examples of each form are given below.

| Integer | Decimal | Exponential |
|:---:|:---:|:---:|
| 7 | 1.5432 | 4.76952E+04 |
| −56 | .72 | 1.54321E−03 |
| 0 | −65.417 | −5.671E−06 |
| 25 | 2.2 | −1.2345E+12 |

*Exponential form,* also called **E-form,** is a form of scientific notation. The expression $1.25347 \times 10^8$ is an example of ordinary scientific notation. In E-form the same number would be expressed as 1.25347E+08.

Some characteristics of E-form are described below.

1. The sign of the number can be either + or −. The + can be omitted when typing a number in E-form. In fact, many computers omit the + when printing the number.
2. This number is equal to or greater than 1 but less than 10. The number of digits here varies from computer to computer.
3. The "E" represents the base, which is ten. (If the number to be printed is very large or very small, some computers print 12 digits with a "D" for "double precision" instead of 6 digits with an "E".)
4. The sign of the exponent can be either + or −. The + can be omitted when typing a number in E-form. In fact, many computers omit the + when printing the exponent.
5. This number is the exponent, which is an integer. Check your manual for your computer's limits for this number.

The following examples illustrate how to change from one form of a number to another.

---

**EXAMPLE 1**

The number in scientific notation: $3.54187 \times 10^{12}$
In decimal form: 3541870000000.0

Multiplying by $10^{12}$ is the same as moving the decimal point to the *right* 12 places.

$$3.54187000000000$$
1 2 3 4 5 6 7 8 9 10 11 12

In E-form: 3.54187E+12

The multiplication symbol and the power of 10 are replaced with an "E" and the exponent.

**EXAMPLE 2**

The number in decimal form: 0.000213547
In scientific notation: $2.13547 \times 10^{-4}$

Multiplying by $10^{-4}$ is the same as moving the decimal point to the *left* 4 places.

$$0.0002.13547$$
4 3 2 1

In E-form: 2.13547E−04

**EXAMPLE 3**

The number in E-form: 6.13578E−05
In scientific notation: $6.13578 \times 10^{-5}$
In decimal form: 0.0000613578

---

The number of digits that are printed varies from computer to computer. Many computers print no more than six digits. Others print nine or more. The following examples show how a computer that prints six digits may round a number having more than six digits.

```
PRINT 1.2345678        PRINT −4.2681422E+08
1.23457                −4.26814E+08
PRINT 546.38942        PRINT 0.2468357
546.389                .246836
```

Rules for rounding may vary slightly from computer to computer. Also, a computer may round differently when a number is the result of computations. You will be asked in the Laboratory Activities to determine the rules your computer uses.

Because of the way computers represent numbers internally and the way they calculate, they can sometimes give very strange results. For example, 25 ↑ 2 and 25 * 25 are exactly the same number, but some computers give 25 * 25 as 625 and 25 ↑ 2 as 625.000001. You should be aware that if your computer output (for a Laboratory Activity for instance) disagrees with the expected output by a very small amount (probably less than .000001 for a computer that gives six digits), the difference may be due to this type of computer error.

The expression 568.72E+12 is not in E-form. Why? In calculator mode, a computer would change it to E-form as follows.

PRINT 568.72E+12
5.6872E+14

On the other hand, PRINT 621.04E+03 would result in the integer 621040 if the computer prints more than five digits.

Numbers may be given in forms other than those shown so far. For example, the population of the United States may be given as 232.9 million, or $232.9 \times 10^6$. This number may be entered into the computer as 232.9E+06. The number is printed by the computer as 2.329E+08 or 232900000. Table 2-1 shows the names of various powers of ten.

**Table 2-1**

| Name | Power of Ten |
|------|--------------|
| quadrillion | $10^{15}$ |
| trillion | $10^{12}$ |
| billion | $10^9$ |
| million | $10^6$ |
| thousand | $10^3$ |
| hundred | $10^2$ |
| ten | $10^1$ |
| one | $10^0$ |
| tenth | $10^{-1}$ |
| hundredth | $10^{-2}$ |
| thousandth | $10^{-3}$ |
| millionth | $10^{-6}$ |

# Exercises

**Write each of the following in BASIC notation.**

1. 0.0156
2. 1,207.0340
3. $1.24 \times 10^2$
4. 132.80
5. $6.78 \times 10^{-3}$
6. −387,042.00
7. −0.0030
8. $2.9807 \times 10^5$
9. $5.34231 \times 10^{-3}$

**Write each of the following in scientific notation and in E-form.**

10. 123,456,000
11. 127.548
12. 0.00024836
13. 0.154326
14. −1,000,000
15. 6,874,005.048
16. −0.00587421
17. 0.00000023
18. 142,000,000,000

Write each of the following in decim[a]

**19.** $1.24 \times 10^7$     **20.** 34.06E+0(

**22.** $3.95402 \times 10^2$     **23.** 8.1819×1(

**25.** 51.421E+07     **26.** .1041E−0[2]

Write each of the following in E-form.

**28.** 2.42 billion     **29.** 4.031 millio[n]

**31.** 40.28 trillion     **32.** 5.34 thousa[n]

**34.** 32.4 hundredths     **35.** 310.45 tenth[s]

Write a BASIC expre[ss]
computer in calcula[

**24.** $123{,}456 \times 1$

**27.** $2^{50}$

**30.** $(3.72$

**32.** $(7$

# Laboratory Activities

### Enter the following commands and note the output.

**1.** PRINT 6.7891457     **2.** PRINT 357.7321436

**3.** PRINT 0.467910389     **4.** PRINT 5.6392256E+02

**5.** PRINT −1.034672154E+10     **6.** PRINT 3.6578193E−05

**7.** Use the results from Activities **1-6** to state the rules your computer uses for rounding. Consult your manual to check your answer.

### Experiment to find the answers to the following questions about your computer.

**8.** What is the greatest number your computer will express without using E-form? The least number?

**9.** What is the least positive number your computer will express without using E-form? The greatest negative number?

**10.** What is the least positive number your computer will express in E-form without rounding to zero? The greatest negative number?

**11.** What is the greatest positive number your computer will express in E-form? The least negative number?

### Use the computer in calculator mode to perform the indicated operations.

**12.** 2E+04+5E+03     **13.** 2E+04−5E+03

**14.** 2E+04*5E+03     **15.** 2E+04/5E+03

**16.** 1.25E−02+3.75E+03     **17.** 1.25E−02−3.75E+03

**18.** 1.25E−02*3.75E+03     **19.** 1.25E−02/3.75E+03

**20.** 34266*87674     **21.** 34266*87674*2635

**22.** 34266/87674+2635     **23.** 1/(34266*87674)

...ssion for each of the following. Then use the
...tor mode to find the value of each expression.

...3,456    **25.** $0.00498^5$    **26.** $1 \div 10{,}000$

     **28.** $0.007^{12}$    **29.** $(4.05 \times 10^{-5}) \times 10^7$

... $\times\ 10^{-4}) \div (-3 \times 10^{-5})$    **31.** $(0.00144 \div 0.00012)^2 \div 4^2 \div 3^2$

...086 $\times 10^7) + (2.41 \times 10^8)$    **33.** $(1.04 \times 10^8) \times (2.01 \times 10^4)$

...sing your computer in calculator mode, do the following activities.

**34.** Find the square of every positive integer from 1 to 30. Record any that show computer error.

**35.** Find $6 \uparrow 2$. Find $6*6$. Find $6 \uparrow 2 - 6*6$. Does your computer give a difference of zero?

**36.** Use the pattern in Activity **35** with every integer from 1 to 10. Does your computer always give a difference of zero?

Use the computer in calculator mode to compute the answers for Activities 37 and 38. Round the results to two significant digits.

**37.** A barrel of oil produces $5.8 \times 10^6$ Btu of energy. How many barrels of oil does the U.S. import if it produces 13.5 quadrillion Btu of energy from imported oil?

**38.** How much money does the U.S. spend on imported oil if one barrel costs $36?

Use the information below for Activities 39-44. Use the computer in calculator mode for computations. Round the results to four significant digits.

| | |
|---|---|
| World Population | 4.8298 billion |
| U.S. Population | 232.9 million |
| Number of Families in U.S. | 57,804 thousand |
| U.S. National Income | $1,161.3 billion |
| U.S. National Savings | $73.8 billion |
| Total U.S. Budget | $563.7 billion |
| U.S. Defense Budget | $130.4 billion |
| U.S. Education Budget | $30.7 billion |

**39.** Find the average income per person in the U.S.

$$\text{average income} = \frac{\text{national income}}{\text{population}}$$

**40.** Find the average number of persons per family in the U.S.

$$\text{average number of persons per family} = \frac{\text{population}}{\text{number of families}}$$

**41.** Find the average amount of savings per family in the U.S.

$$\text{average savings} = \frac{\text{national savings}}{\text{number of families}}$$

**42.** Find the percent of the federal budget spent on defense in the U.S.

$$\text{percent spent on defense} = \frac{\text{defense budget}}{\text{total budget}} \times 100$$

**43.** Find the percent of the federal budget spent on education in the U.S.

$$\text{percent spent on education} = \frac{\text{education budget.}}{\text{total budget}} \times 100$$

**44.** Find the percent the U.S. population is of the world's population.

# 2.3  COMMANDS AND STATEMENTS

A computer can be used much like a typewriter. The PRINT command makes this possible. The example below illustrates how to use a PRINT command to print a name.

**EXAMPLE 1**

PRINT "JOHN LUKASCO"
JOHN LUKASCO  ←——————— This is how the output appears.

In the example above, when the command PRINT "JOHN LUKASCO" is entered into a computer, the computer immediately prints JOHN LUKASCO. In BASIC, a **command** is an instruction which is carried out as soon as it is entered into the computer.

Two PRINT commands can be used to print a person's name and the name of the school on two different lines.

PRINT "JOHN LUKASCO"
JOHN LUKASCO
PRINT "BUCKEYE HIGH SCHOOL"
BUCKEYE HIGH SCHOOL

The expressions in quotation marks (JOHN LUKASCO and BUCKEYE HIGH SCHOOL) are called **strings** and are printed using PRINT commands. Notice that strings are printed in output without quotation marks.

It is possible to print the two lines one after the other, without a PRINT command between them. To do this, each PRINT command is numbered. This changes the PRINT commands to PRINT statements.

10 PRINT "JOHN LUKASCO"
20 PRINT "BUCKEYE HIGH SCHOOL

While the order of the line numbers is important, the numbers themselves are not. It is useful to number successive lines by multiples of ten; then if you want to add a line between two lines, renumbering is not needed. In fact, if you number by multiples of ten, you can add nine lines between any two lines.

Some BASICs require an **END statement** to tell the computer that no more statements follow. Since all BASICs allow an END statement, we will always show one.

Statements, unlike commands, are not carried out as soon as they are entered. A **RUN command** is needed to tell the computer to execute the statements. In BASIC, **statements** are numbered instruction lines that are executed after the RUN command is entered into the computer.

---

**EXAMPLE 2**

10 PRINT "JOHN LUKASCO"
20 PRINT "BUCKEYE HIGH SCHOOL"
30 END
RUN     ←—————————————     **The RUN command tells the**
JOHN LUKASCO     **computer to execute lines**
BUCKEYE HIGH SCHOOL     **10, 20, and 30.**

---

Output can be arranged by using spaces inside the quotation marks as shown in Example 3.

---

**EXAMPLE 3**

10 PRINT "JOHN LUKASCO"
20 PRINT     ←—————————————     **Causes the computer to skip a**
    **line.**

30 PRINT "$\wedge\wedge\wedge\wedge\wedge$BUCKEYE HIGH SCHOOL"     **A $\wedge$ is used to indicate a space.**

40 END
RUN
JOHN LUKASCO

    BUCKEYE HIGH SCHOOL     **Moved to the right by printing**
    **spaces in front of it.**

---

Rules for using spaces in statements and comands vary among BASICs. For example, many BASICs will accept either of the following statements.

    10 PRINT "JOHN LUKASCO" or 10PRINT"JOHN LUKASCO"

However, the first statement is easier to read. You will be asked in the Laboratory Activities to determine the rules your computer uses.

The number of columns in a computer display ranges from 32 to 80. Line printers also vary in the number of columns printed across a page. The following PRINT statements show how a sentence might be arranged for lines of different lengths. Notice that each line ends with a complete word. Words can also be hyphenated in the usual way at the ends of lines.

| Number of Columns | PRINT STATEMENTS |
|---|---|
| 80 | 10 PRINT "THIS SENTENCE IS 80 CHARACTERS LONG AND IN SOME DISPLAYS IT ALL FITS ON ONE LINE" |
| 64 | 10 PRINT "THIS SENTENCE IS 80 CHARACTERS LONG AND IN SOME DISPLAYS IT ALL" <br> 20 PRINT "FITS ON ONE LINE" |
| 40 | 10 PRINT "THIS SENTENCE IS 80 CHARACTERS LONG AND" <br> 20 PRINT "IN SOME DISPLAYS IT ALL FITS ON ONE LINE" |
| 32 | 10 PRINT "THIS SENTENCE IS 80 CHARACTERS" <br> 20 PRINT "LONG AND IN SOME DISPLAYS IT ALL" <br> 30 PRINT "FITS ON ONE LINE" |

Every computer language is governed by a set of rules. When a rule is violated, the computer may give an *error message*. The following statement contains an *error*.

10 PRNT "YOU GOOFED"

PRINT is misspelled PRNT. All *keywords,* such as PRINT, END, RUN, and so on, must be spelled exactly as they are defined in BASIC. Misspelling a keyword is a syntax error and generally causes a SYNTAX ERROR message to be displayed. Error messages vary from computer to computer.

10 PRNT "YOU GOOFED"
20 END
RUN
SYNTAX ERROR IN LINE 10

*Syntax errors* are usually caused by incorrect punctuation, improper use of parentheses, or misspelled keywords. An error can be corrected by retyping the line containing the error.

The following examples illustrate some common syntax errors and typical error messages.

## EXAMPLE 4

10 PRINT 2*3

20 END

RUM           ⟵———————— RUN is misspelled.
SYNTAX ERROR

## EXAMPLE 5

20 PRINT "HELLO GARNET"!  ⟵— The "!" should be between the quota-
30 END                      tion marks.
RUN
SYNTAX ERROR IN LINE 20

It is easy to make errors when using a computer. That is why computers are programmed to give error messages. Do not be afraid to make mistakes. Making mistakes is part of learning.

Statements are stored in read-write memory. Typing new lines erases only previous lines with the same line numbers. Therefore, when entering a new set of statements, first clear the previous set from read-write memory. To do this, enter the command **NEW** (some computers use SCRATCH).

# Exercises

1. What is an expression in quotation marks called?
2. What is one difference between statements and commands?
3. Why is it handy to use line numbers that are multiples of ten?
4. What is the purpose of an END statement?
5. What is the purpose of a RUN command?
6. What statement will cause a line to be skipped?
7. Write a PRINT command that will cause FIVE to be printed beginning 5 spaces from the left side of your screen or the left margin of the paper in your printer.
8. Write a PRINT command that will cause X to be printed 15 spaces from the left side of your screen or the left margin of the paper in your printer.
9. Write a PRINT command that will cause X to be printed 15 spaces from the right side of your screen or the right margin of the paper in your printer.
10. Write a PRINT command that will cause XX to be printed halfway between the left and right sides of your screen or the left and right margins of the paper in your printer.

**Consider the following paragraph for Exercise 11.**

Did you know that the typical automobile costs about $2,000 per year to operate? Car owners not only pay for gas, they also pay for insurance, licenses, maintenance, and repairs.

11. Write PRINT statements so the given paragraph will be printed without breaking any word from line to line.
12. Write a PRINT statement that will cause a syntax error.
13. Name three types of syntax errors.
14. Why is a computer programmed to give error messages?
15. What is the command in your BASIC to erase previous programs from memory?
16. What does the NEW or SCRATCH command do?

# Laboratory Activities ▬▬▬

1. Enter the commands you wrote for Exercises **7-10**. Is the output correct? If not, revise your commands to give the correct output.

2. Enter and run the following statements.

       10PRINT"HOW ARE YOU?"
       20 END

   Did you get an error message? Consult your manual to check your answer and to find out if there are any other rules on spacing.

3. Enter and run the program in Example 4. (Be sure to clear read-write memory first.) What is the error message your computer gives?

4. Enter and run the program in Example 5. (Clear memory first. We will not continue to remind you to do this.) What is the error message your computer gives?

5. Enter and run the PRINT statements you wrote for Exercise **11**.

6. Enter and run the PRINT statement you wrote for Exercise **12**.

**Enter the following PRINT commands. Insert spaces in Activities 8-17 so the numbers will be centered under the headings.**

7. PRINT "NUMBER ∧∧∧∧ SQUARE ∧∧∧∧ CUBE"
8. PRINT "    1          1          1 "
9. PRINT "    2          4          8 "
10. PRINT "    3          9         27 "
11. PRINT "    4         16         64 "
12. PRINT "    5         25        125 "
13. PRINT "    6         36        216 "
14. PRINT "    7         49        343 "
15. PRINT "    8         64        512 "
16. PRINT "    9         81        729 "
17. PRINT "   10        100       1000 "

18. Change the PRINT commands in Activities **7-17** to PRINT statements. Give each statement a different line number. Run the set of statements. What is the difference between using PRINT commands and PRINT statements?

**Use PRINT statements to print the information requested.**

19. Print your name and address on three different lines.

20. Print your name and address on the same line if possible. If it is not possible, use a second line and make sure the first line ends with a complete word or a complete set of numbers.

21. Print your name and address on five lines. Skip a line between your name and street address and between your street address and city and state.

**22.** Print your name on the far left side of the screen on the first line, your street address in the center of the screen on the second line, and your city and state on the far right side of the screen on the third line.

**23.** Print the same information requested in Activity **22** but skip a line after each printed line.

**A business letter can be printed by a computer. Refer to the business letter below and use PRINT statements to complete Activities 24-27. Use a different line number for each statement.**

AAA FOOD CO.
14 E. APPLE DRIVE
PET, OHIO 43210
5 JULY 1982

MS. PAM SPAM
256 N. MAPLE
OAKVILLE, IL 60000

DEAR MS. SPAM:

SORRY TO INFORM YOU THAT THE PRICE OF POODLE DOG FOOD HAS RISEN BY 25%. THE SELLING PRICE IS NOW $13.95 PER CASE.
PLEASE LET US KNOW IF YOU STILL WANT YOUR ORIGINAL ORDER.

SINCERELY,

JAN JONES
PRESIDENT

**24.** Print the name and address of the AAA Food Co. and the date so they are centered as shown.

**25.** Print the name and address of Ms. Pam Spam on the left side of the letter as shown.

**26.** Print the greeting and the body of the letter without breaking any word from line to line.

**27.** Print the ending on the right side of the letter as shown.

**28.** Combine the PRINT statements you wrote for Activities **24-27** to print the entire letter.

**29.** Use PRINT statements to print the following paragraph without breaking any word from line to line. Skip a line after each printed line.

The monies withheld from a paycheck include federal, state, local, and FICA taxes. Other deductions are made for medical and accident insurance, credit unions, and so on.

**Each PRINT statement in Activities 30-38 contains one error. Enter each PRINT statement into the computer with an END statement and run the statements to generate an error message. Then correct the error and run the statements again.**

**30.** A1 PRINT "ERROR"

**31.** 8Ø PRINT 4*5/(2(4+7))

**32.** 9Ø PRINT 12/(3*(3+4)

**33.** 1ØØ WRITE "EDNA, TEXAS"

**34.** 1Ø PRINT 2×(5−7)

**35.** 2Ø PRINT (5+1/6

**36.** 3Ø PINT "YOUR NAME"

**37.** 6Ø "PRINT" 2*3 = 6

**38.** 5Ø PRINT (2+4)/6*7)

# 2.4 VARIABLES AND THE LET STATEMENT

In business, simple interest ($I$) is calculated using the formula $I = P \cdot R \cdot T$. The letters $I$, $P$, $R$, and $T$ are variables.

In most BASICs, a variable may be a single letter of the alphabet. In some BASICs, a variable may also be a letter followed by one of the following.

1. Just one additional character (a letter or a single digit from 0 to 9). Examples of such variables are KM and B3.
2. One or more additional characters (up to a limit that varies with the BASIC), and all characters are read by the computer. Examples of such variables are C29, CIRCLE, and AVG3.
3. One or more additional characters (up to a limit that varies with the BASIC), and only the first two characters are read by the computer. Examples of such variables are TAX, MY23, and ANGLE4.

The example below shows how to tell valid from invalid variables in all three cases mentioned above.

---

**EXAMPLE 1**

|  | **Valid Variables** | **Invalid Variables** |
|---|---|---|
| Case 1 | E | A? ←The ? is not a letter or a digit. |
|  | XX | 2F ←The first character is not a letter. |
|  | K9 | BAT ←Three characters are not allowed. |
| Case 2 and Case 3 | MEAN NUM42 BOY BORROW BO | P*4 ←The * is not a letter or a digit. 3AB ←The first character is not a letter. |

In case 3, only the first two characters in a variable are read by the computer. This means that BOY, BORROW, and BO would all be read as BO by the computer.

---

Using an invalid variable when working with a computer may generate a syntax error.

To a computer, a variable is like the street address of a house. The first time it is used in a program, a **variable** is assigned to a location in the memory of a computer where a value can be stored. This is not the way a variable is used in mathematics.

A **LET statement** is used to assign a value to a variable.

$$10 \text{ LET } I = P*R*T$$

A LET statement has a line number, the keyword LET, and a variable that is assigned a value with an equals sign (=).

In BASIC, the equals sign (=) has a meaning different from its meaning in algebra. The equals sign divides a LET statement into a left-hand part and a right-hand part. The left-hand part must always be a single variable. The right-hand part can be any BASIC expression. It can contain variables, numbers, and operation symbols. A computer finds the value of the expression on the right-hand side of an equals sign and stores that value in a location it assigns to the variable on the left-hand side.

---

**EXAMPLE 2**

10 LET A = 6
The number 6 is stored in a memory location assigned to A.

20 LET M = 5*A
The computer calculates 5 times the contents of A and stores the result in a memory location it assigns to M.

30 PRINT A,M
40 END
The computer prints 6 and 30.

---

## EXAMPLE 3

| | |
|---|---|
| 1∅ LET X = 5 | The computer assigns a memory location to X and stores 5 there. |
| 2∅ PRINT X | The computer prints 5. |
| 3∅ LET X=X+1 | The computer adds 1 to the contents of X and stores the result at X. |
| 4∅ PRINT X | The computer prints 6. |
| 5∅ END | |

In algebra, the equation $X = X + 1$ is not true for any real number. However, in BASIC the definition of $=$ gives the expression meaning for any value of X.

Notice that in line 30 of Example 2 there are two variables in the PRINT statement, separated by a comma. The comma has a special function when used to separate variables or strings in a PRINT statement. The strings and the values of the variables are printed in *zones*. Zones are usually 16 columns wide. In Example 2, the computer would print 6 (the value of A) in *zone one* and 3∅ (the value of M) in *zone two*. The output of the program in Example 2 might look like the following.

$$6 \wedge\wedge\wedge\wedge\wedge\wedge\wedge\wedge\wedge\wedge\wedge\wedge\wedge\wedge 3∅$$

Rules for placement of a number within a zone vary from computer to computer. Check your manual for the rules your computer uses.

It is possible to change line 30 in Example 2 so 6 and 3∅ are printed close to each other. This can be done by using a semicolon between the variables. Line 30 would be written as follows.

$$3∅ \text{ PRINT A;M}$$

The output from this line, depending on the computer, would appear in one of the ways shown below.

$$63∅ \qquad \text{or} \qquad 6\wedge 3∅$$

To put a space between the 6 and the 3∅ in the output on the left, line 30 can be written as follows.

$$3∅ \text{ PRINT A; } ''\wedge'';M$$

The output will now be the same as that on the right above. The semicolons are not necessary in all BASICs, but we will always show them in statements of this type. You will be asked in the Laboratory Activities to determine the rules your computer uses for semicolons.

# Exercises

**Tell whether each variable name is valid or invalid. If invalid, tell why.**

| | | | |
|---|---|---|---|
| **1.** Y | **2.** D2 | **3.** 2X | **4.** # # |
| **5.** AH | **6.** HI | **7.** A+ | **8.** H? |
| **9.** 58 | **10.** (K | **11.** M! | **12.** F* |
| **13.** B | **14.** M | **15.** A6 | **16.** 3 |
| **17.** +B | **18.** TC | **19.** −7 | **20.** DL |

**Write each formula below using a LET statement.**

**21.** $A = \frac{1}{2} \cdot B \cdot H$

**22.** $V = L \cdot W \cdot H$

**23.** $A = S^2$

**24.** $H = VT - 5T^2$

**25.** $R = \frac{F(P + 1)}{N(N + 1)}$

**26.** $A = \frac{F - S}{T}$

**27.** $T = \frac{B}{HW}$

**28.** $V = 0.707(V \div 2)$

**29.** $F = 2.3380(10^{-9}X^2 + 1.5790(10^{-5}X) + 0.9990)$

**30.** $M = \frac{Y_1 - Y_2}{X_1 - X_2}$ (Hint: Use Y1, Y2, X1, and X2 as the variables).

**Identify and correct the error in each LET statement.**

**31.** 10 LET 2*X = A

**32.** 20 LTE A = B*C

**33.** 30 LET 2*L+2*W = P

**34.** 40 LET A = B(C+D)

**35.** 50 LET 1B = A/C

**For each of the following give the value of X after line 20 has been executed.**

**36.** 10 LET X = 10
20 LET X = X+1

**37.** 10 LET X = 5
20 LET X = X↑2+2*X+1

**38.** 10 LET X = 2
20 LET X = 3*X−12/X↑2

**Use each LET statement in Exercises 39-47 and the LET statements below to determine the value of A in each exercise.**

$$10 \text{ LET } K1 = -2$$
$$20 \text{ LET } MN = 2$$
$$30 \text{ LET } P = 0$$
$$40 \text{ LET } X = 1$$

**39.** 50 LET A = (K1+MN+X)*P

**40.** 50 LET A = K1*X

**41.** 50 LET A = MN↑2+X

**42.** 50 LET A = MN/K1−X+MN

**43.** 50 LET A = (MN+X)/(K1+X)

**44.** 50 LET A = (MN+X)↑3

**45.** 50 LET A = MN*K1*X

**46.** 50 LET A = (K1+MN)/X+MN

**47.** 50 LET A = K1↑2+MN↑2/X↑2

**48.** What is the size of a print zone on your computer?

**49.** How many print zones are there on each line on your computer? Is the size of each print zone the same?

**Describe where the following numbers would be printed within a print zone on your computer.**

**50.** 6

**51.** −12

**52.** .34

**53.** −.1234

**54.** −1.28E+08

**55.** 0

# Laboratory Activities

1. Enter and run Example 2.
2. Enter and run Example 3.

**Write the output of each of the following. Then enter and run each activity on your computer. Compare your output with the computer's output.**

**3.**
```
10 LET X = 10
20 LET X = X+1
30 PRINT X,X+1
40 END
```

**4.**
```
10 LET X = 10
20 LET Y = 5
30 PRINT X*Y+X
40 END
```

**5.**
```
10 LET X = 10
20 LET X = X+1
30 PRINT X+1
40 END
```

**6.**
```
10 LET A = 3*4−1
20 LET B = 4↑2+1
30 LET A = A*B
40 LET B = A/B
50 PRINT B
60 END
```

**7.**
```
10 LET A1 = 12↑2
20 LET A2 = 6↑2
30 LET A3 = 3↑2
40 LET A1 = A2/A3
50 PRINT A3
60 END
```

**8.**
```
10 LET MA = 8.24
20 LET TH = 3.39
30 LET MA = TH
40 LET TH = MA
50 PRINT MA*TH
60 END
```

**Combine the PRINT statements in Activities 9-16 with the statements below. Enter and run each set of statements on your computer.**

$$10 \ \text{LET PI} = 3.14$$
$$20 \ \text{LET R} = 6$$
$$30 \ \text{LET A} = \text{PI}*\text{R} \uparrow 2$$
$$50 \ \text{END}$$

**9.** 40 PRINT A,R,PI

**10.** 40 PRINT A;R,PI

**11.** 40 PRINT A;R;PI

**12.** 40 PRINT A;R;"∧";PI

**13.** 40 PRINT A;"∧";R;"∧";PI

**14.** 40 PRINT A
42 PRINT "∧",R
44 PRINT "∧","∧",PI

**15.** 40 PRINT A
42 PRINT "∧";R
44 PRINT "∧";"∧";PI

**16.** 40 PRINT A
42 PRINT "∧";R
44 PRINT "∧∧";PI

**Use your answers to Activities 9-16 to answer the following questions.**

**17.** Which activity contains a statement which caused your computer to print spaces between A, R, and PI?

**18.** What are the rules your computer uses for semicolons? Consult your manual to check your answer.

**Combine the PRINT statements in Activities 19-25 with the statements below. Write the output for your computer, indicating all spaces before and between values. Then enter and run each set of statements on your computer. Compare the output you wrote with the computer's output.**

$$10 \ \text{LET P} = -.23$$
$$20 \ \text{LET Q} = 6$$
$$40 \ \text{END}$$

**19.** 30 PRINT P;Q

**20.** 30 PRINT Q;P

**21.** 30 PRINT P;"∧";Q

**22.** 30 PRINT Q;"∧";P;

**23.** 30 PRINT "∧∧";P;"∧";Q

**24.** 30 PRINT "∧∧";Q;"∧∧";P

**25.** 30 PRINT "∧∧";Q,"∧∧";P

# PASCAL

# NUMBER NOTATION

There are similarities and differences between number notation in *Pascal* and in BASIC.

Integers in *Pascal* are written without commas or decimal points.

| Valid integers | Invalid integers |
|---|---|
| 0 | 0. |
| 25 | 25. |
| 29043 | 29,043 |

In *Pascal*, there is a maximum and a minimum value allowed for integers. The value varies among computers. Exceeding these limits causes an error message.

In BASIC, 25*2.5 is a valid expression. *Pascal* does not allow operations between an integer and a number in any other form.

There are two forms of real numbers used in *Pascal*. The first is decimal form. A real number in decimal form is written without commas and with a decimal point. There must be at least one digit before a decimal point and at least one digit after a decimal point.

| Valid decimals | Invalid decimals | |
|---|---|---|
| 39.0 | 39. | No digit follows the decimal point. |
| 0.3167 | .3167 | No digit precedes the decimal point. |
| 2367.5 | 2,367.5 | Comma not allowed. |

The second form of a real number in *Pascal* is similar to E-form in BASIC.

| Scientific Notation | *Pascal* E-form |
|---|---|
| $2.6374 \times 10^7$ | 2.6374E7 |
| $-5 \times 10^{-12}$ | −5.0E−12 |
| $7.5 \times 10^{10}$ | 7.5E10 |

Since mixed real number and integer expressions are not allowed in *Pascal*, it is important to be aware of the acceptable forms of these numbers.

## Exercises

Tell whether each of the following is valid or invalid in *Pascal*. If invalid, tell why.

1. .5
2. 3.E10
3. 0.14732
4. 26000
5. $1.32 \times 10^{-4}$
6. 1,000,000
7. .000000125
8. 1.3E15
9. .154E10
10. −4.321E−15
11. 3,678.6
12. 643.

13. How would you write a valid *Pascal* expression for the BASIC expression 25*2.5?

# 2.5 COMPUTER PROGRAMS

Kaleb Fisher's father loaned him money to buy a car. Kaleb found the car he needed for $1,864, including tax. His father loaned him the money at 5% interest and gave him two years to pay back the loan. How much interest will Kaleb pay his father over the two year period? How much will Kaleb actually pay for the car including the interest?

Problems of this type can be solved using a computer program. A **program** is a sequence of instructions to a computer for solving a problem. The following example shows a program which will solve the problem stated above.

---

**EXAMPLE 1**

| | |
|---|---|
| 10 LET P = 1864 | P represents the principal. |
| 20 LET R = .05 | R represents the annual interest rate. |
| 30 LET T = 2 | T represents the time in years. |
| 40 LET I = P*R*T | I represents the interest. |
| 50 LET TC = P+I | TC represents the total cost. |
| 60 PRINT I, TC | |
| 70 END | |
| RUN | After RUN is entered, the output is |
| 186.4          2050.4 | displayed. |

---

In Example 1, the program was listed and then the output was displayed below the program. It is also possible to erase the program from the screen before the output is printed. This is called *clearing the screen.* The keyword for clearing the screen differs among BASICs. The following example shows the program in Example 1 with a "clear screen" statement.

---

**EXAMPLE 2**

5   Type in the keyword to clear the screen
10 LET P = 1864
20 LET R = .05
30 LET T = 2
40 LET I = P*R*T                    Even though the program will be cleared
50 LET TC = P+I                     from the screen, it still remains in the
60 PRINT I,TC                       computer's memory.
70 END
RUN
186.4          2050.4

---

Kaleb's next door neighbor, Rita Pruitt, made a similar deal with her father to buy a car. Her car cost $2,768, including tax. Her father loaned the money to her at 6% interest and gave her three years to pay back the loan. Kaleb used his computer to figure Rita's interest and total cost. The following example shows how Kaleb modified his program to figure Rita's interest and total cost.

## EXAMPLE 3

```
5    Keyword to clear screen
10 LET P = 2768          Lines 10, 20, and 30 are changed to
20 LET R = .06           use the new data.
30 LET T = 3
40 LET I = P*R*T
50 LET TC = P+I
60 PRINT I, TC
70 END
RUN
498.24              3266.24
```

Rita and Kaleb decided to write a program to do both problems and to identify each person's interest and total cost in the output.

## EXAMPLE 4

```
5    Keyword to clear screen
10 LET P = 2768
20 LET R = .06
30 LET T = 3
40 LET I = P*R*T
50 LET TC = P+I
60 PRINT "RITA'S INTEREST AND TOTAL COST"
70 PRINT I, TC
80 LET P = 1864
90 LET R = .05
100 LET T = 2
110 LET I = P*R*T
120 LET TC = P+I
130 PRINT "KALEB'S INTEREST AND TOTAL COST"
140 PRINT I, TC
150 END
RUN
RITA'S INTEREST AND TOTAL COST
498.24              3266.24
KALEB'S INTEREST AND TOTAL COST    The computer does not print the
186.4               2050.4          final zeros in either number.
```

# Exercises

1. What is a purpose of the "clear screen" statement?
2. What is the keyword in your BASIC for the "clear screen" statement?

**Use the following program to answer Exercises 3-7.**

```
10 Keyword to clear screen
20 LET X = 25
30 LET S = X↑2
40 PRINT X,S
50 END
```

3. What is the purpose of line 10?  4. What value is stored in X?
5. What value is stored in S?        6. What is the purpose of line 50?
7. What is the output of this program?

**Use the following program to answer Exercises 8-12.**

```
10 Keyword to clear screen
20 LET C = 32.67          C represents the cost of 9 lb of coffee.
30 LET L = 9              L represents pounds.
40 LET Z = 16            Z represents ounces.
50 LET P = C/L           P represents the cost per pound.
60 LET U = P/Z           U represents the cost per ounce.
70 PRINT C
80 PRINT P
90 PRINT U
100 END
```

8. What value is stored in P?        9. What value is stored in U?
10. What is the output of this program?
11. What line numbers could be used to insert a line between lines 70 and 80?
12. Change the program so a line will be skipped after each line printed.

**Use the problem below to answer Exercises 13-18.**

Martha Meder wanted to write a program to compute her wages each week. One week she worked 40 hours and made $5.38 an hour. Her total deductions for the week were $43.04.

13. Write three LET statements to represent Martha's hourly wage (H), total hours worked(T), and total deductions for the week (D). Number the lines 10, 20, and 30.
14. Use the formula G=T*H in a LET statement to compute Martha's gross pay. Number the line 40.

**15.** Use the formula N=G−D in a LET statement to compute Martha's net pay. Number the line 50.

**16.** Write a PRINT statement that will print Martha's gross pay for the week. Number the line 60.

**17.** Write a PRINT statement that will skip a line. Number the line 70.

**18.** Write a PRINT statement that will print Martha's net pay for the week. Number the line 80.

**Write the output of each program.**

**19.**
```
10 LET A = 15
20 LET B = 3
30 LET C = (A+B)/B
40 PRINT C
50 END
```

**20.**
```
10 LET A = 15
20 LET B = 3
30 LET C = (A−B)/B
40 PRINT C
50 END
```

**21.**
```
10 LET A = 15
20 LET B = 3
30 LET C = (A+B)/B↑2
40 PRINT C
50 END
```

**22.**
```
10 LET W = 4
20 LET X = 3
30 LET Y = 2
40 LET Z = (Y−W)*(Y+X)
50 PRINT Z
60 END
```

**23.**
```
10 LET W = 3
20 LET X = W↑2
30 LET Y = 2*W
40 LET Z = W+X+Y
50 PRINT Z
60 END
```

**24.**
```
10 LET W = 3
20 LET X = 4*W
30 LET Y = X↑3
40 LET Z = Y/(X−W)
50 PRINT Z
60 END
```

# Laboratory Activities

1. Enter and run the program for Exercises **3-7**. Use the output to check your answers to Exercises **5** and **7**.

2. Enter and run the program for Exercises **8-12**. Use the output to check your answers to Exercises **8-10**.

3. Enter the statements you wrote for Exercises **13-18** into your computer. Add an END statement and a statement to clear the screen. Run the program. Without reentering the program, run it again.

4. Change LET statements 10, 20, and 30 in Activity **3** using T=35, H=8.75, and D=61.25. Run the program.

**Enter and run each of the programs in Activities 5-8. Check your output against the output shown below each program.**

**5.** NEW
    5 **Keyword to clear screen**
    10 LET T1 = 87
    20 LET T2 = 93
    30 LET T3 = 72
    40 LET TA = (T1+T2+T3)/3
    50 PRINT TA
    60 END
    RUN
    84

**6.** NEW
    5 **Keyword to clear screen**
    10 LET P = 810.25
    20 LET R = .08
    30 LET I = P*R
    40 LET T = P+I
    50 PRINT I
    60 PRINT T
    70 END
    RUN
    64.82
    875.07

**7.** NEW
    5 **Keyword to clear screen**
    10 LET A = 3
    20 LET B = 5
    30 LET C = (A+B)*(A−B)
    40 LET D = C ↑ 2/(A+B) ↑ 2
    50 LET E = (A+B)/(A−B)
    60 PRINT D
    70 PRINT E
    80 END
    RUN
    4
    −4

**8.** NEW
    5 **Keyword to clear screen**
    10 LET X = 2
    20 LET Y = 3
    30 LET P = X ↑ Y
    40 LET Q = (X+1) ↑ Y
    50 LET R = (X+1) ↑ Y/Y
    60 PRINT P
    70 PRINT Q, R
    80 END
    RUN
    8
    27             9

**9.** The weekly salaries of five workers are listed below in LET statements 10-50.

    10 LET A1 = 328.75
    20 LET A2 = 388.20
    30 LET A3 = 400.00
    40 LET A4 = 300.80
    50 LET A5 = 450.25

Write and run a program that will compute the average pay of the five workers (average = sum of wages of all workers divided by the number of workers). Have the computer print each wage on a separate line and print the average of the wages on the last line.

**10.** The following program computes the area (A) of a rectangle where the length (L) and the width (W) are given.

    10 LET L = 17
    20 LET W = 12
    30 LET A = L*W
    40 PRINT L,W,A
    50 END

Enter and run the program.

11. Using Activity **10** as a model, write and run a program to compute the volume (V) of a box. The length (L) of the box is 8 ft, the width (W) is 4 ft, and the height (H) is 6 ft.

12. Write and run a program to compute the area (A) of a triangle. The base (B) is 6 cm and the height (H) is 9 cm.

13. Write and run a program to compute the average (A) of five test scores. The scores are 89, 87, 72, 93, and 84.

14. Write and run a program to compute a yearly interest (I) on a bank account. The principal (P) is $2,899.32. The interest rate (R) is $6\frac{3}{4}$% (0.0675).

15. Write and run a program to compute an electric bill (B) for one month. The cost (C) of electricity is $0.097 per kWh. The amount (A) of electricity used during the month is 610 kWh.

# 2.6  EDITING AND DEBUGGING PROGRAMS

The command LIST will be one of the most useful commands you learn. Entering the **LIST command** causes all program lines stored in read-write memory to scroll onto the screen in numerical order.

## EXAMPLE 1

```
10 LET N = 2
20 LET R = N+1
30 PRINT N,R
40 END
LIST
10 LET N = 2
20 LET R = N+1
30 PRINT N,R
40 END
```

**Lines 10–40 are entered.**

**The LIST command causes the program to scroll onto the screen just as you entered it. (On some computers the spacing may change.)**

Entering the command LIST causes the program lines to be displayed in numerical order, and the computer executes them in that order. However, you can type and enter lines in any order, as long as they are numbered in the order in which they should be executed.

---

**EXAMPLE 2**

30 PRINT N,R
10 LET N = 2                          Lines 10-40 are entered in any order.
40 END
20 LET R = N+1
LIST                                  The program scrolls onto the screen
10 LET N = 2                          exactly as in Example 1.
20 LET R = N+1
30 PRINT N,R
40 END

---

Errors in a program are called **bugs** and correcting them is called **debugging**. The command LIST is useful when you are debugging a program. If an error is detected by the computer, the computer will usually tell you the kind of error and the line it is in. However, not all computers give the same error messages. The following examples show some typical error messages.

---

**EXAMPLE 3**

10 LET X = 1/(4−2*2)
20 PRINT X
30 END
RUN
DIVISION BY ZERO IN 10               An expression in line 10 has a divisor of
                                     zero.

This error can occur because a zero is entered as a divisor, as a result of a calculation, or because a variable divisor was not assigned a value.

---

**EXAMPLE 4**

10 LET D = 1000 ↑ 100
20 PRINT D
30 END
RUN
OVERFLOW ERROR IN 10                 The result of a calculation in line 10 is too
                                     large for the computer to express in
                                     BASIC number notation.

Not all computers handle the same range of numbers, so a result that causes an overflow in one computer may not cause an overflow in another.

---

If the result was too small to express in BASIC notation, it would be given as 0 and no message would appear.

## EXAMPLE 5

Suppose the program in Example 4 is in memory, and the command
LIST 20 is entered.

```
LIST 20
20 PRINT D
```

LIST 20 causes just line 20 to be displayed.

---

Suppose a program with line numbers from 10 to 150 was in memory.
The command LIST 30, 70 (or, in some BASICs, LIST 30–70) would cause
lines 30 and 70 and all lines with numbers between 30 and 70 to be
displayed.

> LIST causes all numbered lines in read-write memory to be
> displayed.
> LIST *n* causes line *n* to be displayed.
> LIST *m,n* ( or LIST *m-n*) causes lines *m*, *n*, and all lines with numbers
> between *m* and *n* to be displayed.

After a line is displayed, and you have located the bug and decided how to
correct it, you can do one of the following.

1. Retype the entire line correctly. (This is good for short, simple
   lines but not so good for long or complicated lines.)
2. Edit the displayed line.

With some computers, editing is done by moving the cursor to the
beginning of the line and using the copy and delete keys. Other computers
have special editing modes or keys.

*Many programming errors do not produce error messages and can only
be found by careful testing.* This is done using values for which the correct
result is known. The computer result is then compared with the known result.
Testing may take days for a large business or scientific program, but it is a
very important method of debugging.

---

## EXAMPLE 6

The program on the right has the
known values N = 0, P = 0 and
N = 2, P = 14.

```
10 LET N = 0
20 LET M = 9
30 LET P = N*(N−M)
40 PRINT P
50 END
```

Test N = 0 to see if P = 0.
RUN
0 ←———— Correct value

Test N = 2 to see if P = 14
10 LET N = 2  **Retype line 10.**
RUN
−14 ←———— Incorrect value

To get the known value for P in both cases, line 30 should read as
follows.             30 LET P = N*(M−N)

You know that there are certain keys, especially on a time-sharing terminal, that you should not use, and others that you should use with caution. There are also certain words in BASIC that must be used with caution. One of these, of course, is NEW (or SCRATCH), which erases any program in memory. DEL (or DELETE) and CLEAR can also have unfortunate results in many computers, and there may be other words that should be used with caution with your particular computer.

If your BASIC allows more than two characters in variable names, you can use names that remind you of what the variable stands for. However, with many computers, you must be careful that BASIC keywords, such as END, LIST, PRINT, and so on, do not occur within the variable names. This is because the computer reads these character combinations and takes them as commands. Such keywords in BASIC are called **reserved words** because they have special uses for which they are reserved.

---

**EXAMPLE 7**

```
10 LET SON = 1000
20 PRINT SON
30 END
RUN
SYNTAX ERROR IN LINE 10
LIST 10
10 LET S ON = 1000
```

**ON is a reserved word.**

**Some computers set off the reserved word when the line is listed.**

---

# Exercises

1. What command tells a computer to display program lines?
2. Does the command in Exercise **1** cause the computer to display the lines in the order in which they were entered?
3. What is the order in which a computer executes program lines?
4. What are bugs?
5. What does debugging a program accomplish?
6. What command tells a computer to display just one program line?
7. What command tells a computer to display two program lines and all lines with numbers between their numbers?
8. What are two ways to correct a bug?
9. What method of editing can you use with your computer?
10. How can you find an error in a program when an error message is not produced?

**11.** Why must some BASIC commands be used with caution?

**12.** What is a reserved word in BASIC?

**13.** Which of the following are important for a program to be run successfully?

**a.** syntax

**b.** removing bugs

**c.** the order in which lines are entered

**d.** the order in which lines are executed

**e.** correcting typing errors

**f.** testing with values that give known results.

# Laboratory Activities

**1.** Enter and run the programs in Examples 1-5 and compare your results with those given.

**Combine the statements in Activities 2-4 with the statements below. Enter and run each set of statements. Tell what error message your computer gives.**

```
10 LET S = 10
30 PRINT T
40 END
```

**2.** 20 LET 1/S = T

**3.** 20 LET T = S/(5−2*2.5)

**4.** 20 LET T = S ↑ (S ↑ 3)

**Enter each program in Activities 5-8 as shown. List the program and correct any typing errors. Then run the program and tell what error message is displayed and why.**

**5.** 20 LET X = 1/(M*2−2*M)
30 PRINT X
40 END
10 LET M = 6

**6.** 10 LET A = 999
30 PRINT A,B
40 END
20 LET B = A ↑ A

**7.** 20 LET N = 10 ↑ D
10 LET D = 10 ↑ 10
30 PRINT N
40 END

**8.** 10 LET R = T+2
30 END
8  LET T = 1/S
2  PRINT R

**Enter each program in Activities 9-12 as shown. List the program and correct any typing errors. Then run the program and correct the bug indicated by the error message. Run the corrected program.**

**9.** 10 LET A = 3
20 LET A+B = C
30 PRINT C ·
15 LET B = 2
40 END

**10.** 10 LET S = T ↑ D/T
20 LET T = 10
30 LET D = 30
40 PRINT S
50 END

**11.** 10 LET X = 5
20 LET Y = X/Z
40 END
30 PRINT Y

**12.** 20 LET A = (A+C)C
30 PRINT A
15 LET A = 2
10 LET C = 6
40 END

**Enter each program in Activities 13-16 as shown. Test each program using the given known values. If there is a bug in the program, find and correct it, and then test the corrected program.**

**13.** C = 9, D = 9, A = 0
C = 9, D = 6, A = −1
10 LET C = 9
20 LET D = 9
30 LET A = (C−D)/3
40 PRINT A
50 END

**14.** X = 5, Y = 1, Z = 3125
X = 4, Y = 2, Z = 16
10 LET X = 5
20 LET Y = 1
30 LET Z = X ↑ X/Y
40 PRINT Z
50 END

**15.** M = 2, N = 5, P = 4
M = 6, N = 2, P = 30
10 LET M = 2
20 LET N = 5
30 LET P = M*(10/N)
40 PRINT P
50 END

**16.** A = 3, B = 3, C = 3
A = 4, B = 2, C = 8
10 LET A = 3
20 LET B = 3
30 LET C = B ↑ 2/A
40 PRINT C
50 END

**17.** Find out from your manual or your teacher what words must be used with caution with your computer. Make a list of these words.

**18.** If your BASIC has reserved words, find out from your manual or your teacher what they are and make a list of them. If your BASIC allows more than two characters in variable names, list for each reserved word at least one longer word that contains the reserved word. Use some of these longer words (one at a time) to replace SON in the program in Example 7. Record how the computer prints each word.

## Vocabulary

PRINT (33)

E-form (36)

command (41)

string (41)

END (42)

RUN (42)

statement (42)

NEW (44)

variable (48)

LET (48)

program (54)

LIST (59)

bug (60)

debug (60)

reserved words (62)

## Chapter Summary

1. Some symbols in BASIC differ from those in arithmetic. For example, 2∗3 means 2 times 3, 2/3 means 2 divided by 3, and 2 ↑ 3 means 2 raised to the power 3. Addition (+) and subtraction (−) symbols are the same in BASIC and arithmetic.

2. The order of operations in BASIC and arithmetic is the same. The order of operations is given below.

   All operations in parentheses are performed first, from the innermost parentheses outward, using the three steps below. If no parentheses appear in an expression, use the three steps in order.

   **First:**    Evaluate powers.

   **Second:**  Do multiplications and divisions from left to right.

   **Third:**    Do additions and subtractions from left to right.

3. A computer can be used in calculator mode to evaluate expressions using PRINT as a command. For example, entering PRINT 2∗3/6 would cause a computer to display a 1.

4. The three forms of numbers used in BASIC are integer form, decimal form, and exponential form, or E-form. Numbers in BASIC are *never* written with commas. Changing numbers from one form to another is a necessary skill for computer users.

5. A PRINT command can be used to display a string, such as a name. The string must be within quotation marks. A more practical way to print a string is with a PRINT statement. (A PRINT command with a line number is called a PRINT statement.) An entire letter can be displayed using several PRINT statements.

6. An END statement tells the computer that no more statements follow. It is the last line in a program.

7. The RUN command is a signal to a computer to execute a program.

8. Misspelling keywords such as PRINT, END, and RUN, using incorrect punctuation, or using parentheses improperly usually causes a syntax error message to be printed.

9. The NEW command is used to clear read-write memory.

10. In most BASICs, a variable may be a single letter of the alphabet. In some BASICs, a variable may also be a letter followed by one of the following.

    1. Just one additional character (a letter or a single digit from 0 to 9).
    2. One or more additional characters (up to a limit that varies with the BASIC), and all characters are read by the computer.
    3. One or more additional characters (up to a limit that varies with the BASIC), and only the first two characters are read by the computer.

11. A LET statement has a line number, the keyword LET, and a variable that is assigned a value with an equals sign (=). In BASIC, the equals sign has a meaning different from its meaning in algebra. A computer finds the value of the expression on the right-hand side of an equals sign and stores that value in a location it assigns to the variable on the left-hand side.

12. When used in PRINT statements, the comma (,) and the semicolon (;) have different functions. When strings, expressions, variables, or values are separated by commas, the output is printed in zones; when they are separated by semicolons, the output is printed close together.

13. The keyword for clearing the screen can be used to clear a program from the screen before the output is printed.

14. The LIST command causes all program lines stored in the read-write memory to scroll onto the screen in numerical order.

15. Debugging is a process of locating and correcting errors (bugs).

16. Some error messages in BASIC are OVERFLOW, DIVISION BY 0, and SYNTAX ERROR.

17. A bug can be corrected by retyping the entire line correctly or by editing the line.

## Chapter Test

**Write an expression in BASIC for each of the following.**

**1.** $3 + 7(5-6)$ 

**2.** $4 \cdot 3^2$

**3.** $\dfrac{5 - 3}{3 \times 4}$ 

**4.** $3^5 \times 4 \div (5+6)$

## Evaluate each BASIC expression.

**5.** 3+4/2+5      **6.** 2↑3*2−3+12/4

**7.** 6−(3+4↑2)+2*(−4)−12      **8.** 3*(6↑2/3)+10*4

## Write each number in BASIC notation.

**9.** 1,387      **10.** 0.2357

**11.** $2.65 \times 10^6$      **12.** $-1.11238 \times 10^{-4}$

## Write each number in scientific notation and E-form.

**13.** −2,000,000      **14.** 0.0000000143

**15.** 365.387      **16.** 10,000

## Write each number in decimal form and in E-form.

**17.** $0.6503 \times 10^6$      **18.** $6.003 \times 10^{-4}$

**19.** $-0.000367514 \times 10^8$      **20.** $-278.375 \times 10^3$

**21.** What is the difference between the PRINT statement and the PRINT command?

**22.** What is a purpose of the END statement? Is it necessary in all BASICs?

**23.** What is the purpose of the RUN command?

**24.** Write PRINT statements that would display the following output in the form shown.

        THIS IS

              PRINTED ON

                      THREE LINES.

## Find and correct the errors in the following PRINT statements.

**25.** 1Ø PRINT A      **26.** 1Ø PRENT X,Y

**27.** 2Ø PRINT "WHY"?      **28.** 3Ø WRITE 2

**29.** 4Ø PRINT 3(6+4)      **30.** 5Ø PRINT 36/(3*(5+6)

## Tell whether each variable name is valid or invalid. If invalid, tell why.

**31.** A*      **32.** A1      **33.** 1A

**34.** A      **35.** AA      **36.** A+

## Write each formula below using a LET statement.

**37.** $C = (3.14)r$      **38.** $A = \frac{1}{2}h(b_1+b_2)$

**39.** $S = \frac{a-b}{c-d}$      **40.** $y = x^2+3x+4$

**41.** $m = (n-2)(n+3)^2$      **42.** $V = \frac{1}{3}(3.14)r^2A$

**Find and correct the errors in the following LET statements.**

**43.** $10$ LET $3 \uparrow Y = X$

**44.** $50$ LET $A = 2(M+N)$

**45.** $40$ LET $P = Q \div S$

**46.** $20$ LIT $B = 3+C$

**Find the value of X in line 20 for each of the following.**

**47.** $10$ LET $X = 5$
$20$ LET $X = 2*X+X$

**48.** $10$ LET $A = -7$
$15$ LET $B = A+3$
$20$ LET $X = -3*A+-5*B$

**49.** $10$ LET $Y = 4$
$15$ LET $Z = Y*2$
$20$ LET $X = -3*(Z/Y) \uparrow 3$

**50.** $5$ LET $M = -10$
$10$ LET $N = M \uparrow 2$
$20$ LET $X = ((N/M)*2)-M$

**Write the output for each of the following PRINT statements, indicating all spaces.**

**51.** $10$ PRINT "MY", "NAME", "IS"
**52.** $10$ PRINT "MY"; "NAME"; "IS"

**53.** Write the output for the following program, indicating all spaces.

$10$ LET $A1 = 12$
$20$ LET $B1 = -5$
$30$ LET $B2 = 0$
$40$ LET $A2 = 1$
$50$ LET $A3 = A1+A2$
$60$ LET $A4 = A1/A2$
$70$ LET $B1 = B1+A1*B2$
$80$ LET $A5 = B2+1$
$90$ PRINT $A1,A2,A3$
$100$ PRINT $B1;"\wedge";B2$
$110$ PRINT $A4$
$120$ PRINT $"\wedge",A5$
$130$ END

**54.** Change the program in problem **53** so a line will be skipped after each printed line.

**55.** What is the purpose of the NEW command?

**56.** Write a program to compute the perimeter (P) of a rectangle. The length (L) is 24 cm and the width (W) is 35 cm. Have the computer print the values for P, L, and W in zones on one line.

**57.** Change the program in problem **56** so the values for P, L, and W will be printed on three lines.

**58.** Write a program to compute the area (A) of a square. The length of each side (S) is 7 cm. Have the computer print the values for A and S in zones on one line.

59. Write a program to compute the average (AV) of four bowling scores. The scores are 112, 97, 132, and 103.

60. What does it mean to "debug" a program?

61. When an error in a program does not produce an error message, how can the error be found?

62. Write the statements below in the order they would scroll onto the screen if they were followed by a LIST command.

$$25 \text{ LET } X = X+1$$
$$10 \text{ LET } X = 0$$
$$30 \text{ PRINT } X,A$$
$$50 \text{ END}$$

63. The program in problem 62 contains an error. Identify the error and correct it.

**Use each line in problems 64-67 with the lines below. Write the error message that your computer would print if the program were entered and run.**

$$10 \text{ LET } X = 20$$
$$30 \text{ PRINT } Y$$
$$40 \text{ END}$$

64. $20 \text{ LET } Y = X/(X-20)$

65. $20 \text{ LET } Y+1 = X+20$

66. $20 \text{ LET } Y = X \uparrow X \uparrow X$

67. $20 \text{ LET } X*5 = Y$

**Each of the programs below contains an error. Identify the error and correct it. Then write the output of the corrected program.**

68.
```
10 LET R = 150
20 LET T = R*3
30 LET S = (T-R)/2*3)
40 LET V = T-S
50 PRINT S
60 PRINT
70 PRINT V
80 END
```

69.
```
10 LET T1 = 100
20 LET T2 = 95
30 LET T3 = 84
40 LET T4 = 81
50 LET A = (T1+T2+T3+T4)/4
60 PRNT A
70 END
```

70.
```
10 LET X = 5
20 LET Y = X ↑ 2
30 LTE Z = 2*Y+X
40 PRINT Y;Z
50 END
```

71.
```
30 LET B = 10
50 LET B*X = N
10 LET X = -3
20 LET A = 4
40 LET M = A*X ↑ 2
60 LET Y = M+N+X
70 PRINT Y
80 END
```

# COMPUTER LITERACY

Internally a digital computer uses only two digits—0 and 1. These two digits (bits) are used in a base two, or binary, number system.

**Powers of Two**

$2^0 = 1$     $2^4 = 16$
$2^1 = 2$     $2^5 = 32$
$2^2 = 4$     $2^6 = 64$
$2^3 = 8$     $2^7 = 128$

In this binary system, each place-value position is a power of two. To find the value of a binary number in base ten, multiply the bit in each place value by the corresponding power of two, and add.

$$(101011)_2 = (1 \times 2^5) + (0 \times 2^4) + (1 \times 2^3) + (0 \times 2^2) + (1 \times 2^1) + (1 \times 2^0)$$
$$= (1 \times 32) + 0 + (1 \times 8) + 0 + (1 \times 2) + (1 \times 1)$$
$$= 32 + 8 + 2 + 1$$
$$= 43$$

Thus the binary number 101011 is the same as 43 in base ten.

Bits are the alphabet of machine language. To see how a computer uses this language, a simple analogy will help.

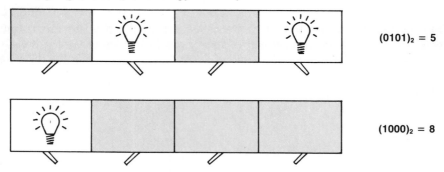

$(0101)_2 = 5$

$(1000)_2 = 8$

Imagine that a light bulb is used to represent a bit. When the bulb is on (current is flowing) it represents one, and when it is off (current is not flowing) it represents zero.

If several bulbs are arranged in a row, then each bulb can stand for a place-value position. In this way, the row of bulbs is used to represent different numbers.

This rather simple concept is the basis of modern computers. Of course, a computer does not contain rows of light bulbs. But it does contain a large number of tiny electronic switches.

# BINARY NUMBERS

Imagine that a computer is instructed to add two numbers, 5 and 8. The switches representing the two numbers are arranged as shown below.

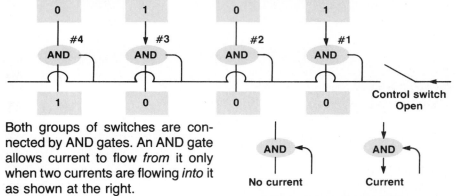

Both groups of switches are connected by AND gates. An AND gate allows current to flow *from* it only when two currents are flowing *into* it as shown at the right.

When the control switch is closed, current is sent into each AND gate. Since AND gates two and four only receive current through the control switch, no current flows from them. But AND gates one and three receive current through the control switch *and* the upper group of switches. Current flows from these gates causing two of the lower switches to change as shown below.

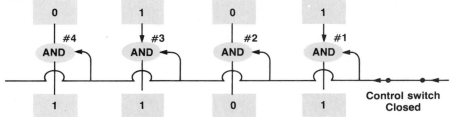

Notice that the bottom row of switches now represents 13, the sum of 5 and 8.

A computer is actually far more complex than this simple arrangement of AND gates and switches. (The above arrangement does not even have a 'carry' needed to do many addition problems.) However, this is basically how a computer works.

Computers are used in weather centers to help monitor and predict weather conditions. Many different computer programs are used in such centers, and each program may be used many times. Using computers helps the weather center provide better service to the public.

# PUTTING THE COMPUTER TO WORK

If a new program had to be written each time a calculation was to be performed, computers would not be very useful. However, one program can be written to solve a large number of similar problems. The program can then be stored on a magnetic tape or disk so it can be used again. In this chapter you will learn how to write some programs of this type and how to store the programs on a tape or disk.

## 3.1 READ/DATA STATEMENTS

There are several ways to enter information into a computer. In Chapter 2, LET statements were used to enter numbers into a computer. **READ/DATA statements** can also be used to enter numbers.

---

**EXAMPLE 1**

| **Program using**<br>**LET statements** | **Program using**<br>**READ/DATA statements** |
|---|---|
| 10 LET P = 1864 | 10 READ P,R,T |
| 20 LET R = .05 | 20 DATA 1864, .05, 2 |
| 30 LET T = 2 | 40 LET I = P*R*T |
| 40 LET I = P*R*T | 50 PRINT I |
| 50 PRINT I | 60 END |
| 60 END | |

---

In the example above, lines 10, 20, and 30 in the program on the left are replaced by lines 10 and 20 in the program on the right. Both programs have the same output.

In a program using READ/DATA statements, the variables in the READ statement are assigned locations in memory, and the numbers in the DATA statement are stored, in order, at those locations. In the example the first number, 1864, is stored at the location assigned to the first variable, P, the second number, .05, is stored at R, and the third number, 2, is stored at T.

Some important facts about READ/DATA statements are given below.

| **READ** | **DATA** |
|---|---|

1. Variables appear in READ statements.

| | | |
|---|---|---|
| 10 READ A,B,C | right |
| 10 READ 5,4,2 | wrong |

1. Values for variables appear in DATA statements.

| | | |
|---|---|---|
| 20 DATA 4,9 | right |
| 20 DATA 4,A | wrong |

2. Variables are separated by commas.

| | | |
|---|---|---|
| 10 READ X,Y,Z,E | right |
| 10 READ X Y Z;E | wrong |

2. Values are separated by commas.

| | | |
|---|---|---|
| 20 DATA 1,2,3,4 | right |
| 20 DATA 1,2 3,4 | wrong |

3. A comma is not used after READ.

| | | |
|---|---|---|
| 10 READ X,Y | right |
| 10 READ, X,Y | wrong |

3. A comma is not used after DATA.

| | | |
|---|---|---|
| 20 DATA 50,23,25 | right |
| 20 DATA, 50,23,25 | wrong |

4. A line number is required.

| | | |
|---|---|---|
| 10 READ X | right |
| READ X | wrong |

4. A line number is required.

| | | |
|---|---|---|
| 20 DATA 1,5,8,9 | right |
| DATA 1,5,8,9 | wrong |

5. The READ statement must be in the logical place for assigning values to the variables.

5. DATA statements may appear anywhere in a program prior to the END statement.

6. If there is a READ statement, there must be at least one DATA statement.

6. If there is a DATA statement, there must be at least one READ statement.

7. Any number of READ statements may be used, as long as there are no more variables in READ statements than there are values in DATA statements.

7. Any number of DATA statements may be used, as long as there are at least as many values in DATA statements as there are variables in READ statements.

| | |
|---|---|
| 10 READ X1,X2,X3 <br> 20 DATA 5,6,10 | right |
| 10 READ X1,X2,X3 <br> 20 DATA 5,6 | wrong |

Money in a savings account generally earns compound interest. Using READ/DATA statements, a program can be written to calculate the interest earned on $1,000, if the annual rate is 6%, the time invested is one year, and the interest is compounded semiannually (twice a year).

## EXAMPLE 2

The following program can be used to figure the interest for the first six months.

| | |
|---|---|
| 10 LET AI=1000 | **AI represents the amount invested.** |
| 20 READ P,R,T | **P, R, and T represent principal, rate, and** |
| 30 DATA 1000,.06,.5 | **time.** |
| 40 LET I=P*R*T | |
| 50 LET NP=P+I | **I represents the interest for 6 months.** |
| 60 LET TI=NP−AI | **NP represents the new principal.** |
| 70 PRINT NP,I,TI | **TI represents the total interest.** |
| 80 END | |
| RUN | |
| 1030      30      30 | |

To use the same program to figure the interest for the next 6 months, the value for P(principal) in line 30 must be replaced with the value of NP.

| | |
|---|---|
| 30 DATA 1030,.06,.5 | **1030 replaces 1000.** |
| RUN | |
| 1060.9      30.9      60.9 | **The total interest is $60.90 .** |

Since only one value, the value for P, is changed, it is a good idea to put it in a separate DATA statement.

| | |
|---|---|
| 30 DATA 1000  ←——————————— | **Only this value is replaced.** |
| 35 DATA .06,.5  ←——————————— | **There is no need to retype these also.** |

# Exercises

1. What information should appear after the keyword READ? After the keyword DATA?

2. Where in a program may a READ statement be located? Where may a DATA statement be located?

**Find and correct the error in each of the READ/DATA statements below.**

3. 10 DATE 6.5,3.4,7.3
   20 READ A,B,C

4. 10 DATA 10,2,4
   10 READ X,Y,Z

5. 10 READ X1,Y1,Z1,A1
   20 DATA 5,10,15

6. 10 READ A,B,C,D,E,
   20 DATA 1,2,3,4,5

7. 10 READ, M,N,P,Q,R
   20 DATA 10,9,8,7,6

8. 10 DATA A,B,C
   20 READ 20,30,40

9. 10 DATA $1,$2,$3
   20 READ D1,D2,D3

10. 10 READ A,B,C,D
    20 DATA 13,32 15,33

11. READ M,N
    DATA 7.2,9.8

12. 10 DATA 6,4,10
    20 READ A;B;C

### Find and correct the error in each of the following programs.

**13.** 10 LET A=3*Y
20 LET D=X−6
30 READ X,Y
40 DATA 3,4
50 PRINT A;D
60 END

**14.** 10 READ X,Y
20 LET W=X+Y
30 LET X=(W−Y)↑2
40 PRINT W,X
50 DATA,2,3
60 END

### Rewrite each of the following programs using READ/DATA statements.

**15.** 10 LET A=3
20 LET B=4
30 LET C=B↑A
40 LET D=C/8
50 PRINT D
60 END

**16.** 10 LET A=3
20 LET B=4
30 LET C=5
40 LET D=(B+C)/A
50 PRINT D
60 END

**17.** 10 LET M=16
20 LET N=M*3
30 LET P=N/12
40 LET Q=M+N+P
50 PRINT Q,P,N
60 END

**18.** 10 LET M=5
20 LET N=2
30 LET Q=4
40 LET R=(M*N)↑Q
50 PRINT R
60 END

### Give the output of each of the following programs.

**19.** 10 READ R,Q,S
20 DATA 1,2,3
30 LET T=Q+R−S
40 PRINT T
50 END

**20.** 10 DATA 3,5,4
20 READ S,R,T
30 LET Q=S−R
40 PRINT T,Q
50 END

**21.** 10 DATA 51,17,4,3
20 READ Q,R,S,N
30 LET A=(Q+R+S)/N
40 PRINT "AVERAGE IS"
50 PRINT A
60 END

**22.** 10 READ A
20 PRINT A
30 READ V
40 PRINT V
50 LET C=A*V
60 PRINT C
70 DATA 4,5
80 END

**23.** 10 READ P,R,T
20 DATA 12000
30 DATA .1,2
40 LET I=P*R*T
50 PRINT "PRINCIPAL AND INTEREST ARE"
60 PRINT P,I
70 END

# Laboratory Activities ▬▬▬▬▬

1. Enter and run the programs in Example 1. Compare the outputs.

2. Enter and run the program in Example 2. Then replace the DATA statement as suggested in the example. What advantages are there in using the two DATA statements?

3. Enter and run each set of statements in Exercises **3-12.** Add a PRINT statement and an END statement. Record any error messages. Check your answers to the exercises by correcting each set and running it again.

4. Enter and run each program in Exercises **15-18.** Then check your answers to the exercises by entering and running each program as you rewrote it.

5. Enter and run each program in Exercises **19-23.** Use the output to check your answers to the exercises.

6. Rewrite the READ statement in the second program in Example 1 so the variables appear in the order R,P,T. Enter and run the program, making any other changes necessary to give the correct output.

7. Change the program in Example 2 so the output includes the following and, on the next line, only the value of TI. Enter and run the program.

$1000 AT 6% EARNS

8. Use the program in Example 2 to figure the interest on $1000 at 6% over 1.5 years, if the interest is compounded semiannually. (*Hint:* Change the DATA statement or statements twice.)

9. Use the program from Activity **7** to figure the interest over 2 years. Enter and run the program.

10. Change the program in Example 2 so the interest can be computed at 5%, 6%, or 7%. (*Hint:* Put the rate in a separate DATA statement.) Enter and run the program for each interest rate.

**Write a program using READ/DATA statements to solve each of the following problems. Enter and run each program.**

11. Find the average number of kilometers a car can be driven on a liter of gasoline if the car uses 28 liters in 350 km.

12. The formula for finding a pitcher's earned run average (ERA), given earned runs scored (ES) and innings pitched (P), is ERA=9·ES÷P. Find the ERA for pitchers with the following records: 2 runs in 9 innings; 7 runs in 54 innings; 42 runs in 70 innings. (*Hint:* Write a program to find one ERA, then change the DATA statements to find the others.)

13. Tickets for the school play cost $3 for students and $5.50 for adults. What is the total cost of 5 student tickets and 3 adult tickets? (Write the program so that either the cost of tickets or the number of tickets can be changed easily.)

# 3.2 INPUT STATEMENTS

An **INPUT statement** allows data to be entered into a computer during the execution of a program. When a computer comes to an INPUT statement, it stops executing the program and prints a question mark (?) to indicate that data should be entered. After the data are entered, the computer continues executing the program. The format of an INPUT statement is similar to that of a READ statement.

---

**EXAMPLE 1**

**Program using** | **Program using an**
**READ/DATA statements** | **INPUT statement**

```
10 READ P,R,T                10 INPUT P,R,T
20 DATA 1864,.05,2           30 LET I=P*R*T
30 LET I=P*R*T               40 PRINT I
40 PRINT I                   50 END
50 END                       RUN
RUN                          ? 1864.,05,2
186.4                        186.4
```

In the programs above, lines 10 and 20 in the program on the left are replaced by line 10 in the program on the right. The data for the program on the right are entered after the question mark and are separated by commas.

---

The data for the INPUT statement must be entered in the same order as the corresponding variables are listed in the INPUT statement. If not enough values are entered, the computer continues to print question marks until it is given enough data. If too many values are entered, the computer uses the first values entered and ignores the rest.

To change data in a program that uses READ/DATA statements, the DATA statements must be reentered. However, to change data in a program that uses INPUT statements, new values can be entered each time the program is run.

When INPUT statements are used, it is helpful to tell the person running the program what kinds of data are needed and in what order to enter them. This can be done using PRINT statements. The following examples show two ways of including such instructions in the program from Example 1.

---

**EXAMPLE 2**

```
5 PRINT "ENTER THE PRINCIPAL, RATE, AND TIME"     Final periods are often
7 PRINT "SEPARATED BY COMMAS"                      omitted.
```

```
10 INPUT P,R,T
30 LET I=P*R*T
40 PRINT I
50 END
RUN
ENTER THE PRINCIPAL, RATE, AND TIME
SEPARATED BY COMMAS
?1864,.05,2
186.4
```

Lines 5 and 7 cause these
instructions to be printed.

## EXAMPLE 3

```
5 PRINT "ENTER THE PRINCIPAL"
8 INPUT P
10 PRINT "ENTER THE RATE AS A DECIMAL"
15 INPUT R
18 PRINT "ENTER THE TIME IN YEARS"
20 INPUT T
30 LET I=P*R*T
40 PRINT I
50 END
RUN
ENTER THE PRINCIPAL
?1864
ENTER THE RATE AS A DECIMAL
?.05
ENTER THE TIME IN YEARS
?2
186.4
```

Each value is entered separately.

# Exercises

1. What happens when a computer comes to an INPUT statement?
2. What follows the keyword INPUT?
3. How should data for an INPUT statement be separated?
4. What is the advantage of using INPUT statements if new data are used each time a program is run?
5. How can a person running a program be told what data are needed and in what order they should be entered?

Write INPUT statements to replace each of the following sets of statements and tell what data should be entered.

**6.** 10 READ A,B,C
20 DATA 6,−5,4.3

**7.** 10 READ X1,X2,X3,X4
20 DATA 1000,.08,.5,10

**8.** 10 READ BC
20 DATA 2000

**9.** 10 READ P,R
20 DATA 1.3E−04,3.14E+10

**10.** 10 LET A=.4
20 LET B=.04

**11.** 10 LET X1=−50
20 LET Y1=50
30 LET Z1=0

**12.** 10 LET KK=1000

**13.** 10 LET A=1E+06
20 LET BA=3.33333E−12

Find and correct the error in each INPUT statement below.

**14.** 10 INPTU A,B

**15.** 10 INPUT X1 X2 X3

**16.** 10 INPUT 1.2,3.14,7.8

**17.** 10 INPUT A,B&C

**18.** 10 INPUT A;B

**19.** 10 INPUT,X,Y,Z

**20.** INPUT A,B,C

**21.** 10 INPUT 1A,1B

Rewrite each program using INPUT statements.

**22.** 10 READ X
20 DATA 10
35 LET S=X↑2
40 PRINT X,S
50 END

**23.** 10 LET T1=85
20 LET T2=90
30 LET T3=92
40 LET A=(T1+T2+T3)/3
50 PRINT A
60 END

**24.** 10 READ C,L
20 DATA 44.1,9
30 LET P=C/L
40 LET U=P/16
50 PRINT C,L
60 PRINT P
70 PRINT U
80 END

**25.** 10 LET M=100
20 LET M=M+1
30 LET N=200
40 LET N=N−1
50 LET P=M*N
60 PRINT P,M,N
70 END

# Laboratory Activities

**1.** Enter and run the programs in Example 1. Compare the outputs.

**Enter the second program in Example 1. Run the program for each of the following activities. Enter input as instructed.**

**2.** Enter only 1864. What happens? Now enter .05. What happens? Enter 2. What happens?

**3.** Enter 1864,.05. What happens? Now enter 2. What happens?

**4.** Enter 1864,.05,2,10,100. What happens?

**5.** Enter and run the program in Example 2.

**6.** Add PRINT and END statements to each set of statements given in Exercises **6-13**. Enter and run each program. Then replace the given statements with the INPUT statement you wrote and run each program again. Compare the output to the first output.

**7.** Enter and run each INPUT statement in Exercises **14-21**. (Add an END statement if necessary.) Use any values as input. Record any error messages. Check your answers to the exercises by entering and running your corrected statements.

**Enter and run the program from the exercise listed. Then enter the program you wrote for the exercise and run it using the data given. Finally, add statements to your program so instructions are printed before the data are entered.**

**8.** Exercise **22:** 10      25      -378      .000756      1E+10      1      0      3.14

**9.** Exercise **23:** 85,90,92      66,81,63      90,100,83

**10.** Exercise **24:** 44.1,9      55,10      100,21

**11.** Exercise **25:** 100,200      50,40      95,35

**12.** Enter and run the program in Example 3. What is the advantage of using separate INPUT statements? Do you see any disadvantage?

**Write a program to solve each problem. Use INPUT statements, and also include instructions. Enter and run each program.**

**13.** Compute the cube of whatever number is entered as input.

**14.** Find the area of a circle $(A \approx 3.14r^2)$ when the radius is entered as input.

**15.** Find the circumference of a circle $(C \approx 3.14d)$ when the diameter is entered as input.

**16.** Find the perimeter of a rectangle when the lengths of two unequal sides are entered as input.

**17.** Find the interest on $12,000 invested at 16% compounded semiannually. Write the program so it can be rerun to find the total interest for a given number of years. Why should you not include a statement to clear the screen in this program?

**18.** In professional football, a touchdown counts 6 points, an extra point after a touchdown counts 1 point, a safety counts 2 points, and a field goal counts 3 points. Find the total score (TS) for one team, if the numbers of touchdowns (TD), safeties (S), extra points (EP), and field goals (F) are entered as input.

# PASCAL ASSIGNMENT STATEMENT

*Pascal* has a statement that corresponds to a LET statement in BASIC. It is called an assignment statement.

| LET statements in BASIC | Corresponding assignment statements in *Pascal* |
|---|---|
| 20 LET PI = 3.14 | PI: = 3.14; |
| 30 LET C = PI*D | CIRCUMFERENCE: = PI*DIAMETER; |

In the statement PI: = 3.14;, the value 3.14 is assigned to a storage location named PI.

Notice that in a *Pascal* assignment statement a colon (:) is placed in front of the equals sign, and a semicolon (;) is placed at the end of the statement.

In *Pascal,* the operational symbols for real numbers ($+$, $-$, $*$, and $/$) are the same as in BASIC.

## Exercises
**Write *Pascal* assignment statements for each of the following LET statements. If you recognize formulas, use variable names that will clarify their meaning.**

**1.** 10 LET A = 3.14*R*R
**2.** 20 LET P = 2*L+2*W
**3.** 30 LET A = L*W
**4.** 40 LET A = S*S
**5.** 50 LET V = L*W*H
**6.** 60 LET AV = (A1+A2+A3)/3
**7.** 70 LET A = .5*B*H
**8.** 80 LET A = .5*H*(B1+B2)
**9.** 90 LET I = P*R*T
**10.** 100 LET V = 3.14*R*R*H
**11.** 110 LET V = 1/3*L*W*H
**12.** 120 LET F = 9/5*C+32
**13.** 130 LET C = 5/9*(F−32)
**14.** 140 LET NP = GP−TX
**15.** 150 LET ST = R*C
**16.** 160 LET FT = YD*3

**Write *Pascal* assignment statements that will make the following conversions.**

**17.** millimeters to centimeters
**18.** centimeters to decimeters
**19.** meters to kilometers
**20.** meters to centimeters
**21.** inches to feet
**22.** gallons to quarts
**23.** milliliters to liters
**24.** kilograms to grams

# 3.3 USING EXTERNAL MEMORY

Switching off a computer erases everything in read-write memory. Therefore programs and data that are to be saved must be stored outside the computer. **Tape recorders** and **disk drives** are used to copy programs or data from read-write memory onto **tapes** or **disks.** Even when the recorder or disk drive is switched off, the information stored on the tape or disk remains.

Before entering a program to be saved, remember to use the NEW command. You should do this even if you are the first person to use the computer after it is switched on. To store a program on tape or disk, a **SAVE command (CSAVE** in some BASICs) is used. For disks (and, with some computers, for tapes) the command SAVE must be followed by a program name. The name should not be used for any other program on the disk or tape, and it should remind you of what the program does.

The general procedure for entering a program and saving it on a tape or disk is given below.

1. Enter NEW to erase any programs in read-write memory.
2. Enter the program into the computer. (It is a good idea to list the program to check for typing errors and to run the program to check the output.)
3. Enter SAVE (or CSAVE), and a program name if necessary, to store the program.

This procedure is illustrated in the following example.

---

**EXAMPLE 1**

```
NEW
10 INPUT P,R,T
20 LET I=P*R*T
30 PRINT I
40 END
LIST                          List the program and check for errors.
10 INPUT P,R,T
20 LET I=P*R*T
30 PRINT I
40 END
RUN                           Run the program and check the output.
? 1864,.05,2
186.4
SAVE                          SAVE tells the computer to store the
or                            program on disk or tape. The program
SAVE SIMPLE INTEREST          still remains in read-write memory.
```

A program stored on tape or disk can be *copied* into read-write memory using the **LOAD command (CLOAD** in some BASICs), followed by the program name if one was used in saving it. The program remains on the tape or disk even though it has been loaded into memory. Unfortunately, a program stored on tape or disk using one computer usually cannot be loaded into a computer made by a different manufacturer.

The general procedure for loading a program into memory from tape or disk is given below.

1. Enter NEW to erase any programs in read-write memory.
2. Enter LOAD (or CLOAD), and a program name if necessary, to copy the program into read-write memory.

The program is now ready to list or run. The loading procedure is illustrated in the following example.

---

**EXAMPLE 2**

NEW
LOAD or LOAD SIMPLE INTEREST    The command LOAD causes the program
                                to be copied from tape or disk into read-
                                write memory.

LIST                            You can now list the program or run it.

10 INPUT P,R,T
20 LET I=P*R*T
30 PRINT I
40 END

---

It is possible to erase or replace a program stored on a tape or disk. The procedure depends on the BASIC and the type of external storage.

# Exercises

1. Why is external storage necessary?
2. Why should NEW be used before a program is loaded or typed?
3. What is the procedure for entering and saving a program?
4. What is the procedure for copying a program from tape or disk?
5. How can you check to see whether a program has been loaded properly from tape or disk?

# Laboratory Activities ▬▬▬▬▬▬▬▬▬

**Consult your manual or teacher to answer the following questions for your system.**

1. What type of external storage is available?
2. What keyword is used to save programs? Must a program name be used?
3. What keyword is used to load programs? Must a program name be used?
4. Is there a procedure for verifying that a program has been saved or loaded successfully? If so, find out how to use the procedure.

**If you are responsible for handling tapes or disks, find out how to do the following.**

5. Save programs on tape or disk.
6. Load programs from tape or disk.
7. Erase an unwanted program from a tape or disk.
8. Replace a program with another program.
9. "Write protect" a tape or disk.

**If you will be using disks, find out how to do the following.**

10. Initialize a disk.          11. "Boot" a disk.

12. Enter and save the program in Example 3, page 79. If a name is required call the program SIMPLE INTEREST.

**Enter and save the program you wrote for the exercise or activity listed. Each program will be referred to in this book by the name given here.**

13. Activity **13,** page 81; CUBE
14. Activity **14,** page 81; AREA CIRCLE
15. Activity **15,** page 81; CIRCUMFERENCE
16. Activity **16,** page 81; PERIMETER RECTANGLE
17. Activity **17,** page 81; COMPOUND INTEREST
18. Activity **18,** page 81; FOOTBALL TEAM TOTAL
19. Exercise **24,** page 80; PRICE OF COFFEE

20. Write and run a program to find the average of up to 10 numbers. (*Hint:* Include an instruction to enter the numbers and then, if there are fewer than 10, to enter zeros. Also have the quantity of numbers entered as input.) Save the program as AVERAGE TEN.

# 3.4 OUTPUT

There are many ways to control the placement of output. The following is a list of some you have already learned to use.

1. PRINT statements, to avoid breaking words at ends of lines.
2. PRINT, to leave a blank line.
3. Spaces inside quotation marks (alone or with characters), to shift output to the right.
4. *Commas* in PRINT statements, to print output in zones.
5. *Semicolons* in PRINT statements, to print output close together.

A PRINT statement like the following can be used to space output.

$$30 \text{ PRINT X;" ";Y}$$

The spaces inside the quotation marks, like characters inside quotation marks, are a string. A string that does not contain characters is called a *null string*. Strings that appear in the same PRINT statement with variables do not have to be null strings. However, all strings must be in quotation marks and the variables for which values are to be printed must *not* be in quotation marks.

---

**EXAMPLE 1**

```
10 READ X
20 DATA 20
30 LET S=X↑2
40 PRINT "THE SQUARE OF ";X;" IS ";S      Extra spaces are not needed
50 END                                     in some BASICS.
RUN
THE SQUARE OF 20 IS 400
```

---

A comma or semicolon can be used at the end of a PRINT statement to control where the output of the next PRINT statement appears. That output is printed in the next zone (if a comma is used) or close to the previous output (if a semicolon is used), as if only one PRINT statement had been used.

---

**EXAMPLE 2**

```
10 READ P,R,T
20 DATA 5000,.13,5
30 LET I=P*R*T
40 PRINT "PRINCIPAL",
42 PRINT "RATE",
44 PRINT "TIME",
46 PRINT "INTEREST"
```

```
50 PRINT P,R,T,I
60 END
RUN
PRINCIPAL    RATE     TIME      INTEREST
5000          .13      5         3250
```

**EXAMPLE 3**

```
10 READ X,Y
20 DATA 5,15
30 LET S=X+Y
40 PRINT "X+Y=";
45 PRINT S
50 END
RUN
X+Y=20
```

Most BASICs have a **TAB function** that can be used in PRINT statements to control the spacing of output. The format of the TAB function is TAB(X). The expression in parentheses may be either a whole number (some BASICs do not allow zero) or a variable whose value is a whole number. There are limits to the size of this number.

TAB (X) may be preceded and followed by any expression or string allowed in a PRINT statement. An expression or string following TAB(X) is printed beginning in column X. If output has already been printed in column X, the TAB instruction is ignored. Some computers call the first column on the left column 1, and others call it column 0. We will call it column 1.

The following example shows how the TAB function can be used to print headings. Notice that headings make the output easier to read.

**EXAMPLE 4**

```
10 READ P,R,T
20 DATA 5000,.13,5
30 LET I=P*R*T
40 PRINT "PRINCIPAL";TAB(12);"RATE";TAB(18);
45 PRINT "TIME";TAB(24);"INTEREST"
50 PRINT P;TAB(12);R;TAB(18);T;TAB(24);I
60 END
RUN
PRINCIPAL    RATE     TIME      INTEREST
5000          .13      5         3250
```

**Printing started in the first column.**   **Printing started in column 12.**   **Printing started in column 18.**   **Printing started in column 24.**

# Exercises

1. What kind of number must X be in TAB(X)?
2. What is the effect of using a comma at the end of a PRINT statement?
3. What is the effect of using a semicolon at the end of a PRINT statement?
4. What is the effect of TAB(X) if output has already been printed in column X?
5. What kind of expression can follow or precede TAB(X)?
6. In a PRINT statement, what must be in quotation marks? What must not be in quotation marks?

**Rule a sheet like the one shown below but use the same number of columns as your computer prints.**

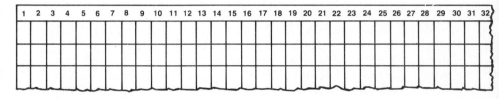

**Use the PRINT statements in Exercises 7-20 with the following READ/DATA statements. On the ruled sheet, show the output for the resulting program in the appropriate columns. Use the same print zones that your computer uses.**

```
10 READ A,B
20 DATA 55,-75
60 END
```

**7.** 30 PRINT A,B

**8.** 30 PRINT A;B

**9.** 30 PRINT A,
40 PRINT B

**10.** 30 PRINT A;
40 PRINT B

**11.** 30 PRINT A
40 PRINT B

**12.** 30 PRINT "A="A,"B="B

**13.** 30 PRINT "A=" ;A;"B=";B

**14.** 30 PRINT "A=",A,"B=",B

**15.** 30 PRINT "A=",A;"B=",B

**16.** 30 PRINT TAB(10);A;TAB(20);B

**17.** 30 PRINT TAB(10);"A=";A,
40 PRINT TAB(20);"B=";B

**18.** 30 PRINT TAB(10);"A=";A
40 PRINT TAB(10);"B=";B

**19.** 30 PRINT TAB(10);"A=";
40 PRINT TAB(25);"B="
50 PRINT TAB(10);A;TAB(25);B

**20.** 30 PRINT TAB(01);"A=";TAB(25);"B="
40 PRINT
50 PRINT TAB(01);A;TAB(25);B

**For Exercises 21-30, write PRINT statements that will print the output shown. If the TAB function is available, use it only in Exercises 27-30. Use the READ/DATA statements below to complete the exercises.**

10 READ X,Y,Z
20 DATA −1.2,2.3,−3.4

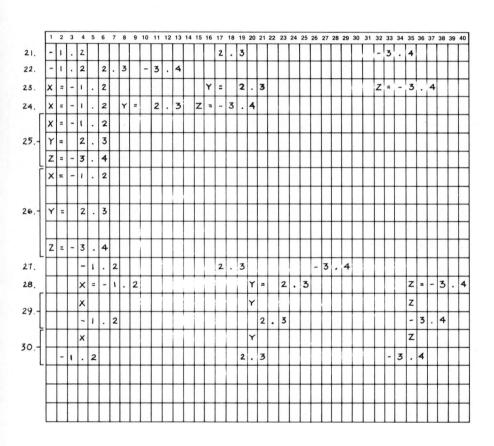

# Laboratory Activities

1. If your computer has a TAB function, enter the following program. Do not add a command to clear the screen.

   ```
   10 PRINT "ENTER A VALUE FOR X IN TAB(X)"
   20 INPUT X
   30 PRINT TAB(X);X
   40 END
   ```

   Experiment with various values of X in this program to find the maximum value allowed in your system.

2. Is the value of X in TAB(X) limited to the number of columns printed by your computer? What happens when X is greater than the number of columns?

3. Experiment with the program in Activity **1** to find the minimum value allowed for X. Does your computer allow TAB(0)? If so, what is its effect?

4. If your computer does not have a TAB function, find out what happens when you try to use TAB(X) in a PRINT statement.

5. In the program in Example 1, replace line 40 with four PRINT statements so that the output is the same as shown in the example.

6. If your BASIC has a TAB function, enter and run the program in Example 4.

7. Enter and run each program from Exercises **7-15** to check your answers to the exercises.

8. If your BASIC has a TAB function, enter and run each program from Exercises **16-20** to check your answers to the exercises.

9. Load FOOTBALL TEAM TOTAL (Activity **18**, page 85). Add statements to the program to arrange the output in five columns. Label the columns TDS, EXTRA PTS, SAFETIES, FIELD GOALS, and SCORE. Use two lines for labels containing two words. Have the values printed on one line below the labels. Use the TAB function in your program if it is available. Run the program, using any input values. Save the program as FOOTBALL WITH HEADINGS.

**If your BASIC has a TAB function, do the following activities. Enter and run the statements in each set. Then replace line 10 with a PRINT statement using TAB functions so the output is the same as the original output.**

10. ```
    10 PRINT 2,-70,3.14
    20 END
    ```

11. ```
    10 PRINT -30;.123;12
    20 END
    ```

12. Use the TAB function in a program to print the business letter on page 46. Enter and run the program.

# 3.5 DOCUMENTING PROGRAMS

The PRINT statements that give instructions for INPUT statements are a form of documentation. *Documentation* is part of any well-written computer program. It is used to give the name, author, and purpose of the program, as well as other information about the program. Documentation can be done *within a program,* in **REM statements,** and *in output,* using PRINT statements. Many commercial programs come with printed sheets or booklets of documentation that tell how the program works and how to use it.

REM statements are not printed in output. When a computer encounters the keyword REM during execution of a program, it ignores the rest of the line. REM statements are for the benefit of a person looking at a listing of the program. They often tell how the program works.

On the other hand, documentation that is printed as output during execution of a program usually tells a person running the program how to use the program.

The following is an example of a program that uses both types of documentation.

---

**EXAMPLE 1**

```
10 REM PROGRAM AUTHOR: DEREK ELLIS
20 REM PROGRAM NAME: RECTANGLE PERIMETER AND AREA
30 PRINT "TO FIND PERIMETER AND AREA OF RECTANGLE"
50 PRINT "ENTER THE LENGTH AND WIDTH"
60 PRINT "SEPARATED BY A COMMA"
80 REM L=LENGTH AND W=WIDTH
90 INPUT L,W
100 REM P=PERIMETER
110 LET P=2*L+2*W
120 REM A=AREA
130 LET A=L*W
140 PRINT "LENGTH";TAB(8);"WIDTH";
150 PRINT TAB (14);"PERIMETER";TAB(24);"AREA"
160 PRINT L;TAB(8);W;TAB(14);P;TAB(24);A
180 PRINT "IF YOU WANT TO DO ANOTHER PROBLEM TYPE RUN"
190 END
RUN
TO FIND PERIMETER AND AREA OF RECTANGLE
ENTER THE LENGTH AND WIDTH
SEPARATED BY A COMMA
?5,3
LENGTH   WIDTH   PERIMETER   AREA
5        3       16          15
IF YOU WANT TO DO ANOTHER PROGRAM, TYPE RUN
```

Documentation can be very extensive. The example below illustrates another way to figure compound interest. Documentation is used to explain the formula.

---

**EXAMPLE 2**

```
10 REM PROGRAM AUTHOR: MARIA HERNANDEZ
20 REM PROGRAM NAME: COMPOUND INTEREST
30 PRINT "COMPOUND INTEREST PROGRAM BY MARIA HERNANDEZ"
60 PRINT "ENTER PRINCIPAL, RATE AS A DECIMAL,"
70 PRINT "TIME IN YEARS, AND HOW OFTEN INTEREST IS COMPOUNDED"
80 PRINT "(USE 2 FOR SEMIANNUALLY, 4 FOR QUARTERLY, "
85 PRINT "12 FOR MONTHLY, AND 365 FOR DAILY)"
90 PRINT "TYPE COMMAS BETWEEN THE NUMBERS"
100 INPUT P,R,T,CP
110 REM THE EXPONENT N IS CALCULATED BY MULTIPLYING THE
115 REM TIME IN YEARS TIMES THE NUMBER FOR
116 REM HOW OFTEN INTEREST IS COMPOUNDED
120 LET N=T*CP
130 REM PR IS THE RATE FOR EACH TIME SPAN
140 REM FOR EXAMPLE: IF THE RATE IS 12% AND INTEREST
145 REM IS COMPOUNDED QUARTERLY THEN
146 REM PR=.12/4=.03 (3% INTEREST FOR 3 MONTHS)
150 LET PR=R/CP
155 REM STATEMENT 160 IS THE COMPOUND INTEREST FORMULA
160 LET I=P*((1+PR)↑N-1)
190 PRINT "PRINCIPAL";TAB(11);"RATE";TAB(16);"TIME";
195 PRINT TAB(21);"COMPOUNDED";TAB(32);"INTEREST"
210 PRINT P;TAB(11);R;TAB(16);T;
211 PRINT TAB(21);CP;TAB(32);I
220 PRINT
240 PRINT "IF YOU WANT TO WORK ANOTHER PROBLEM TYPE RUN"
250 END
RUN
COMPOUND INTEREST PROGRAM BY MARIA HERNANDEZ
ENTER PRINCIPAL, RATE AS A DECIMAL,
TIME IN YEARS, AND HOW OFTEN INTEREST IS COMPOUNDED
(USE 2 FOR SEMIANNUALLY, 4 FOR QUARTERLY,
12 FOR MONTHLY, AND 365 FOR DAILY)
TYPE COMMAS BETWEEN THE NUMBERS
? 1000,.12,1,12
```

| PRINCIPAL | RATE | TIME | COMPOUNDED | INTEREST |
|-----------|------|------|------------|----------|
| 1000 | .12 | 1 | 12 | 126.823 |

```
IF YOU WANT TO WORK ANOTHER PROBLEM TYPE RUN
```

# Exercises

1. What are some uses of documentation in computer programs?
2. What statements can be used to include documentation within a program?
3. What statements can be used to document a program in output?

**Find the errors in the following programs.**

**4.** 10 A. DONEY
20 PROGRAM: READ AND WRITE
30 READ A
40 PRINT A
50 DATA 50
60 END

**5.** 10 REM NAME: SAM RANK
20 PRINT: TAB PROGRAM
30 READ X,Y
40 DATA 150,300
50 PRINT TAB(2);X;TAB(10);Y
60 END

**6.** REM NAME G. LEWIS
REM PROGRAM: TRIANGLE AREA
10 READ B,H
20 LET A=1/2*B*H
30 PRINT B,H,A
40 DATA 25,30
50 END

**7.** 10 REM R. SANCHEZ
20 REM PRODUCT PROGRAM
30 READ A,B
40 DATA 7,8
50 LET C=A+B
60 PRINT C
70 END

# Laboratory Activities

1. Enter and run the program in Example 1. Use any values as input. Save the program. We will refer to it as RECTANGLE PERIMETER AND AREA.
2. Enter and run the program in Example 2. Use any values as input. Replace COMPOUND INTEREST with this program.
3. Enter, list, and run the following program.
   ```
   10 REM MY NAME IS (type your name here)
   20 REM THIS IS AN EXPERIMENT
   30 PRINT "MY NAME IS (type your name here)
   40 PRINT "THIS IS AN EXPERIMENT
   50 END
   ```
   Which lines appear in a listing? Which appear in output?
4. Enter and debug each program in Exercises **4-7**.

**Load each program named in Activities 5-11. List the program and add documentation. Replace the program saved earlier with the documented program.**

**5.** CUBE

**6.** AREA CIRCLE

**7.** CIRCUMFERENCE

**8.** AVERAGE TEN

**9.** SIMPLE INTEREST           **10.** PRICE OF COFFEE

**11.** FOOTBALL WITH HEADINGS

**12.** Write a program to compute a weekly salary (40 hours a week) and a yearly salary (52 weeks a year) if the hourly salary is entered as input. Document the program with REM statements and in the output. Enter and debug the program. Save this program as SALARY.

# 3.6 FLOWCHARTS

When a task can be done in a sequence of steps, a **flowchart** can be used to plan the steps and to show how they are related. The example below shows a computer program and the corresponding flowchart.

**EXAMPLE 1**

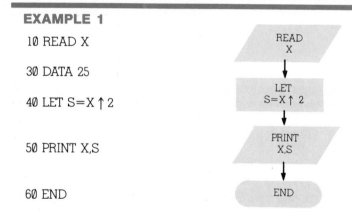

```
10 READ X

30 DATA 25

40 LET S=X ↑ 2

50 PRINT X,S

60 END
```

DATA statements are usually not included in a flowchart.

Some of the symbols used in flowcharts are shown in Example 1. The meanings of the symbols are given below.

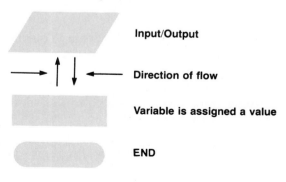

Input/Output

Direction of flow

Variable is assigned a value

END

Often, making a flowchart is the first step in writing a program. *Coding the program* (writing it in a computer language) is the next step. The following example shows a flowchart of the steps in finding the total hours worked in a week and the average number of hours worked each day, using the given data.

---

**EXAMPLE 2**

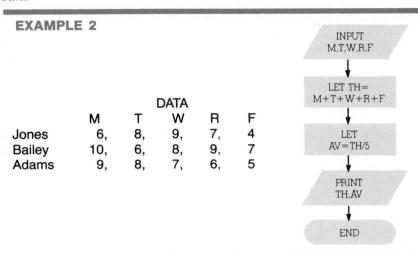

|  | **DATA** |  |  |  |  |
|---|---|---|---|---|---|
|  | M | T | W | R | F |
| Jones | 6, | 8, | 9, | 7, | 4 |
| Bailey | 10, | 6, | 8, | 9, | 7 |
| Adams | 9, | 8, | 7, | 6, | 5 |

---

The problem in Example 2 can now be written in BASIC.

---

**EXAMPLE 3**

```
2 REM PROGRAM: HOURS WORKED
10 INPUT M,T,W,R,F
20 LET TH=M+T+W+R+F
30 LET AV=TH/5
40 PRINT TH,AV
50 END
RUN
? 6,8,9,7,4
34              6.8
RUN
? 10,6,8,9,7
40              8
RUN
? 9,8,7,6,5
35              7
```

---

Statements should be added to this program to clear the screen and to give more documentation, the purpose of the program if the title does not make it clear, definitions of the variables, input instructions, and labels for the output.

# Exercises

**1.** What is a flowchart used for?

**2.** Is every line in a computer program accounted for in the flowchart?

**3.** Write the additional statements mentioned as being needed in the program in Example 3.

**Code a program for each flowchart below. Fully document each program within the program and in output.**

**4.** CELSIUS TO FAHRENHEIT
C represents degrees Celsius.
F represents degrees Fahrenheit.

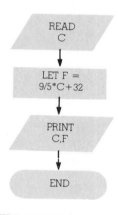

**5.** BATTING AVERAGE
AB represents times at bat.
H represents the number of hits.
AV represents the batting average.

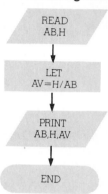

**6.** SPHERE VOLUME
R represents length of the radius.
PI represents the constant $\pi$.
V represents volume of the sphere.

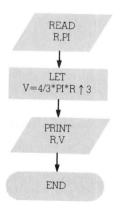

**7.** GAS MILEAGE
D represents distance in miles.
GA represents number of gallons of gas.
GM represents gas mileage (miles per gallon).

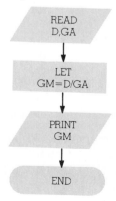

**8.** WAGES

HW represents regular hours worked.

HP represents hourly pay.

OH represents overtime hours worked.

W represents wages for regular hours.

OW represents overtime wages.

TW represents total wages.

TH represents total hours worked.

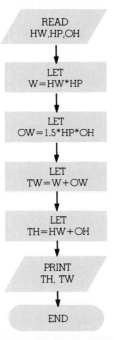

**9.** BUDGET

MI represents monthly income.

PH represents percent (in decimal form) of income spent on housing.

PF represents percent (in decimal form) of income spent on food.

H represents amount spent on housing.

F represents amount spent on food.

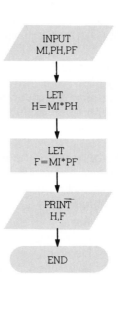

# Laboratory Activities

**1.** Enter the program in Example 3. Add your statements from Exercise **3**. Run the program, using the data given in the example. Debug and save the program. For reference, call it HOURS WORKED.

2. Enter and run the programs from Exercises **4-9.** Use any values for data. Debug the programs and save them. Each program will be referred to by the name given in the exercise.

**Load each program named below. List the program, and make a flowchart of the steps.**

| | |
|---|---|
| **3.** CUBE | **4.** AREA CIRCLE |
| **5.** CIRCUMFERENCE | **6.** FOOTBALL WITH HEADINGS |
| **7.** PRICE OF COFFEE | **8.** AVERAGE TEN |
| **9.** SALARY | **10.** RECTANGLE PERIMETER AND AREA |
| **11.** SIMPLE INTEREST | **12.** COMPOUND INTEREST |

**Make flowcharts for programs to solve the following problems. Code each program and fully document it. Enter, run, and debug each program, using the given data as input. Then save the program. A name is given with each activity for reference.**

**13.** BASKETBALL PERCENTAGE: Compute the winning percentage (WP) of a basketball team if the number of wins (W) and the number of losses (L) are entered as input. (WP = 100·W÷games played.) The output should show the number of games won, lost, and played, and the winning percentage.

| Team | Wins | Losses |
|---|---|---|
| Kansas City | 34 | 20 |
| Denver | 30 | 27 |
| Milwaukee | 24 | 34 |
| Indiana | 22 | 33 |
| Chicago | 22 | 35 |

**14.** SALES TAX: Compute sales tax (ST) if the cost of an item (C) and the tax rate (TR) are entered as input. (ST = TR·C, where TR is expressed as a decimal.) The output should show the item cost, sales tax, and total cost.

| Item | Cost | Tax Rate |
|---|---|---|
| Toaster | $34.98 | $5\frac{1}{4}\%$ |
| Electric skillet | $25.95 | 6% |
| Iron | $19.30 | $4\frac{1}{2}\%$ |
| Lamp | $93.69 | 7% |
| Blender | $46.99 | $6\frac{3}{4}\%$ |

# Vocabulary

# Chapter Summary

1. READ/DATA statements can be used to enter information into a computer. A READ statement must be accompanied by at least one DATA statement. Variables in a READ statement and values in a DATA statement must be separated by commas.

2. The INPUT statement is another way to enter data into a computer. The data are entered from the keyboard after a "?" is displayed on the screen. The data must be separated by commas unless they are entered one at a time.

3. When a computer is switched off, programs in read-write memory are lost. External memory devices, such as tape recorders and disk drives, are used to store programs on tapes or disks.

4. The SAVE (CSAVE in some BASICs) command is used to store a program on a tape or disk. The LOAD (CLOAD in some BASICs) command is used to copy a program from a tape or disk into read-write memory.

5. When a comma is used at the end of a PRINT statement, the computer prints the output of the next PRINT statement in the next zone. When a semicolon is used at the end of a PRINT statement, the computer prints the output of the next PRINT statement on the same line. (The space between the outputs depends on the rules your computer uses for semicolons.)

6. Strings and values for variables or expressions can be printed using the same PRINT statement. The strings must be in quotation marks and the variables or expressions for which values are to be printed should not be in quotation marks.

7. In most BASICs, the TAB function can be used in a PRINT statement to control the spacing of output. Expressions that precede or follow a TAB(X) statement can be any expressions allowed in a PRINT statement.

8. A computer program should have documentation. REM statements can be used for documentation within a program. (REM statements are not printed in output.) Documentation can be printed in output by using PRINT statements.

9. A flowchart can be the first step in writing a program. A flowchart can be used to show the logical flow of a program. Some of the symbols used in flowcharts are shown below.

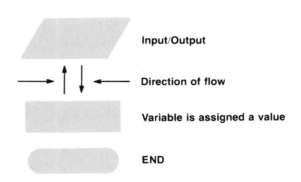

Input/Output

Direction of flow

Variable is assigned a value

END

## Chapter Test

**Write READ/DATA statements that can be used in place of the following LET statements.**

**1.** 10 LET X = 4
20 LET Y = 3

**2.** 15 LET M = −1
20 LET N = 10

**3.** 10 LET A = 2
20 LET B = 3
30 LET C = 4

**4.** 10 LET R = −2
20 LET S = 5
30 LET T = 1
40 LET U = −6

**Find and correct the error(s) in each of the READ/DATA statements below.**

**5.** 10 DATA A1,B1,C1
20 READ 2.3,3.5,4.6

**6.** 10 READ X Y Z
20 DATA 1,2,3

**7.** 10 REED M,N
20 DATA −1,−2

**8.** 10 DATA 3%,5%
20 READ H,I

**Find the value of X in each of the following programs.**

**9.** 10 READ A,B
20 DATA 10,20
30 LET X = B/A
40 PRINT X
50 END

**10.** 10 DATA 6,3
20 READ M,N
30 LET R = (M−N) ↑ N
40 LET X = R/N
50 PRINT X
60 END

**11.** What is an advantage of using an INPUT statement over using READ/ DATA statements?

**Write INPUT statements and the corresponding data that can be used in place of the following READ/DATA statements.**

**12.** 10 READ X,Y
20 DATA 2,4

**13.** 10 READ A,B,C
20 DATA 1.3,2.6,−7.1

**14.** 10 READ RS,T
20 DATA −10,7

**15.** 10 DATA 2.1,3.2,−4.3,5.7
20 READ AA,BB,CC,DD

**Find and correct the error in each INPUT statement below.**

**16.** 10 INPTU A,C,E
**18.** 10 INPUT,M,N

**17.** 10 INPUT X;Y;Z
**19.** 10 INPUT 3,5,6

**Rewrite each program using INPUT statements.**

**20.** 10 READ R,S
20 DATA 15,5
30 LET T = (R/S) ↑ 2
40 PRINT T
50 END

**21.** 10 LET A = 4
20 LET B = .5
30 LET C = −1
40 LET D = A*C
50 LET E = D/B
60 PRINT D,E
70 END

**22.** Name two types of external memory devices.
**23.** What is the purpose of the SAVE command?
**24.** What is the purpose of the LOAD command?
**25.** List the steps for storing a program on a tape or disk.
**26.** List the steps for loading a program back into memory from a tape or disk.

**Combine the PRINT statements in problems 27-35 with the statements below. Write the output as your computer would print it.**

10 READ X,Y,Z
20 DATA −4,9,3.667
60 END

**27.** 30 PRINT Z,Y,X
**28.** 30 PRINT Y
40 PRINT Z
50 PRINT X
**29.** 30 PRINT Z;X;Y
**30.** 30 PRINT " ";Y;" ";X;" ";Z
**31.** 30 PRINT TAB(5);X;TAB(10);Y;TAB(18);Z
**32.** 30 PRINT "FIRST ";X;"SECOND ";Z;"THIRD ";Y

**33.** 30 PRINT X,
40 PRINT Y,
50 PRINT Z

**34.** 30 PRINT Y;TAB(15);
40 PRINT X;TAB(20);
50 PRINT Z

**35.** 30 PRINT "X = ";X;TAB(20);"Y = ";Y;TAB(30);"Z = ";Z

**36.** Describe a difference between documentation within a program and in output.

**37.** What is the purpose of a REM statement?

**Find and correct the errors in the following programs.**

**38.** REM B. NIES
REM DIVISION
20 READ A,B
30 DATA 10,−2
40 LET D = A/B
50 PRINT D
60 END

**39.** 10 REM "NAME:T. MCCLAIN"
20 PRINT PROGRAM:SQUARES
30 DATA 5
40 READ B
50 LET S = B↑2
60 PRINT S
70 END

**Give the flowchart symbols used for each of the following.**

**40.** Input/Output

**41.** Direction of flow

**42.** Variable is assigned a value

**43.** END

**Draw a flowchart for each of the following programs.**

**44.** 10 REM FEET TO INCHES
20 READ F
30 DATA 4
40 LET I = 12*F
50 PRINT F,I
60 END

**45.** 10 REM CIRCUMFERENCE
20 READ R
25 DATA 12
30 LET PI = 3.14
40 LET D = 2*R
50 LET C = PI*D
60 PRINT C
70 END

**46.** 10 REM VOLUME OF A PYRAMID
20 INPUT B,H
30 LET V = 1/3*B*H
40 PRINT B,H
50 PRINT V
60 END

**47.** 10 REM TIP
20 READ P1,P2,P3,R
30 DATA 13.95,8.35,4.5,.15
40 LET PT = P1+P2+P3
50 LET T = PT*R
60 LET TB = PT+T
70 PRINT PT
80 PRINT T
90 PRINT TB
100 END

**Code a program for each flowchart below. Use REM statements to give the name of the program and the meanings of the variables as shown above the flowcharts.**

**48.** METRIC CONVERSIONS

M represents meters.
DM represents decimeters.
CM represents centimeters.

**49.** COST OF CARPET

L represents floor length.
W represents floor width.
A represents floor area.
C represents cost per yard.
TC represents total cost.

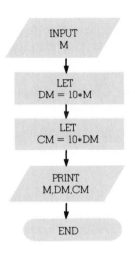

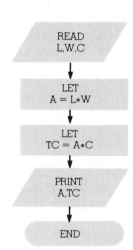

**Draw flowcharts for problems 50 and 51. Then code the program and write the output for the given data.**

**50.** Compute the total cost of an order at a fast food restaurant. The output should include the total cost of the order.

| Item | Cost | Number ordered |
|---|---|---|
| Hamburger | 90¢ | 6 |
| French fries | 55¢ | 4 |
| Soft drink | 40¢ | 5 |

**51.** Compute the total service charge on a checking account. The output should include the charge per check, the number of checks written, the charge per month, and the total service charge.

| Charge per check | Number of checks | Charge per month |
|---|---|---|
| $0.08 | 23 | $2.25 |
| $0.12 | 15 | $3.50 |

# COMPUTER LITERACY

Computers are widely used in today's society. The use of computers helps improve the quality of life in many ways.

In the medical field, computers are used to help improve health care. A computer can help a doctor make faster and more accurate diagnoses. It can analyze a patient's health history and the results of laboratory tests. A computer can help medical researchers study the effects of drugs and procedures before they are used on patients. Computers make record-keeping and accounting in hospitals and doctor's offices easier and more efficient.

In businesses of all kinds, computers are used to help with paperwork, record-keeping, and information retrieval. When such tedious jobs as these are given to the computer, people can concentrate on other jobs that are more challenging to them.

Computers are used to store and analyze data collected when polls are taken. Poll results are used to predict election outcomes, possible future trends (such as sales of popular records), public opinion, and so on. This information is used by businesses, government agencies, and other organizations to improve the services which they provide.

Drawings, music, sculpture, and poetry are being generated by computers. Computer-made music is currently being used in popular songs along with man-made music. Computers are also being used to produce special effects in movies and animated films.

PLT(51)(-60.,130..20000.,,,)
#COL C0;_

**A computer being used to generate a drawing of a building.**

# USES IN SOCIETY

Computers are used to improve the quality of air and space travel. At airports, computers help control air traffic. In the area of space travel, computers are used to simulate space flights and the conditions encountered on such flights. Computers also help control the actual flight.

Many forms of land and water transportation are controlled by computers. Computers help control engines on ships, and aid in navigation. Computers are used by railroad companies to help keep track of which freight cars are in use and their location. Some automobiles come equipped with small computers that keep track of oil pressure, gasoline, voltage, engine temperature, and other needed information.

Society has come to depend on computers in many ways. They can be useful tools that help make life safer and more enjoyable.

**Computers being used to control air traffic at an airport.**

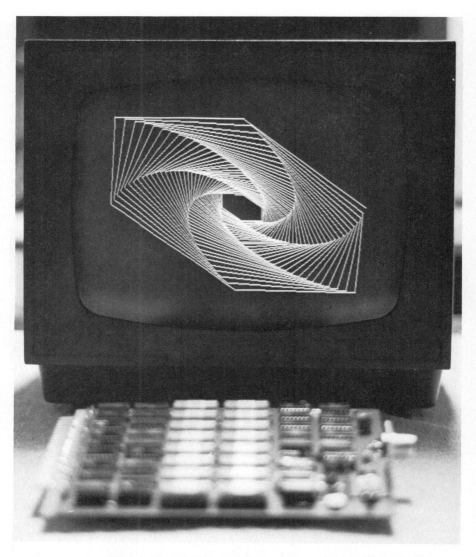

A computer can be programmed to draw pictures containing branches and loops. It can also be programmed to execute branches and loops so that a part of a program or an entire program can be executed again and again.

# BRANCHES AND LOOPS

If program statements are executed in strict numerical order, the only way to use part of a program again is to repeat the statements or to run the entire program again. However, these problems can be avoided by using program branches and loops.

## 4.1 UNCONDITIONAL BRANCHES

A **branch** is used to transfer control of a program from the line containing the branch statement to another line. There are two kinds of branches, unconditional and conditional. An **unconditional branch** is taken every time it is read by the computer.

An unconditional branch starts with a **GOTO statement.** The format of a GOTO statement is GOTO *n,* where *n* is the number of the line to be executed next. The computer then continues executing the program from line *n.*

Some BASICs allow a space between the words GO and TO. The following tests will tell you whether this space is allowed, or even needed, in the BASIC you are using.

---

**TEST 1**

```
10 PRINT "BRANCHING TEST"
20 GOTO 40
30 REM ERROR MESSAGE MEANS TEST FAILED
40 PRINT "TEST PASSED"
50 END
```

**TEST 2**

Change line 20 in Test 1 to the following.

```
20 GO TO 40
```

---

In Tests 1 and 2 the branch is forward to a higher-numbered line. A GOTO statement can also cause a branch back to a lower-numbered line.

---

**EXAMPLE 1**

```
10 PRINT "THIS PROGRAM BRANCHES BACK"
20 PRINT "FROM LINE 40 TO LINE 30"
30 PRINT "HERE WE GO AGAIN!"
40 GOTO 30
50 END
```

Line 50 is never executed. Do you see why? The program goes into an *infinite loop* that can be stopped by causing a break. (Check to see what method your system uses for breaks.)

---

The following is a flowchart for the program in Example 1. Notice that the GOTO statement is represented only by an arrow.

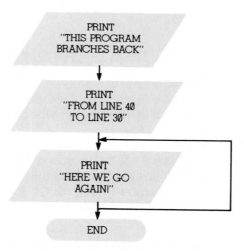

If the line number in the GOTO statement is not the number of a program line, most computers print an error message.

---

**EXAMPLE 2**

```
10 PRINT "BAD BRANCH PROGRAM"
20 GOTO 40
30 END
RUN
BAD BRANCH PROGRAM
UNDEFINED STATEMENT ERROR IN 20
```

To keep programs reasonably short, some of the documentation, the statement to clear the screen, and PRINT statements to space output will be omitted in this book. You should add the missing statements before you save a program.

# Exercises

1. What is the purpose of a branch statement?
2. What kind of branch is always taken?
3. What is the format of an unconditional branch statement?
4. What happens if GOTO is followed by a line number that is not in the program?
5. On your computer, how can you stop the execution of a program like the one in Example 1?
6. Which of the statements shown would allow the program below to be used repeatedly without being rerun?

   **a.** 60 GOTO 40    **b.** 60 GOTO 30    **c.** 60 GOTO 60    **d.** 60 GOTO 25

   ```
   10 PRINT "TO CHANGE METERS TO KILOMETERS"
   20 PRINT "ENTER NUMBER OF METERS"
   30 INPUT M
   40 LET KM=M/1000
   50 PRINT M;" METERS  = ";KM;" KILOMETERS"
   70 END
   ```

# Laboratory Activities

1. Use the programs in Tests 1 and 2 to find out whether your BASIC uses GO TO or GOTO, or both.
2. Enter and run the program in Example 1.
3. Enter and run the program in Example 2. What error message does your computer give?
4. Load RECTANGLE PERIMETER AND AREA and make the following change.

   180 GOTO 90

   Run the program using the following input.

   | 7,18 | 1.5,3.4 | 1340,2100 |

   When you are out of input, stop the program.

5. Write a program that prints your name again and again until you cause a break. Enter and run the program.

6. Write and run a program that prints your name and address once and then scrolls them off the top of the screen.

7. Enter and run the program from Exercise **6.** Check your answer to the exercise by inserting your choice for line 60. Then run and debug the program and save it as METERS TO KILOMETERS.

**Use the program from Activity 7 to find out how many kilometers there are in the given number of meters.**

**8.** 5,762 m      **9.** 10,196 m      **10.** 1,320 m      **11.** 25,765 m

**Enter and run each of the following programs.**

**12.** 10 PRINT "***** ⋀";
   20 GOTO 10
   30 END

**13.** 10 PRINT " ⋀### ⋀#";
   20 GOTO 10
   30 END

14. Write and run three programs to print designs of your own. Experiment with different letters and characters and with the effects of commas and semicolons.

15. Using one input statement and a GOTO statement, write a program that could replace the one in Example 4, page 55. The output should include both Rita's and Kaleb's interest and total cost.

16. Write and run a program to change kilometers to meters (1 km = 1,000 m). Save the program as KILOMETERS TO METERS.

17. Use the program from Activity **16** to check your answers to Activities **8-11.** (Be sure to allow for computer and rounding errors.)

# 4.2 CONDITIONAL BRANCHES

Conditional program branches are like railroad branches that are controlled by switches. Whether a train takes a branch, or does not, depends on whether the switch is open or closed. Whether or not a computer takes a conditional branch depends on whether a statement (the condition) is true or false.

A **conditional branch** uses an **IF-THEN statement.** Example 1 shows a program that contains an IF-THEN statement, and the flowchart for the program. Notice that conditional and unconditional branches may be used in the same program.

## EXAMPLE 1

10 PRINT "WHAT IS 2+2?"

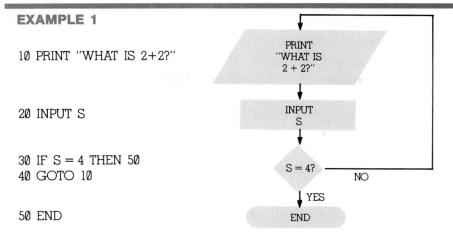

20 INPUT S

30 IF S = 4 THEN 50
40 GOTO 10

50 END

Line 30 calls for a decision to be made. (A decision is shown in a flowchart by a diamond-shaped box). If S = 4 is true, then the rest of line 30 is executed, and the program branches to line 50. If S = 4 is false, then the rest of line 30 is ignored and the program "drops through" to line 40 (the next line).

Here are some BASIC symbols that may be used in stating *conditions.*

| | | | |
|---|---|---|---|
| < | less than | = | equal to |
| > | greater than | <> | not equal to |
| <= | less than or equal to (not greater than) | >= | greater than or equal to (not less than) |

In many BASICS, the order of the parts of a double symbol is not important. If this is true in your BASIC, statements like those below may be used.

## EXAMPLE 2

IF 0 <> 1 THEN 50        IF 0 >< 1 THEN 50
IF 0 <= 1 THEN 50        IF 0 =< 1 THEN 50
IF 1 >= 0 THEN 50        IF 1 => 0 THEN 50

Every BASIC allows one or more of the forms shown below for an IF-THEN statement.

## EXAMPLE 3

IF 1+1 = 2 THEN 50
IF 1+1 = 2 THEN GOTO 50
IF 1+1 = 2 GOTO 50

Some BASICs allow more than one condition to control a conditional branch. The conditions are joined by **AND** if both conditions must be true to cause the branch, or by **OR** if only one of the conditions must be true to cause the branch.

---

**EXAMPLE 4**

20 IF S = 4 AND N = 1 THEN 50      The branch is taken if S = 4 is true and
                                    N = 1 is true.

20 IF S = 4 OR N = 1 THEN 50       The branch is taken if either S = 4 is
                                    true or N = 1 is true.

---

If your BASIC allows more than one condition in an IF-THEN statement, then each of the test programs below should produce the same result.

---

**TEST 1**

50 PRINT "ENTER A NUMBER FROM 1 TO 10"
60 INPUT N
70 IF N < 1 THEN 50          The branch is taken if N is less than 1
75 IF N > 10 THEN 50         or greater than 10.
80 PRINT N
90 END


**TEST 2**

Change line 70 in Test 1 to the following.
70 IF N < 1 OR N > 10 THEN 50
(Delete line 75)


**TEST 3**

Change lines 70 and 75 in Test 1 to the following.
70 IF N >= 1 AND N <= 10 THEN 80
75 GOTO 50

---

# Exercises

1. What statement is used in a conditional branch?
2. Where is the condition stated for a conditional branch?
3. Where is the line number given for a conditional branch?

4. In a flowchart, what shape is the box that indicates a decision?
5. What do the symbols =, <, and > stand for?
6. What do the symbols <=, >=, and <> stand for?
7. What causes a program to branch if two conditions are joined by AND?
8. What causes a program to branch if two conditions are joined by OR?

**For each statement below, write yes or no to tell if program control will be transferred to line 40.**

9. 10 IF 1 = 1 THEN 40
10. 10 IF 0 = 1 THEN 40
11. 10 IF 2 > 3 THEN 40
12. 10 IF 2 < 3 THEN 40
13. 10 IF 5+2 <> 7 THEN 40
14. 10 IF 5+2 = 7 THEN 40
15. 10 IF 6 <= 4+2 THEN 40
16. 10 IF 6 >= 5+1 THEN 40
17. 10 IF 5 >= 9 THEN 40
18. 10 IF 0 <= −4 THEN 40
19. 10 IF 5 = 5 AND 8 = 9−1 THEN 40
20. 10 IF 7 = 5+2 AND 4 > 7 THEN 40
21. 10 IF 5 = 5 OR 4 > 7 THEN 40
22. 10 IF 4 = 3 AND 2 < 1 THEN 40
23. 10 IF 4 = 3 OR 2 < 1 THEN 40
24. 10 IF 9 = 9 OR 5 < 3 THEN 40

# Laboratory Activities

1. Enter and run the program in Example 1. Test the effect of correct and incorrect answers to the question.

**Write and run a short test program to find out which symbol of the given pair your BASIC allows, or whether it allows both.**

2. <>   ><
3. <=   =<
4. >=   =>

5. Write and run a short test program to determine which forms your BASIC allows for IF-THEN statements.
6. Enter and run the program in Test 1. Use input values to test each branch and to avoid branching.
7. Use Test 2 to find out whether your BASIC allows conditions joined by OR.
8. Use Test 3 to find out whether your BASIC allows conditions joined by AND.

9. Enter the set of lines below. Then enter the line from each of Exercises **9-18,** and run the resulting program to check your answers to the exercises.

    20 PRINT "PROGRAM CONTROL WAS NOT SENT TO LINE 40"
    30 GOTO 50
    40 PRINT "PROGRAM CONTROL WAS SENT TO LINE 40"
    50 END

10. If your BASIC allows more than one condition to control a conditional branch, use the set of lines for Activity **9** and enter the line from each of Exercises **19-24.** Run the resulting program to check your answers to the exercises.

11. Enter and run the following program.

    10 LET C = 0
    20 PRINT "## ∧∧** ∧∧?";
    30 LET C = C+1
    40 IF C = 23 THEN 60
    50 GOTO 20
    60 END

12. Write and run three programs to print designs of your own. Experiment with using more than one PRINT statement to construct the design.

13. Change the program in Test 1 to accept any number except a number from 1 to 10. Enter and run the program.

14. If your BASIC allows more than one condition to control a branch, rewrite your program from Activity **13** to combine the conditions using OR. Then rewrite it to combine them using AND. Enter and run the programs.

# 4.3 USING BRANCHES

DATA statements can be used to supply more than one set of values for the variables in a READ statement. A conditional branch can send program control back to a READ statement until all data have been used.

### EXAMPLE 1

10 PRINT "EXAMPLE OF READING MULTIPLE SETS OF DATA"
20 DATA 1,31,2,28,3,31,4,30,5,31,6,30
30 DATA 7,31,8,31,9,30,10,31,11,30,12,31
40 PRINT "MONTH", "NUMBER OF DAYS"
50 READ A,B
60 PRINT A,B

The data are read and printed in pairs.

```
70 IF A <> 12 THEN 50          When A equals 12, the program ends.
90 END
RUN
EXAMPLE OF READING MULTIPLE SETS OF DATA
MONTH          NUMBER OF DAYS
1              31
2              28
3              31
4              30
5              31
6              30
7              31
8              31
9              30
10             31
11             30
12             31
```

When a READ statement is executed, the computer locates the data and reads them in the order in which they are listed. After each variable has been assigned a value, the computer "marks" its place in the list of data. Then, when the READ statement is executed again, or when another READ statement is executed, the computer finds the marker and continues reading data from where it left off.

Each time the computer reads data, it reads as many values as there are variables in the READ statement. If there are two variables, the total number of data must be a multiple of two. If there are three variables, the total number of data must be a multiple of three, and so on.

A branch can depend on actual data, as in Example 1, or on **dummy data** added after the last usable data.

**EXAMPLE 2**

The following lines can be used in the program in Example 1.

```
35 DATA 0,0                    The branch is taken as soon as the
55 IF A = 0 THEN 90            dummy values are read; they are not used
70 GOTO 50                     as data.
```

The dummy data do not have to be in a separate statement, as long as they are the last data. There must be a complete set of dummy data; if there are two variables, there must be two dummy values, if three variables, three dummy values. The dummy values must not be the same as any of the usable values or the branch may be taken before all the data are read.

---

**EXAMPLE 3**

| Wrong | Right |
|-------|-------|
| 10 DATA 2,4,0,5,6,3,0,0 | 10 DATA 2,4,0,5,6,3,999,999 |
| 20 READ X,Y | 20 READ X,Y |
| 30 IF X = 0 THEN 90 | 30 IF X = 999 THEN 90 |

The branch will be taken when the third value is read.

The branch will not be taken until the dummy data are read.

---

You know how to use PRINT statements to give the person who is running a program instructions about input. It is also a good idea to force the person, if you can, to enter the correct type of input. In Test 1 on page 112 the program will not continue past line 75 if the instructions are not followed. However, it is even better if the person using the program is told why the values typed were rejected by the computer. This makes the program easier to use.

---

**EXAMPLE 4**

Lines 70 and 75 in the program in Test 1 on page 112 could be replaced by the following lines.
62 IF N < 1 THEN 68
64 IF N > 10 THEN 72
66 GOTO 80
68 PRINT "THAT NUMBER IS LESS THAN 1"
70 GOTO 50
72 PRINT "THAT NUMBER IS GREATER THAN 10"
74 GOTO 50

---

The messages in lines 68 and 72 can be longer or shorter, but always keep in mind that their purpose is to be helpful.

If the user is expected to enter an integer, the INT (integer) function can be used to test the input.

**INT**(X) is the greatest integer that is not greater than X.

| | |
|---|---|
| INT(3.1412) = 3 | INT(.316) = 0 |
| INT(5) = 5 | INT(−1.36) = −2 |
| INT(−4) = −4 | INT(− .345) = −1 |

Notice that when X is an integer, X = INT(X). This fact can be used to force a person to enter an integer as input.

---

**EXAMPLE 5**

10 PRINT "EXAMPLE OF INTEGER INPUT TEST"
20 PRINT "ENTER AN INTEGER"
30 INPUT I

```
40 IF I = INT(I) THEN 70
50 PRINT "THAT WAS NOT AN INTEGER"
60 GOTO 20
70 LET OI = −I
80 PRINT "THE OPPOSITE OF ";I;" IS ";OI
90 END
```

A conditional branch can be used to give the person using the program a choice between rerunning the program and quitting. A *quit option,* similar to the one in the example below, can be added to any program in which it might be useful.

## EXAMPLE 6

The following lines can be used in the program in Example 5.

```
82 PRINT "RUN AGAIN? ENTER 1 FOR YES"
84 PRINT "OR ANY OTHER NUMBER TO QUIT"
86 INPUT E
88 IF E = 1 THEN 10
```

A quit option will not work with a program that has READ/DATA statements. Remember that the computer uses a marker to keep track of data. A program with READ/DATA statements can only be reused after a command, such as RUN, sends the marker back to the beginning of the data.

# Exercises

1. In what order are data read?
2. If a program has five variables in READ statements, how many data must there be? How many may there be?
3. What are dummy data? How are they used?
4. What values should not be used for dummy data? Why?
5. What is the purpose of the message included with an input test?
6. What is the purpose of a quit option?
7. Can a quit option always be used? Why or why not?
8. What will the output be in Example 1 if the number of line 70 is changed to 55?

**Give the value of each of the following.**

9. INT(19.274)
10. INT(−9.11)
11. INT(0)
12. INT(−13)
13. INT(−4.71)
14. INT(.75)

# Laboratory Activities

1. Enter and run the program in Example 1. Compare your output with the output shown.
2. Change the program in Activity **1** as directed in Example 2. Run the program. Compare the output with that from Activity **1.**
3. Add the statements in Example 6 to the program in Activity **1.** Run the program. Enter 1 (for yes) in the quit option. Describe the result.
4. Write and run a program to show the result when the statements on the left in Example 3 are executed. Then use the statements on the right in the example in your program. Compare the results.
5. Enter the program from Test 1 on page 112. Make the changes described in Example 4. Run the program using both correct and incorrect input values.
6. Enter and run the program from Example 5, using both correct and incorrect input values.
7. Use the statements shown in Example 6 in your program from Activity **6** and run the program again. (Notice how much easier the program is to use.)
8. Use the computer in calculator mode to check your answers to Exercises **9-14.**
9. Load COMPOUND INTEREST (see page 93). Make the following changes and additions. Save the revised program and call it COMPOUND INTEREST 2.

   ```
   102 IF P <= 0 THEN 114
   104 IF R <= 0 THEN 114
   106 IF T <= 0 THEN 114
   108 IF CP < 1 THEN 114
   110 IF CP > 365 THEN 114
   112 GOTO 120
   114 PRINT "SORRY, BAD INPUT, TRY AGAIN"
   116 GOTO 100
   240 PRINT "MORE INPUT? ENTER 1 FOR YES"
   250 PRINT "OR ANY OTHER NUMBER TO QUIT"
   260 INPUT E
   270 IF E = 1 THEN 60
   280 END
   ```

10. Run COMPOUND INTEREST 2 and use it to complete the following table.

    | PRINCIPAL | RATE | TIME | COMPOUNDED | INTEREST |
    |-----------|------|------|------------|----------|
    | 1250 | .08 | 2 | 4 | |
    | 900 | .1 | 1 | 2 | |
    | 3245 | .075 | 3 | 4 | |
    | 630 | .0525 | 2.5 | 2 | |

**Load the program named. Add appropriate input tests and messages. Run and debug the program and save it in place of the earlier version.**

| | |
|---|---|
| **11.** CUBE | **12.** AREA CIRCLE |
| **13.** CIRCUMFERENCE | **14.** HOURS WORKED |
| **15.** BASKETBALL PERCENTAGE | **16.** SIMPLE INTEREST |
| **17.** FOOTBALL WITH HEADINGS | **18.** SALARY |
| **19.** RECTANGLE PERIMETER AND AREA | **20.** BATTING AVERAGE |
| **21.** CELSIUS TO FAHRENHEIT | **22.** SPHERE VOLUME |
| **23.** GAS MILEAGE | **24.** WAGES |
| **25.** BUDGET | **26.** SALES TAX |
| **27.** METERS TO KILOMETERS | **28.** KILOMETERS TO METERS |

**29.** Write and run a program to find the value of the expression $3x^2 + xy - 10y^2$. Use the following DATA statement.

> 10 DATA 4,5,6,10,1,2,3,4,0,0

Use the last two values as dummy data.

**30.** Write and run a program to calculate the perimeter (P) of a triangle if the lengths of the three sides (A, B, and C) are entered as input. Include input tests and a quit option. Save the program and call it TRIANGLE PERIMETER.

# 4.4 COUNTING AND REPEATED OPERATIONS

Sometimes you may know how many times you want the computer to execute certain statements. You can use a conditional branch and a *counter* to control the number of times a program, or part of a program, is executed. In Example 1, C is the counter.

**EXAMPLE 1**

```
10 PRINT "THIS PROGRAM ";
15 PRINT "COUNTS TO 10"
20 LET C = 0                C is given a starting value.
30 LET C = C+1              Every time line 30 is executed, 1 is
40 PRINT C;"⋀";             added to C.
50 IF C < 10 THEN 30        As long as C is less than 10, program
60 END                      control returns to line 30.
RUN
THIS PROGRAM COUNTS TO 10
 1    2    3    4    5    6    7    8    9    10
```

Assigning a starting value to a variable is called **initializing** the variable. It is important to initialize every variable whose value will change during execution of a program. Then, if the program is run more than once, each variable is reassigned the correct starting value at the beginning of each new run. (In some BASICs, commands such as RUN and CLEAR reset all variables to 0.)

A counter can count from any number to any other number. It can count by twos, by threes, or by any number you wish. It can count forwards or backwards. In each example below, the lines given can be used in the program in Example 1.

---

**EXAMPLE 2**

```
15 PRINT "COUNTS TO 10 BY TWOS"
30 LET C = C+2                    Every time line 30 is executed, 2 is
                                  added to C.
```

**EXAMPLE 3**

```
15 PRINT "COUNTS FROM 10 TO 20"
20 LET C = 9
50 IF C < 20 THEN 30             As long as C is less than 20, program
                                 control returns to line 30.
```

**EXAMPLE 4**

```
15 PRINT "COUNTS BACKWARDS FROM 0 TO −10"
20 LET C = 1
30 LET C = C−1                   Every time line 30 is executed, 1 is
                                 subtracted from C.

50 IF C > −10 THEN 30            As long as C is greater than −10,
                                 program control returns to line 30.
```

---

A counter is often used to keep track of how many times lines are executed.

---

**EXAMPLE 5**

```
10 PRINT "THIS PROGRAM FINDS AN AVERAGE"
20 PRINT "ENTER ONE NUMBER AT A TIME"
30 LET S = 0
40 LET C = 0
50 INPUT N
60 LET S = S+N           S represents the sum of the numbers entered so far.
70 LET C = C+1           C is the counter.
80 PRINT "MORE NUMBERS?"
90 PRINT "YES = 1, NO = ANY OTHER NUMBER"
100 INPUT A
110 IF A = 1 THEN 50
```

120 LET AV = S/C
130 PRINT "THE AVERAGE IS ";AV
140 END

In this program, the counter C keeps track of how many numbers are entered. The final value of C is used in finding the average.

# Exercises

1. What can be used to control the number of times a program, or part of a program, is executed?
2. What does it mean to initialize a variable?
3. Why should a starting value be assigned to any variable whose value will change during program execution?
4. In Example 5, what will happen if line 110 transfers control to line 40?

**Tell what changes must be made in the program in Example 1 to make a program that counts as described in each of the following.**

5. From 2 to 13
6. From 5 to 15
7. From 25 to 10
8. From 10 to 0
9. From 10 to 0 by twos
10. From 8 to 38 by twos
11. From 0 to 15 by threes
12. From 15 to 0 by threes

13. What will the output be if the program in Example 1 is changed by entering the lines below?

                50 IF C = 10 THEN 60
                55 GOTO 30

**Complete line 58 in each of the following so that, if the lines are added to the program in Example 1, the revised program will give the result suggested by line 52.**

14. 51 PRINT
52 PRINT "WANT THE NEXT NUMBER?"
54 PRINT "YES = 1, NO = 2"
56 INPUT E
58 IF E = 1 THEN

15. 51 PRINT
52 PRINT "RUN AGAIN?"
54 PRINT "YES = 1, NO = 2"
56 INPUT E
58 IF E = 1 THEN

# Laboratory Activities ▬▬▬▬▬

1. Enter and run the program in Example 1. Compare your output with the output given.

2. Make the changes described in Examples 2-4. Run and debug the resulting programs.

3. Enter and run the programs you wrote for Exercises **5-12.**

4. Enter the program in Example 1. Make the changes described in Exercise **13** and run the program.

5. Add lines 52-58 from Exercises **14** and **15** to the program in Example 1. Run the revised programs to check your answers to the exercises.

6. Change the program in Example 5 so that only positive numbers are accepted as input. (Include a suitable message.) Run and debug the program.

7. Change the program in Activity **6** to give the person using the program the option of quitting or running the program again. Run the program and then save it under the name AVERAGE.

8. Use AVERAGE to compute an average monthly electric bill using the data given below.

| Month | Bill | Month | Bill |
|---|---|---|---|
| January | $91.13 | July | $26.12 |
| February | $83.62 | August | $27.94 |
| March | $71.43 | September | $31.21 |
| April | $52.14 | October | $45.70 |
| May | $30.40 | November | $68.82 |
| June | $29.16 | December | $89.50 |

9. Using the data given below and AVERAGE, compute the average number of hours worked per week by employees of the Graham Company.

| Employee | Hours worked |
|---|---|
| J. Smith | 43 |
| R. Haas | 51 |
| T. Morris | 39 |
| D. Craig | 28 |
| C. Lewis | 36 |
| M. Munoz | 48 |
| K. Trinter | 54 |
| B. Morlani | 45 |

10. Write and run a program to compute the sum of the integers from 1 to 10.

11. Write and run a program to compute the sum of the even integers from 2 to 30.

# PASCAL                                    PRINTING

Printing in *Pascal* can be done using a WRITELN (meaning "write a line") statement. In many ways the WRITELN statement is similar to the PRINT statement in BASIC.

Strings can be printed using WRITELN statements as shown below.

WRITELN ('PASCAL IS EASY TO LEARN');

Notice that a single quotation mark is used at the beginning and end of a string.

The example below shows a program segment using a WRITELN statement.

HOURLYWAGE:=6.35;
HOURSWORKED:=45.0;
WRITELN (HOURLYWAGE, HOURSWORKED);

The output will appear as follows.

6.35000  4.50000E1

There is a way to control output in *Pascal.* The results are similar to those for TAB(X) in BASIC.

A:=−7.3;
WRITELN ('THE NUMBER IS':15,A:5:1);

The following diagram of the output shows the spacing.

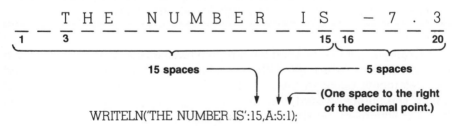

## Exercises

Diagram the WRITELN statements in Exercises 1-4 to show the output. Use the following assignment statements.

A:=−3.7;
B:=12.86;
C:=0.58;

1. WRITELN ('FIRST IS',A:5:1, ' SECOND IS', B:6:2, ' THIRD IS',C:5:2);
2. WRITELN ('PROGRAMMING':13, 'IN':5, 'PASCAL':8);
3. WRITELN ('A':10, 'B':10);     4. WRITELN (A:5:1, ' IS LESS THAN':14, C:6:2);
   WRITELN (A:10:1, B:10:2);

# 4.5 LOOPS

A **loop** occurs when program control returns to lines that have already been executed. A branch can cause a loop, but the word loop more often refers to a group of lines controlled by **FOR/NEXT statements.** The loop is introduced with a FOR statement and ends with a NEXT statement.

---

**EXAMPLE 1**

```
10 PRINT "THIS PROGRAM COUNTS TO A NUMBER OF YOUR CHOICE"
20 PRINT "HOW HIGH SHOULD IT COUNT?"
30 PRINT "ENTER A POSITIVE INTEGER"
40 INPUT N
50 IF N < 1 THEN 30          Test for positive input
60 IF N <> INT(N) THEN 30    Test for integer input
```

```
70 FOR C = 1 TO N  ⎤
80     PRINT C;"⋀";  ⎬ ⟶  FOR/NEXT loop
90 NEXT C          ⎦
```

```
95 PRINT
100 PRINT "THAT'S ALL!"
110 END
```

The statements between FOR and NEXT are often indented, as shown above, to emphasize the loop. If N = 10, this program produces the same result as the program in Example 1 on page 119.

---

In Example 1, if C = N when the program reaches the NEXT statement, the program goes on to line 100. Otherwise, the value of C is increased by 1 and the statements between the FOR and the NEXT statements are executed again. The number added to C can be changed by putting a **STEP** value in the FOR statement, as shown in Example 2.

---

**EXAMPLE 2**

Replacing line 70 in the program in Example 1 changes the way the program counts.

```
70 FOR C = 1 TO N STEP 2     To count by twos
70 FOR C = N TO 0 STEP −1    To count backwards
```

---

Often, either a loop or a conditional branch can be used to do the same job, as shown in the next example.

## EXAMPLE 3

In Example 1 on pages 114 and 115 either of the following has the same effect.      70 IF A <> 12 THEN 50      45 FOR C = 1 TO 12
70 NEXT C

The names of the parts of a FOR statement are given below.

10    FOR    C    =    2    TO    20    STEP    2

**Index**    **Initial**    **Final**    **Increment**
**value**    **value**

The index can be any legal variable. In most BASICs, the initial and final values and the increment can be represented by numbers, variables, or expressions. (STEP 1 has the same effect as not giving a step value.)

FOR statements and NEXT statements are always used in pairs. A FOR statement without a matching NEXT statement assigns the first value to the index, but does not loop back to assign the second value. A NEXT statement without a matching FOR statement, or NEXT followed by a variable different from the index in the matching FOR statement, produces an error message in most BASICs. However, in some BASICs, NEXT need not be followed by any variable.

## EXAMPLE 4

```
20 FOR N = 1 TO 10        10 LET M = 3
30 LET PR = N*23          20 PRINT M ↑ N
40 PRINT PR               30 NEXT N
50 END                    40 END
RUN                       RUN
23                        1
                          NEXT WITHOUT FOR ERROR IN 30
```

Sometimes a loop is used to delay execution of the lines that follow.

## EXAMPLE 5

```
10 PRINT "DELAY LOOP EXAMPLE"
20 LET N = 0
30 LET C = 0
40 PRINT "WHAT'S THE HURRY?"
50 FOR C = 1 TO 500
60 NEXT C
70 LET N = N+1
80 IF N = 20 THEN 100
90 GOTO 30
100 END
```

# Exercises

1. What statement introduces a loop? What statement ends a loop?
2. How can you change the amount added to the index value in a loop?
3. What statement should always appear after a FOR statement?
4. What statement must always appear before a NEXT statement?
5. In Example 1, why is the input tested before the loop is executed?

**Give the NEXT statement that goes with each of the following FOR statements.**

6. 20 FOR I = 3 TO 9 STEP 3
7. 15 FOR C = 1 TO 5
8. 30 FOR J = N TO 10 STEP 2

**Find and correct the error in each loop.**

9. 10 FOR C = 1 TO 10
   20    PRINT C,
   30 END

10. 10 LET X = 1
    20 PRINT X,I
    30 NEXT I
    40 END

11. 10 READ A,C
    15 IF A = 0 THEN 60
    20 FOR D = A TO 10 STEP C
    30    PRINT D
    40 NEXT A
    45 GOTO 10
    50 DATA 1,1,2,2,0,0
    60 END

12. 10 LET Y = 1
    20 FOR X = 5 TO Y
    30    PRINT X
    40 NEXT X
    50 END

**Rewrite each program using a FOR/NEXT loop.**

13. 10 LET C = 0
    20 LET C = C+2
    30 PRINT C
    40 IF C < 10 THEN 20
    50 END

14. 10 LET C = 10
    20 LET C = C−2
    30 PRINT C
    40 IF C > 0 THEN 20
    50 END

15. 10 LET X = −15
    20 LET X = X+5
    30 PRINT X
    40 IF X < 10 THEN 20
    50 END

16. 10 LET N = 4
    20 LET N = N−4
    30 PRINT N
    40 IF N > −20 THEN 20
    50 END

**Write the output for each of the following programs.**

17. 10 FOR C = 1 TO 10
    20    LET M = .015*C
    30    PRINT C, M
    40 NEXT C
    50 END

18. 10 READ N
    20 DATA 12
    30 FOR C = 1 TO N
    40    PRINT C*5
    50 NEXT C
    60 END

**19.** 10 READ X
20 DATA 5,15,25,35
30 FOR C = 0 TO X STEP X
40     PRINT C,X
50 NEXT C
60 IF X < 35 THEN 10
70 END

**20.** 10 READ A,B,C
20 DATA 1,5,1,2,16,2,0,0,0
30 IF A = 0 THEN 100
40 LET S = 0
50 FOR I = A TO B STEP C
60     LET S = S+I
70 NEXT I
80 PRINT S
90 GOTO 10
100 END

**21.** 10 READ X,Y,Z
20 DATA 9,21,2,3,21,4,999,999,999
30 IF X = 999 THEN 80
40 FOR J = X+1 TO Y−1 STEP Z
50     PRINT J
60 NEXT J
70 GOTO 10
80 END

**22.** 10 READ I
20 DATA 0,3,−10
30 IF I = −10 THEN 80
40 FOR T = 3 TO 18 STEP I+3
50     PRINT T
60 NEXT T
70 GOTO 10
80 END

# Laboratory Activities

1. Enter the program in Example 1. Run the program several times, using a different input value each time. Experiment with input values less than and equal to zero.
2. Replace line 70 in Example 1 with each line 70 given in Example 2. (Be sure to change line 10 also.) Run the revised programs.
3. Remove the input test from the program in Example 1. Experiment with various values for N to see what output they produce.
4. Remove the input tests from the programs in Activity **2**. Experiment with various values for N to see what output they produce.
5. Change the program in Example 1 on pages 114 and 115 by using the FOR/NEXT loop given in Example 3. Run the program. Is the output the same as the original output?
6. Enter and run each program in Example 4. Compare your output to the output given. Debug the programs and run them again.
7. Enter the programs in Exercises **9-12**. Run and debug the statements to check your answers to the exercises.
8. Enter and run the programs in Exercises **13-16**. Then enter and run the program you wrote for each exercise. Are the outputs the same?
9. Enter and run the programs in Exercises **17-22**. Use the output to check your answers to the exercises.

10. Load COMPOUND INTEREST 2 (see page 118). Make the following changes and additions. Save the revised program and call it COMPOUND INTEREST 3. (Delete lines 60-70, 102-104, and 195-211. )

```
20 PRINT "THIS PROGRAM COMPUTES INTEREST"
30 PRINT "ON $100 AT RATES FROM 5% TO 10%"
40 PRINT "ENTER TIME IN YEARS AND HOW COMPOUNDED"
100 INPUT T,CP
112 GOTO 118
118 LET P = 100
130 PRINT "PRINCIPAL = $";P
140 PRINT "RATE", "INTEREST"
145 FOR R = .05 TO .1 STEP .005
170 PRINT 100 * R;"%",
180 PRINT "$";I
190 NEXT R
270 IF E = 1 THEN 40
```

11. Use COMPOUND INTEREST 3 to make a table comparing the annual interest on $100 when interest is compounded quarterly, monthly, and daily.

12. Enter the program in Example 5. Run the program several times, using a stopwatch to time each delay caused by the loop. Does the length of the delay vary from run to run?

13. Change the final value to 1,000 in line 50 of the program used in Activity **12** and repeat the experiment described in that activity. Then try to find a final value that gives a delay of exactly 1 second. Change line 40 to print the number of seconds that have passed. (You may want to remove line 80 so your clock will not stop every 20 seconds and have to be restarted.)

# 4.6 NESTED LOOPS

Almost any statement can be used inside a loop. Even a loop can be used inside a loop. Such loops are called **nested loops.** In Example 1, the inner loop is indented more than the outer loop. (The circular symbol used in Example 1 is called a connector. It is used to connect two symbols in a flowchart.)

## EXAMPLE 1

```
10 PRINT "NESTED LOOP STRUCTURE"
20 PRINT "LOOP", "VALUE C", "VALUE D"
```

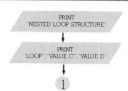

```
25 REM BEGIN OUTER LOOP
30 FOR C = 1 TO 4

40    PRINT "OUTER",C
45    REM BEGIN INNER LOOP
50    FOR D = 1 TO C

60        PRINT "INNER","   ",D
70    NEXT D
75    REM INNER LOOP EXIT
80 NEXT C
85 REM OUTER LOOP EXIT
90 END
```

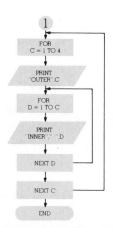

Notice that one loop is completely inside the other. The loops must not cross. Each time the outer loop is executed once, the inner loop is executed completely.

Transferring control from inside a loop to outside a loop without allowing the loop to be fully executed makes it hard to keep track of the values of variables. The first program in Example 2 shows how this problem can occur. The second program shows how to use nested loops to avoid the problem.

**EXAMPLE 2**

```
5 LET I = 0
10 FOR R = I TO 9
20    LET N_1
30    LET P = R*N
40    PRINT R;"X";N;" = ";P
50    LET N = N+1
60    IF N > 12 THEN 90
70    GOTO 30
80 NEXT R
90 LET I = I+1
100 IF I < = 9 THEN 10
110 END
```

Control is transferred to line 90 when N > 12. Line 80 is skipped.

The following program gives the same output as the one above.

```
10 FOR R = 0 TO 9
20    FOR N = 1 TO 12
30        LET P = R*N
40        PRINT R;"X";N;" = ";P
50    NEXT N
60 NEXT R
70 END
```

A program can have an unlimited number of nested loops. However, at some point the computer may give an error message, such as OUT OF MEMORY ERROR.

# Exercises

1. What are nested loops?
2. With nested loops, which is executed more often, the inner loop or the outer loop?
3. Can the outer loop's NEXT statement come before the inner loop's NEXT statement?
4. Is there a limit to the number of loops that can be nested?

**Write the output for each of the following programs.**

**5.**
```
10 FOR A = 6 TO 9
20    FOR B = 2 TO 9
30       LET C = A*B
40       PRINT A;"X";B;" = ";C
50    NEXT B
60    PRINT
70 NEXT A
80 END
```

**6.**
```
10 FOR X = 2 TO 10 STEP 2
20    PRINT "X = ";X
30    FOR Y = 1 TO 9 STEP 2
40       PRINT "Y = ";Y
50    NEXT Y
60    PRINT
70 NEXT X
80 END
```

**7.**
```
10 FOR I = 2 TO 5
20    FOR J = 3 TO 5
30       FOR K = 4 TO 5
40          PRINT I,J,K,I*J*K
50       NEXT K
60       PRINT
70    NEXT J
80 NEXT I
90 END
```

**8.**
```
10 FOR M = 2 TO 4
20    FOR N = 1 TO M
30       LET P = M−N
40       PRINT M;"−";N;" = ";P
50    NEXT N
60    FOR R = N TO 5
70       LET S = N−R
80       PRINT N;"−";R;" = ";S
90    NEXT R
100 NEXT M
110 END
```

# Laboratory Activities

1. Enter and run the program in Example 1.
2. Enter and run both programs in Example 2. Compare the outputs.

3. Add a delay loop inside the inner loop of the second program in Example 2. Run the statements and describe the effect of the delay loop.

4. Enter and run the programs in Exercises **5-8**. Use the output to check your answers to the exercises.

5. Load COMPOUND INTEREST 3 (see page 128). Make the following changes and additions. Save the revised program and call it COMPOUND INTEREST 4.

   30 PRINT "ON AMOUNTS FROM $100 TO $500 AT RATES FROM 5% TO 10%"
   112 GOTO 120
   **(Delete lines 118 and 130)**
   140 PRINT "PRINCIPAL","RATE","INTEREST"
   147 FOR P = 100 TO 500 STEP 100
   167    PRINT "$";P,
   185 NEXT P

6. Run the interest program in Activity **5**. Use at least six different pairs of input values. Experiment with illegal values to be sure the input tests are valid.

**Enter and run the following programs. Record the output. Then debug the programs and run them again.**

**7.** 10 FOR A = 1 TO 5
    20    FOR B = 1 TO 10
    30       PRINT A+B
    40    NEXT A
    50    PRINT
    60 NEXT B
    70 END

**8.** 10 READ R,S
    20 DATA 1,5
    30 FOR T = R TO S
    40    PRINT R,T,S
    50    FOR U = 1 TO S
    60      PRINT U
    70    NEXT U
    80 NEXT S
    90 END

**Enter and run the following programs.**

**9.** 10 FOR R = 1 TO 3
    20    FOR C = 1 TO 7
    30      FOR N = 1 TO C
    40        PRINT "&";
    50      NEXT N
    60      PRINT
    70    NEXT C
    80 NEXT R
    90 END

**10.** 10 FOR T = 1 TO 10
    20    PRINT TAB(16−T);"?"
    30 NEXT T
    40 FOR T = 10 TO 1 STEP −1
    50    PRINT TAB(16−T);"?"
    60 NEXT T
    70 END

11. Write and run three programs to print designs of your own. Be sure to use FOR/NEXT loops and nested loops in your programs.

12. Experiment with adding delay loops in various places in the design programs in Activities **9-11**.

**13.** Load AVERAGE. Replace line 20 to have the user enter as input the number of values (C) to be averaged. Add a line for input instructions. Then replace lines 40 and 70 to form a loop that includes lines 50, 60, 75, and 77. (Lines may have to be renumbered.) Add input instructions. Line 72 and lines 80-110 should be deleted. Run the program, using the data from Activities **8** and **9** on page 122. Save the program in place of the previous program called AVERAGE.

**14.** Write a program to print a temperature chart. In one column show temperatures in degrees Celsius every ten degrees from −40 to 100. In another column, show the equivalent temperatures in degrees Fahrenheit. The columns should be labeled. (See CELSIUS TO FAHRENHEIT for the formula).

**15.** Rewrite the program in Example 1 on pages 114 and 115 so the numbers of the months are generated by a FOR/NEXT loop and the numbers of days are read from a DATA statement.

# 4.7  SUBROUTINES

The usefulness of a computer comes largely from the fact that it can do the same thing many times and very rapidly. Rerunning an entire program is one way to take advantage of this capability. Within a program, loops, and sometimes branches, can cause program lines to be executed repeatedly. Another way to use a line or a group of lines more than once is to put the lines into a **subroutine.**

Program control is sent to a subroutine by a **GOSUB statement.** A **RETURN statement** sends control back to the line following the GOSUB statement.

---

**EXAMPLE 1**

```
10 PRINT "SIMPLE INTEREST"
20 READ P,R,T
30 DATA 1000, .06, .5
40 PRINT "AFTER";TAB(11);"PRINCIPAL";TAB(22);
45 PRINT "INTEREST";TAB(33);"INTEREST"
46 PRINT TAB(33);"TO DATE"
50 LET M = 6
60 GOSUB 110          Control goes to the subroutine starting on line 110.
```

```
70 LET P = NP
80 LET M = 12
90 GOSUB 110
100 GOTO 160
110 LET I = P*R*T
120 LET TI = TI+I
130 LET NP = P+I
140 PRINT M;" MONTHS"; TAB(11);P;TAB(22);I;
145 PRINT TAB(33);TI
150 RETURN
160 END
```

**Control returns to this line.**

**Control goes back to the subroutine.**

**Control returns to this line and then goes to the END statement.**

**Control returns to line 70 after the first use and to line 100 after the second use.**

The program in Tests 1 and 2 on page 107 can be changed to discover whether a space between GO and SUB is allowed or needed in your BASIC.

The branch to a subroutine can be made conditional in several ways. Every version of BASIC allows one or both of the forms shown below for a conditional branch to a subroutine.

**EXAMPLE 2**

```
IF 1 = 1 THEN GOSUB 40
IF 1 = 1 GOSUB 40
```

Example 3 shows how a conditional branch to a subroutine works.

**EXAMPLE 3**

```
10 PRINT "CONDITIONAL BRANCH TO A SUBROUTINE"
20 IF 1 = 1 THEN GOSUB 50
30 PRINT "NOW DO REST OF PROGRAM"
40 GOTO 70
50 PRINT "BRANCH SUCCESSFUL"
60 RETURN
70 END
```

The branch to the subroutine can also be made conditional by branching around the GOSUB statement, as shown in Example 4. Notice that in Example 3, the subroutine is executed if the condition is true; in Example 4, it is executed if the condition is false.

**EXAMPLE 4**

Replace line 20 in Example 3 with the following lines.

```
20 IF 1 <> 1 THEN 30
25 GOSUB 50
```

An error message may result if GOSUB is followed by a line number that is not used in the program or if a RETURN statement is used without a matching GOSUB statement. However, GOSUB without a matching RETURN usually has the same effect as GOTO.

---

### EXAMPLE 5
```
10 PRINT "GOSUB EXAMPLE"
20 GOSUB 40
30 PRINT "NO LINE 40"
50 END
RUN
GOSUB EXAMPLE
UNDEFINED STATEMENT IN 40
```

### EXAMPLE 6
The following statements can be used in the program in Example 5.
```
20 PRINT "RETURN WITHOUT GOSUB"
30 RETURN
RUN
GOSUB EXAMPLE
RETURN WITHOUT GOSUB
RETURN WITHOUT GOSUB ERROR IN 30
```

### EXAMPLE 7
The following statements can be used in the program in Example 5.
```
30 PRINT
40 PRINT "GOSUB WITHOUT RETURN"
RUN
GOSUB EXAMPLE
GOSUB WITHOUT RETURN
```

---

# Exercises

1. Which of the following take advantage of the computer's capability to do the same thing many times?

    **a.** loops           **b.** branches
    **c.** subroutines    **d.** rerunning

2. What kind of statement causes a program to branch to a subroutine?

3. What statement sends program control from a subroutine back to the main program?

**4.** When control is returned from a subroutine to the main program, to what line in the main program is control returned?

**5.** May a branch to a subroutine be conditional?

**6.** Must a branch to a subroutine be conditional?

**7.** What usually happens if GOSUB is followed by a line number not used in the program?

**8.** What usually happens if RETURN does not have a matching GOSUB?

**9.** What usually happens if a GOSUB does not have a matching RETURN?

**10.** Identify each subroutine in the program below by giving the numbers of the first and last lines. Then tell the purpose of the subroutine.

```
10 PRINT "FOR SQUARES OF SUCCESSIVE INTEGERS"
12 PRINT TAB(8);"THIS PROGRAM GIVES"
14 PRINT "THE ACTUAL VALUE OF THE SQUARE"
16 PRINT "THE VALUE AS GIVEN IN COMPUTER OUTPUT"
18 PRINT "THE ERROR IN THE VALUE COMPUTED"
19 PRINT "AND USED BY THE COMPUTER"
30 PRINT "ENTER SMALLEST INTEGER TO BE SQUARED"
40 INPUT SM
50 IF SM = INT(SM) THEN 80
60 GOSUB 200
70 GOTO 40
80 PRINT "ENTER LARGEST INTEGER TO BE SQUARED"
90 INPUT LG
100 IF LG = INT(LG) THEN 130
110 GOSUB 200
120 GOTO 90
130 IF LG-SM >= 0 THEN 140
132 GOSUB 250
134 GOTO 30
140 PRINT "N"; TAB(5);"SQUARE";TAB(15);"OUTPUT";TAB(28);"ERROR"
150 FOR N = SM TO LG
160     GOSUB 300
170     PRINT N; TAB(5);NM; TAB(13);N2; TAB(25);DN
180 NEXT N
190 GOTO 400
200 PRINT "NOT AN INTEGER—TRY AGAIN"
210 RETURN
250 PRINT "NUMBERS IN WRONG ORDER—TRY AGAIN"
260 RETURN
300 LET NM = N*N
310 LET N2 = N ↑ 2
320 LET DN = N2-NM
330 RETURN
400 END
```

**Write the output for each of the following programs.**

**11.** 10 READ C
20 DATA 12.5
30 LET N = 5
40 GOSUB 80
50 LET N = 3
60 GOSUB 80
70 GOTO 110
80 LET TC = C*N
90 PRINT C,N,TC
100 RETURN
110 END

**12.** 10 READ A,B,C
20 DATA 4,5,6
30 GOSUB 110
40 LET A = B+C
50 GOSUB 110
60 LET B = C+A
70 GOSUB 110
80 LET C = B+A
90 GOSUB 110
100 GOTO 150
110 PRINT "A = ";A,
120 PRINT "B = ";B,
130 PRINT "C = ";C
140 RETURN
150 END

# Laboratory Activities

**1.** Enter and run the program in Example 1. Compare the results with those for the program in Example 2 on page 75.

**2.** Change Tests 1 and 2 on page 107 to find out whether the space between GO and SUB is allowed or needed in your BASIC.

**3.** Write and run a short test program to find out which forms your BASIC allows for a conditional branch to a subroutine.

**4.** Enter and run the program in Example 3.

**5.** Change the program in Activity **4** as described in Example 4. Run the program and compare the output to that from Activity **4**.

**6.** Change the condition in line 20 in the program in Activity **5** so the branch to the subroutine is not taken.

**7.** Enter and run the programs in Examples 5-7. Compare your output with the output shown in the examples.

**8.** Enter and run the program in Exercise **10**. Experiment with various input values, including negative integers, nonintegers, and integers entered in the wrong order. Save the program as COMPUTER ERROR–SQUARES.

**9.** Enter and run the programs in Exercises **11** and **12**. Use the output to check your answers to the exercises.

# Vocabulary

branch (107)

unconditional branch (107)

GOTO (107)

conditional branch (110)

IF-THEN (110)

AND (112)

OR (112)

dummy data (115)

INT (116)

initialize (120)

loop (124)

FOR/NEXT (124)

STEP (124)

index (125)

initial value (125)

final value (125)

increment (125)

nested loops (128)

subroutine (132)

GOSUB (132)

RETURN (132)

# Chapter Summary

1. A branch is used to transfer control of a program from the line containing the branch statement to any other line.

2. An unconditional branch is taken every time it is read by the computer. It is introduced by a GOTO statement.

3. A conditional branch is taken only if the stated condition is met. It starts with an IF-THEN statement.

4. A conditional branch calls for the computer to make a decision. The flowchart symbol for a decision is a diamond-shaped box.

5. The condition for a conditional branch may be stated using one of the symbols $=$, $<$, $>$, $<=$, $>=$, or $<>$.

6. Depending on the BASIC, an IF-THEN statement may have the format IF condition THEN line number, IF condition THEN GOTO line number, or IF condition GOTO line number.

7. Some BASICs allow more than one condition to control a conditional branch. When the conditions are joined by AND, the branch is taken only if all conditions are true. When the conditions are joined by OR, the branch is taken if either condition is true or if both conditions are true.

8. DATA statements can be used to supply more than one value for each variable in a READ statement. A conditional branch sends program control back to the READ statement until all data are read. The branch can depend on actual data or on dummy data.

9. Conditional branches can be used to force the person using the program to enter the correct type of input. When input is rejected, it is helpful to display a message telling why the input is not suitable.

10. INT(X) is the greatest integer that is not greater than X.

11. If X is an integer, then X=INT(X). This fact can be used in a conditional branch to force the person using the program to enter an integer as input.

12. A conditional branch can be used to give an option to use the program again or to quit.

13. A conditional branch and a counter can be used to control the number of times a program, or any part of it, is executed.

14. Any variable whose value will change during execution of a program should be initialized.

15. A counter can count forwards or backwards from any number to any other number by an increment. A counter can also be used to keep track of how many times lines are executed.

16. A loop occurs when control returns to program lines that have already been executed. The word loop usually refers to a set of lines controlled by FOR/NEXT statements.

17. A FOR statement has the format FOR index = initial value TO final value. It may also include STEP increment.

18. A FOR statement always has a corresponding NEXT statement in the form NEXT index.

19. Every time a FOR/NEXT loop is executed, one or the increment following STEP is added to the value of the index. When the value of the index equals the final value, execution drops through to the line following the NEXT statement.

20. A loop may be used to delay execution of the lines that follow.

21. Loops can be nested one inside the other. Each time the outer loop is executed once, the inner loop is executed completely.

22. A line or set of lines that is to be used more than once can be put into a subroutine.

23. Control is sent to a subroutine using a GOSUB statement. The format of a GOSUB statement is GOSUB line number. RETURN sends control from the subroutine back to the line following the GOSUB statement.

24. A branch to a subroutine may be made conditional by using IF condition THEN GOSUB line number or by using an IF-THEN statement to branch around the GOSUB statement.

## Chapter Test

**Match each numbered item with the best lettered choice.**

1. conditional branch
2. unconditional branch
3. quit option
4. loop

**a.** lets person using the program rerun program or quit

**b.** controls or keeps track of how many times lines are executed

5. delay loop
6. counter
7. increment
8. initialize
9. dummy data
10. subroutine
11. infinite loop
12. nested loop

c. assign starting values to variables

d. every time it is read, sends control to the line specified

e. sends control back to lines already executed

f. after execution, sends control back to the line after the line from which control came

g. prevents later lines from ever being executed

h. prevents later lines from being executed immediately

i. is executed completely every time the loop containing it is executed once

j. is added to counter or index each time loop is executed

k. transfers program control if a stated condition is met

l. are used to cause a branch after all usable data are read

**Name the keywords used for each of the following.**

13. conditional branch

14. branch to a subroutine

15. unconditional branch

16. loop

**For each statement or set of statements in problems 17-30, write yes or no to tell if program control will be transferred to line 40.**

**17.** 10 GOTO 40

**18.** 16 GOSUB 40

**19.** 12 IF 1*3 <> 3 THEN 40

**20.** 14 IF 6 = INT (6.1) THEN 40

**21.** 25 IF 7 < 0 THEN 40

**22.** 35 IF −2 = INT(−2) THEN 40

**23.** 50 IF INT(−.63) = −1 THEN 40

**24.** 20 IF 5 = 5 AND 5 <> 6 THEN 40

**25.** 60 IF 6+1 = 7 AND 6 = 7+1 THEN 40

**26.** 15 IF 3 = 2 OR 3 > 2 THEN 40

**27.** 90 IF 3−4 > 1 OR −1 = 4−3 THEN 40

**28.** 18 IF N = 1 OR N <> 1 THEN 40

**29.** 10 READ A,D
20 DATA 9,994
30 IF D = 99 THEN 10
40 PRINT A,D

**30.** 30 GOSUB 50
35 GOTO 70
40 PRINT X
50 PRINT Y
60 RETURN
70 PRINT Z

## Give the value of each of the following expressions.

**31.** INT(3.7)

**32.** INT(13)

**33.** INT(−3.14)

**34.** INT(.9)

**35.** INT(−8)

**36.** INT(−.05)

**37.** INT(0)

**38.** INT(82.9999)

**39.** −INT(−7.0002)

**40.** −INT(23.08)

## In each FOR statement below, name the increment, the starting value, the index, and the final value.

**41.** 10 FOR C = 4 TO 40 STEP 6

**42.** 20 FOR R = −3 TO 5

**43.** 30 FOR N = 12 TO 0 STEP −2

**44.** 40 FOR P = 30 TO −10 STEP S

**45.** 50 FOR C = A TO 4∗A

**46.** 60 FOR C = D TO E STEP F

## Use the program below to answer problems 47-65.

```
10 REM PROGRAM:FRACTIONS TO DECIMALS
12 REM WRITTEN BY MARIA HARPER
14 PRINT "WHEN YOU ENTER TWO POSITIVE INTEGERS, THIS PROGRAM"
16 PRINT "FINDS THE DECIMAL VALUE OF EVERY FRACTION"
17 PRINT "GREATER THAN 0 AND LESS THAN 1"
18 PRINT "WHOSE DENOMINATOR IS AN INTEGER EQUAL TO"
20 PRINT "OR BETWEEN THE INTEGERS YOU NAME"
30 PRINT "ENTER THE DENOMINATORS IN ANY ORDER"
40 INPUT D1,D2
50 IF D1>D2 THEN GOSUB 200
60 FOR DR = D1 TO D2
70    FOR NR = 1 TO DR−1
80       LET VL = NR/DR
90       PRINT NR;"/";DR;" = ";VL
100   NEXT NR
110 NEXT DR
120 GOTO 300
200 LET D3 = D2
210 LET D2 = D1
220 LET D1 = D3
230 RETURN
300 END
```

**47.** Which lines contain the outer loop?

**48.** Which lines contain the inner loop?

**Identify the following in the outer loop. Then identify them in the inner loop.**

**49.** The initial value

**50.** The final value

**51.** The index

**52.** The increment

**53.** Which line causes a branch to a subroutine? Is it conditional or unconditional?

**54.** Which lines contain the subroutine?

**55.** What line is executed after line 230 is executed?

**For the input values given below, write yes or no to tell whether control is transferred to the subroutine.**

**56.** 2,5          **57.** 7,5          **58.** 20,4          **59.** 5,10

**60.** For the input values listed in each of problems **56-59,** give the values of D1 and D2 in line 40. Then give their values in line 60.

**61.** What is the purpose of the subroutine? Why is it necessary?

**62.** What two input tests should be included?

**63.** Write the missing input tests.

**64.** Write a delay loop to slow down the printing of the output on the screen.

**65.** Write a quit option for the program. Change line 120 so the quit option will be executed.

**66.** Write a program to determine if a number entered as input is a multiple of 7.

**67.** Write a program to compute the sum of the squares of the integers from 1 to 10.

**68.** Change the program you wrote for problem **67** to compute the sum of the squares of the integers between and including two integers entered as input.

**69.** Change the program you wrote for problem **68** to compute the sum of the squares of the even integers between and including two even integers entered as input.

**70.** Change the program you wrote for problem **69** to compute the sum of the squares of the odd integers between and including two odd integers entered as input.

# COMPUTER LITERACY

Computers are used by thousands of businesses, government agencies, educational institutions, and other organizations. Behind all of the work the computers do are the people who program and operate the computers and related equipment.

A problem to be solved using a computer is first given to the systems analyst. The job of the systems analyst is to analyze the problem. A college degree and two or more years of programming experience are usually needed to obtain a job as a systems analyst.

The systems analyst usually works closely with a group of programmers. The group often consists of a senior programmer, who is in charge, programmers, junior programmers, and trainees. This group writes the program and prepares sample data to use in a test run of the program. A programmer usually needs a computer science degree. However, it is possible to be trained to be a programmer.

**Programmers and analysts working together on a problem.**

# CAREERS

The program then goes to the computer operator. The operator sets up the necessary equipment to run the program. While the program is running, the operator makes sure the equipment is working properly. Computer operators usually serve an apprenticeship. Many employers prefer some college background. A college degree is helpful for computer operators who wish to eventually become programmers or systems analysts.

Many businesses use computer systems that read programs and data from punched cards or tape. With this type of system, keypunch operators are needed to keypunch data onto the cards or tape.

Keypunching involves using a keypunch, which is similar to a typewriter keyboard, to punch holes in the cards or tape. The cards or tape are then read by an input device. The job requires an ability to type around 30 to 40 words per minute and a high school education. The training for this job usually takes two to three weeks.

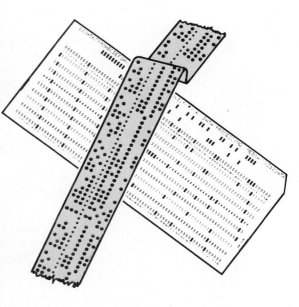

However, you do not need to work in a computer center to use computers on the job. Bank tellers, airline reservation personnel, department store clerks, and supermarket clerks are just a few examples of other people who may use computers on the job.

Today, more organizations than ever are using computers for many purposes. Because of this, the computer industry is growing rapidly and the future is bright for computer-related careers.

**5**

Most people know that engineers and scientists use computers to solve problems. However, computers are also used by many other people. For example, the football coach and team shown above are using a printout from a computer to help them develop a strategy for their next game. Before they could use the computer to help solve their problems, someone had to write a program.

# PROBLEM SOLVING WITH COMPUTERS

Computers can be programmed to solve many different kinds of problems. However, before a computer can solve any kind of problem, someone must tell it what to do and how to do it. In this chapter, you will learn how to examine a problem and how to develop a program to solve the problem.

## 5.1 PLAYING COMPUTER

In order to understand what will happen when a program is run, you can *play computer.* To do this, go through the program line by line, writing down the effect of executing each line. You may have already done this for exercises that called for debugging programs or that asked questions about the output of programs.

When you are *playing computer,* be sure to go through the program several times, using different input values each time. Try to use values that test every line, branch, and subroutine. If you make any changes in the program, retest every line that might be affected by the change.

In Example 1, the computer

    (a) prints the characters that are in quotation marks
    (b) asks for, accepts, and stores input
    (c) tests the input as instructed
    (d) either branches or does not branch, depending on the input test results
    (e) performs arithmetic operations
    (f) displays output

---

**EXAMPLE 1**

| Program line | Result of execution |
|---|---|
| 10 PRINT "THERE ARE 3 NATURAL" | THERE ARE 3 NATURAL |
| 11 PRINT "NUMBERS WHOSE PRODUCT | NUMBERS WHOSE PRODUCT |
| 12 PRINT "AND SUM ARE EQUAL" | AND SUM ARE EQUAL |
| 14 PRINT "WHAT ARE THEY?" | WHAT ARE THEY? |
| 20 PRINT "ENTER YOUR GUESS" | ENTER YOUR GUESS |
| 22 PRINT "WITH COMMAS" | WITH COMMAS |
| 25 PRINT "BETWEEN THE NUMBERS" | BETWEEN THE NUMBERS |
| 30 INPUT A,B,C | ?1,2,5 |
| 40 IF A <= 0 OR B <= 0 OR<br>   C <= 0 THEN 120 | Condition is false;<br>branch is not taken. |
| 50 IF A <> INT(A) OR B <> INT(B)<br>   OR C <> INT(C) THEN 120 | Condition is false;<br>branch is not taken. |
| 60 LET PR = A*B*C | PR = $1 \cdot 2 \cdot 5 = 10$ |
| 70 LET SM = A+B+C | SM = $1 + 2 + 5 = 8$ |
| 80 PRINT "PRODUCT =";PR;", SUM = ";SM | PRODUCT = 10, SUM = 8 |
| 90 IF PR = SM THEN 140 | Condition is false;<br>branch is not taken. |
| 100 PRINT "NO—TRY AGAIN" | NO—TRY AGAIN |
| 110 GOTO 20 | Control returns to line 20. |
| 120 PRINT "ENTER NATURAL NUMBERS" | **Additional input values** |
| 130 GOTO 30 | **should be chosen to test** |
| 140 PRINT "RIGHT! GOOD FOR YOU!" | **each branch.** |
| 150 END | |

---

The tasks performed in Example 1 are all suitable *computer tasks.* However, there are many other tasks a computer can do. For example, you have seen that a computer can check for some errors in the use of BASIC.

What program-related tasks are not suitable for a computer? The following is a list of some things a person can do that a computer cannot do.

1. Gather the data needed for input. (You have learned several ways to supply input.)
2. Decide what requirements the input should meet. (You have learned to use input tests in programs.)
3. Judge the value of the results. (The computer can be instructed that when certain conditions are met it should print "good," "bad," "wrong," "right," or whatever other value the programmer puts on the result.)
4. Know the reason for doing something. (You should know why the computer must do each specific thing you tell it to do.)
5. In general, do anything it has not been told to do. (Someone else has programmed the read-only memory of the computer you are using, and you are learning how to program the read-write memory.)

If you know more than one computer language or more than one version of BASIC, remember to *play computer* in the language (or version) in which the program is written.

The next example shows how *playing computer* can help debug a program. The program below uses the SQR(X) function.

> **SQR(X)** is the principal square root of X, where X is a nonnegative number.

## EXAMPLE 2

| **Program line** | **Result of execution** |
| --- | --- |
| 10 PRINT "IF A*B = N, THEN A AND" | IF A*B= N, THEN A AND |
| 15 PRINT "B ARE FACTORS OF N" | B ARE FACTORS OF N |
| 20 PRINT "THIS PROGRAM FINDS ALL" | THIS PROGRAM FINDS ALL |
| 22 PRINT "POSITIVE INTEGER FACTORS" | POSITIVE INTEGER FACTORS |
| 24 PRINT "OF A POSITIVE INTEGER" | OF A POSITIVE INTEGER |
| 30 PRINT "ENTER A POSITIVE INTEGER" | ENTER A POSITIVE INTEGER |
| 40 INPUT N | ?-4 |
| 45 IF N <> INT(N) THEN 30 | Condition is false; branch is not taken. |
| 50 PRINT "FACTORS OF ";N | FACTORS OF−4 |
| 60 LET SQ = INT(SQR(N)) | Error message; SQR(N) |
| 70　　FOR D = 1 TO SQ | cannot use a negative N. |
| 80　　LET Q = N/D | |
| 90　　IF Q <> INT(Q) THEN 110 | |
| 100　　　PRINT D,Q | |
| 110 NEXT D | |
| 120 PRINT "THAT'S ALL!" | |
| 130 END | |

# Exercises

1. What is the purpose of playing computer?
2. How many times should you play computer with a program that offers you choices? What should you do if you make a change in the program?
3. List five program-related tasks suitable for a computer. List five program-related tasks not suitable for a computer.
4. What does SQR(X) stand for? What restriction is there on X?

**Give the output for each of the commands in Exercises 5-12.**

5. PRINT SQR(16)
6. PRINT SQR(0)
7. PRINT SQR(−25)
8. PRINT SQR(1)

**9.** PRINT −SQR(36)          **10.** PRINT SQR(49)
**11.** PRINT SQR(2)            **12.** PRINT SQR(.36)

## Play computer to debug the following programs.

**13.** 10 PRINT "THIS PROGRAM FINDS HOW MANY GALLONS OF WATER ARE"
15 PRINT "NEEDED TO FILL A RECTANGULAR TANK OR SWIMMING POOL"
20 PRINT "ENTER THE LENGTH, WIDTH, AND DEPTH"
30 INPUT L,W,D
40 IF L <= 0 OR W <= 0 OR D <= 0 THEN 20
50 LET CI = L∗W∗D
60 LET GA = CI/231
70 PRINT "VOLUME IS ";CI;" CUBIC INCHES OR ";G;" GALLONS"
80 END

**14.** 10 PRINT "THIS PROGRAM ROUNDS DECIMALS"
30 PRINT "ENTER YOUR DECIMAL";
40 ENTER D
50 PRINT "NUMBER OF DIGITS NEEDED TO RIGHT OF DECIMAL POINT";
60 INPUT RT
70 LET ND = INT(D∗10 ↑ RT+.5)
80 LET RD = ND/(10 ↑ RT)
90 PRINT D ROUNDS TO RD
100 END

**15.** 10 PRINT "REGULAR POSTAGE RATES APPLY"
15 PRINT "ONLY TO STANDARD SIZED ENVELOPES"
20 PRINT "THIS PROGRAM TELLS IF AN ENVELOPE IS STANDARD"
30 PRINT "ENTER EITHER THE HEIGHT OR LENGTH IN INCHES";
40 INPUT N
50 PRINT "IS THAT (1) THE HEIGHT, OR (2) THE LENGTH?"
55 PRINT "ENTER 1 OR 2";
60 INPUT D
70 IF D = 1 THEN 200
80 IF D <> 2 THEN 50
90 IF N < 5 OR N > 11.5 THEN 300
110 LET HS = N/2.5
120 IF HS >= 3.5 THEN 140
130 LET HS = 3.5
140 PRINT "YOUR ENVELOPE MAY BE FROM ";HS;" INCHES HIGH"
150 LET HL = N/1.3
160 IF <= 6.125 THEN 180
170 LET HL = 6.125
180 PRINT "TO ";HL;" INCHES HIGH"
190 GOTO 310
200 IF N < 3.5 OR N > 6.125 THEN 300
220 LET LS = 1.3∗N
230 IF LS >= 5 THEN 250

```
240 LET LS = 5
250 PRINT "YOUR ENVELOPE MAY BE FROM ";LS;" INCHES LONG"
260 LET LL = 2.5*N
270 IF LL <= 11.5 THEN 290
280 LET LL = 11.5
290 PRINT "TO ";LL;" INCHES LONG"
295 GOTO 310
300 YOUR ENVELOPE IS NOT STANDARD SIZED
310 END
```

# Laboratory Activities

1. Enter and run the program in Example 1. Use input values that test each branch. (If necessary, rewrite lines 40 and 50 to separate the conditions.)
2. Enter and run the program in Example 2. Use input values that test each branch.
3. Add the missing input test to the program in Activity **2**. Run the revised program and test each branch again. Save the program as FACTORS.
4. Enter and run the following program.

```
10 PRINT "FOR SQUARE ROOTS OF PERFECT SQUARES FROM 1 TO 100"
12 PRINT "THIS PROGRAM GIVES THE TRUE VALUE AS"
14 PRINT "GIVEN IN OUTPUT AND THE ERROR IN THE"
16 PRINT "VALUE COMPUTED AND USED BY THE COMPUTER"
20 PRINT "SQUARE";TAB(10);"OUTPUT";TAB(20);"ERROR"
30 FOR N = 1 TO 10
40    LET X = N*N
50    LET Y = SQR(X)
60    LET D = Y-INT(Y)
70    PRINT X;TAB(10);Y;TAB(20);D
80 NEXT N
90 END
```

5. Use your computer in calculator mode to check your answers to Exercises **5-12**.
6. Enter and run the program you debugged in Exercise **13**. Save the program as GALLONS.
7. Enter and run the program you debugged in Exercise **14**. Save the program as ROUND.
8. Enter and run the program you debugged in Exercise **15**. Save the program as ENVELOPE.

# 5.2 ANALYZING PROBLEMS

Even though a computer can do many tasks, there are some it cannot do. Any problem that a computer can help solve must be broken down into human tasks and computer tasks. The first analysis should not go into very much detail.

---

**EXAMPLE 1**

The problem is to paint the walls of a room. A first analysis gives the following list of tasks.

1.1 Decide what color to paint the walls.
1.2 Find out how much paint is needed.
1.3 Buy the required amount of paint.
1.4 Paint the room.

---

There are many things to consider under task 1.1. Different people would consider different things in making their decisions. However, most people would not use a computer to help choose paint colors (although a computer can be programmed to give the programmer's opinions on what colors to use in different rooms of a house).

Unfortunately, the computer cannot paint the room (task 1.4). Tasks 1.2 and 1.3 seem to be the ones with which the computer might be the most help. These tasks should now be analyzed in more detail. (Human tasks should also be analyzed in more detail if instructions on how to do them are needed. However, right now we are interested in the computer tasks.)

---

**EXAMPLE 2**

Task 1.2: Find out how much paint is needed.

2.1 Find the total area of the walls in each room.
2.2 Find out how much wall area each gallon of paint will cover.
2.3 Use the results of tasks 2.1 and 2.2 to find out how many gallons of paint are needed for each room.

Task 1.3: Buy the required amount of paint.

2.4 Find out how much the paint will cost.
2.5 Get the money and make the purchase.
2.6 Transport the paint or have it delivered.

---

Notice that the tasks are not yet clearly separated into human and computer tasks. However, tasks 2.5 and 2.6 do not appear suitable for a computer, so the remaining four tasks should now be analyzed further. We can also begin to determine which tasks the computer can do.

**EXAMPLE 3**                                         **Computer's role**

Task 2.1: Find the total area of the walls in each room.

| | | |
|---|---|---|
| 3.1 | Measure the length and height of each wall. (Assume the room and walls are rectangular.) | accept input |
| 3.2 | For each wall, find the overall area. | do computation |
| 3.3 | Count the number of openings in each wall. | accept input |
| 3.4 | Measure length and height of each opening. (Assume each opening is rectangular.) | accept input |
| 3.5 | For each wall, calculate the area to be painted, allowing for any openings. | do computation |
| 3.6 | Find the wall area to be painted. | do computation |

Task 2.2: Find out how much wall area each gallon of paint will cover.

| | | |
|---|---|---|
| 3.7 | Find out from the manufacturer and/or retailer how much area each gallon will cover and how many coats are needed. | accept input |
| 3.8 | Decide how many coats of paint you will use in each room. | accept input |
| 3.9 | Use results of tasks 3.7 and 3.8 to find wall area each gallon of paint will cover. | do computation |

Task 2.3: Use the results of tasks 2.1 and 2.2 to find out how many gallons of paint are needed for each room.

| | | |
|---|---|---|
| 3.10 | Divide wall area to be painted (from task 3.6) by total wall area each gallon will cover (from task 3.9) to find out how many gallons are needed. | do computation |

Task 2.4: Find out how much the paint will cost.

| | | |
|---|---|---|
| 3.11 | Find total number of gallons needed. | do computation |
| 3.12 | Find how much a gallon of paint costs. | accept input |
| 3.13 | Multiply result of task 3.11 by result of task 3.12 to find total cost of paint. | do computation |
| 3.14 | Find the rate for any sales tax. | accept input |
| 3.15 | Find the sales tax and add it to the cost found in task 3.13. | do computation |

We now have separated the original problem into two sets of tasks—the human tasks and the computer tasks. The computer tasks must be analyzed even further before a program can be written. We could continue the analysis in list form, but may people prefer to make flowcharts. The following example is a flowchart of tasks 3.1 through 3.15 from Example 3.

**EXAMPLE 4**

3.1    INPUT
       For each wall: length, height

3.2    For each wall: find overall area.

3.3    INPUT
       For each wall: number of openings

3.4    INPUT
       For each opening in each wall: length, width

3.5    For each wall: find area to be painted.

3.6    Find wall area to be painted.

3.7    INPUT
       Area 1 gallon covers

3.8    INPUT
       Number of coats

3.9    Find net area 1 gallon covers.

3.10   Find gallons of paint needed. (Divide wall area from
       task 3.6 by area covered by 1 gallon from task 3.9.)

3.11   Find total gallons of paint needed.

3.12   INPUT
       Cost per gallon

3.13   Find total cost of paint. (Multiply total gallons
       from task 3.11 by cost per gallon from task 3.12.)

3.14   INPUT
       Rate for any sales tax

3.15   Find sales tax and add to total cost from task 3.13.

While there do not seem to be any major gaps in the solution so far, the steps are not very detailed. There are no steps for output and there are no details for most of the computations. However, the original problem, which was to paint the walls of a room, has been broken down into human tasks and computer tasks, and the computer tasks are well on their way to becoming a program.

There are many ways to analyze any problem. Some ways lead to useful solutions and some do not. Some ways are better than others if a computer is to be used to help solve the problem. Unless the problem is very simple, analyzing it requires much thought, some trial and error, perhaps some going back to make changes, and then going forward again. Do not be fooled by the fact that this process is not obvious in the analysis shown in this section. This is exactly how it was done. You will understand the process better when you analyze a problem yourself.

# Exercises

1. If a computer is to be used to help solve a problem, into what two kinds of tasks must the problem be broken?
2. Might a human task like painting walls need more analyzing before a person would know what to do and how to do it? Why were the human tasks not analyzed in more detail in the examples?
3. In analyzing a problem, is it necessary to have the same detail for each task at every stage of the analysis?
4. Would you expect everyone who solves problems to analyze them in the same way?
5. In analyzing a problem, is it important to get each step exactly right before going on to the next one?

6. The problem is that Joan wants to buy an aquarium for her room. Which of the following, A or B, seems to be the better first analysis?

| A | B |
|---|---|
| I. Find out what size and shape tank she can buy that will fit her space. | I. Decide how much money she has to spend. |
| II. Find out the cost of each tank, including the cost of extra equipment, fish, and operation. | II. Buy the largest tank (with all equipment) she can afford. |
| III. Choose a tank that fits her room and budget. | III. Find out whether the tank will fit her room; if not, find another place for it. |
| IV. Buy the tank, fill it, and stock it with fish. | IV. Fill the tank and stock it with fish. |

7. Which tasks in analysis **A** in Exercise **6** do you think a computer might help with?

8. Which tasks in analysis **B** in Exercise **6** do you think a computer might help with?

9. Make your own first analysis of Joan's problem.

10. Choose the tasks in your analysis in Exercise **9** with which a computer might help. Analyze these tasks in more detail, until you have a list of computer tasks.

11. Draw a flowchart showing the relationships between the computer tasks in your list from Exercise **10.**

12. Mario has a checking account at a local bank. Every month he deposits his paycheck, he writes checks to pay his bills, and the bank pays him interest. Mario's problem is to keep track of the amount in his checking account. Make a first analysis of Mario's problem.

13. Choose the tasks in your analysis in Exercise **12** with which a computer might help and analyze them in more detail.

14. Draw a flowchart to show the relationships between the computer tasks in your analysis in Exercise **13.**

# 5.3 THE FINAL ANALYSIS

It would be possible to write a program using the analysis in the last section. However, it would not be easy, because the computer tasks have not been described in enough detail. The program would probably need a lot of debugging. Additional flowcharts can be used to show how the analysis of the problem might continue.

To avoid confusion later, it is a good idea to start choosing variables for the program now. You should keep a list of variables and their meanings as you choose them. Also, use variables that remind you of their meanings. One and two character variables are used in the examples because they are allowed in all versions of BASIC.

Now it is time to start *playing computer.* (The right-hand column in the following examples tells the meaning of each variable and lists other reminders.)

## EXAMPLE 1

This includes an analysis of task 3.1 in Example 4 on page 152.

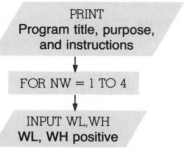

Rectangular room, walls, and openings; use same units of measurement throughout.

For wall number NW, tell user to enter Wall Length and Wall Height.

Notice that "for each" in the original flowchart on page 152 is replaced with a loop.

The next step in the flowchart in Example 4 on page 152 says "For each wall find overall area." FIND is not a keyword in BASIC, so this step needs more analysis. "For each wall" indicates that we are still in the FOR NW loop. The overall area of a rectangular wall can be found by multiplying the length by the height.

## EXAMPLE 2

This is an analysis of tasks 3.2, 3.3, and 3.4 in Example 4 on page 152.

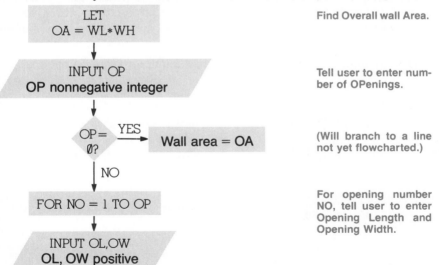

Find Overall wall Area.

Tell user to enter number of OPenings.

(Will branch to a line not yet flowcharted.)

For opening number NO, tell user to enter Opening Length and Opening Width.

The number of times the FOR NO loop should be executed depends on the value of OP, which will be supplied as input.

To find the area to be painted, subtract the total area of the openings in the wall from the overall area of the wall. Since the total area of all openings in the wall is needed, keep a "running total." That is, start with zero and add the area of each opening as it is found. Then close the FOR NO loop.

---

## EXAMPLE 3

This is an analysis of task 3.5 in Example 4 on page 152.

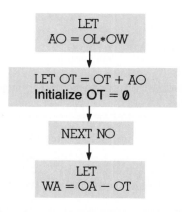

| | |
|---|---|
| LET<br>AO = OL*OW | **Find Area of this Opening.** |
| LET OT = OT + AO<br>**Initialize OT = 0** | **Find running Total for Opening area.**<br>**Initialize OT for each wall.** |
| NEXT NO | **Close inner loop. Now OT is total wall opening area.** |
| LET<br>WA = OA − OT | **Find Wall Area to be painted.** |

---

The next step in the flowchart says "Find wall area to be painted." To find the total wall area in a room, add the areas of all the walls. Again, start with zero and add each wall area as it is found. Then close the FOR NW loop.

---

## EXAMPLE 4

This is an analysis of tasks 3.6, 3.7, and 3.8 in Example 4 on page 152.

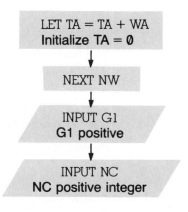

| | |
|---|---|
| LET TA = TA + WA<br>**Initialize TA = 0** | **Find running Total for wall Area.**<br>**Initialize TA at beginning.** |
| NEXT NW | **Close outer loop. Now TA is wall area of room.** |
| INPUT G1<br>**G1 positive** | **Tell user to enter area 1 Gallon covers.** |
| INPUT NC<br>**NC positive integer** | **Tell user to enter Number of Coats needed.** |

The next step says to "find net area 1 gallon covers", but does not tell how to do it. The net area 1 gallon covers is found by dividing G1 by NC. (For example, if 1 gallon will cover 100 square units with one coat, it will only cover 100/2 or 50 square units with two coats.)

---

**EXAMPLE 5**

This is an analysis of tasks 3.9 and 3.10 in Example 4 on page 152.

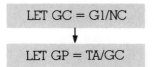

Find net area 1 Gallon covers.

Find Gallons of Paint needed.

---

If the paint can only be purchased in gallons, and if GP is not an integer, then GP needs to be rounded up to the next gallon before going on. For example, if it takes 3.7 gallons of paint to paint a room, you must buy 4 gallons.

To round any number N up to the next integer, use the following statement.

$$\text{LET } N = \text{INT}(N)+1$$

The analysis of the room-painting problem can be continued for the rest of the computer tasks. As before, the "find" steps need more detail.

# Exercises

1. Is it possible to write a computer program without drawing a detailed flowchart? What advantage is there to drawing one?
2. What is one advantage of choosing variables before writing the program? A disadvantage?
3. Is there any connection between the variables used in the examples and the quantities they represent? What advantage does this have?
4. What is included on the second line of each input step in the flowchart?
5. In each example, what kind of BASIC statement corresponds to the words "for each"?
6. What must be done when steps in the analysis do not use BASIC statements or operations?

7. What information could be given as output each time the FOR NW loop is executed? After the loop is closed?

8. What additional information could be given as output after the last step shown in Example 5?

9. Does it matter in what units (meters, feet, or inches) the walls are measured for the room-painting program?

10. When the flowchart in this section is coded into a program, what should come just before each INPUT line?

**In Exercises 11-25 refer to the examples and your variable list.**

11. Write PRINT statements to give information about the program as indicated in the first step of the flowchart in Example 1.

12. Complete the input tests shown below for WL and WH. (Notice that statements are used temporarily where program line numbers will be put later.)

$$IF\ WL <=\quad THEN\ (INPUT\ WL)$$
$$IF\ WH\quad 0\ THEN\ (INPUT\ WH)$$

13. Write an input test for negative values of OP. (Use statements in place of line numbers, as shown in Exercise **12**.)

14. Write input tests for OL and OW.

15. For each input step shown in Examples 1, 2, and 4, write instructions to tell the user what to enter as input.

16. Write the branch statement for OP = 0. (Use a statement in place of a line number, as shown in Exercise **12**.)

17. Before which step should the statement LET OT = 0 come?

18. Before which step should the statement LET TA = 0 come?

19. Write input tests for G1 and NC.

20. Write a PRINT statement to follow the last step shown in Example 4 to tell the user the wall area of the room.

21. Write a statement to round GP to the next gallon.

22. For what values of GP do you not want to round to the next integer? (*Hint*: Play computer to see the effect the rounding statement has on various possible values of GP.)

23. Complete the detailed analysis and flowchart for steps 3.11–3.15 of the flowchart on page 152.

24. Draw a detailed flowchart for the problem in Exercises **6-11** on pages 153 and 154.

25. Draw a detailed flowchart for the problem in Exercises **12-14** on page 154.

# PASCAL       PROGRAMS

```
PROGRAM SIMPLEINTEREST;
VAR INTEREST, PRINCIPAL, RATE, TIME: REAL;
BEGIN
     PRINCIPAL : = 1000.0;
     RATE : = 0.12;
     TIME : = 2.0;
     INTEREST : = PRINCIPAL*RATE*TIME;
     WRITELN ('PRINCIPAL RATE TIME INTEREST');
     WRITELN(PRINCIPAL:9:1, RATE:5:2, TIME:5:1, INTEREST:9:2)
END.
```

The output will appear as follows.

```
PRINCIPAL RATE TIME INTEREST
   1000.0   0.12   2.0    240.00
```

Every *Pascal* program contains three parts. Characteristics of the three parts are described below.

**Part One:**    Name of Program       PROGRAM program name ;

The program name can be as long as desired. However, only the first eight characters are read by the computer. The name cannot contain spaces or special characters and must start with a letter. A semicolon is placed after the program name.

**Part Two:**    Declaration of Variables       VAR variable names: REAL;
                                                     VAR variable names: INTEGER;

The variable names are separated by commas. A colon is placed at the end of the variable list and a semicolon follows the keyword REAL or INTEGER. These keywords describe the type of numbers the variables can represent.

**Part Three:**    Body of the Program

The body of the program starts with the *Pascal* keyword BEGIN and concludes with the keyword END. (A period must follow the "D" in "END".) Semicolons designate the end of each program statement line except the one preceding the END. statement.

## Exercises    Write programs in *Pascal* for each of the following.

**1.** Example 1, page 54        **2.** The program for Exercises **8-12,** page 56
**3.** Exercise **21,** page 57        **4.** Activity **5,** page 58
**5.** Activity **10,** page 58

# 5.4 WRITING PROGRAMS

The detailed flowchart from the examples in Section 5.3 and your answers for the exercises on pages 157 and 158 can now be used in writing the first part of a program to help solve the room-painting problem. Some lines of the program are given in the example below, while other lines are only indicated by REM statements. REM statements can also be added to give the meanings of variables not described in input instructions.

| EXAMPLE 1 | Refer to |
|---|---|
| 10–18 REM **PRINT** statements | Exercise **11** |
| 20 FOR NW = 1 TO 4 | Example 1 flowchart |
| 30     REM **Instructions for WL,WH** | Exercise **15** |
| 40     INPUT WL,WH | Example 1 flowchart |
| 50     IF WL <= 0 THEN 30 | Exercise **12** |
| 60     REM **Input test for WH** | Exercise **12** |
| 70     LET OA = WL*WH | Example 2 flowchart |
| 80     REM **Instructions for OP** | Exercise **15** |
| 90     INPUT OP | Example 2 flowchart |
| 100    REM **Input test for OP** | Exercise **13** |
| 110    IF OP = 0 THEN (line number of wall area calculation) | Example 2 flowchart **(Cannot be completely written yet.)** |
| 120     FOR NO = 1 TO OP | Example 2 flowchart |
| 130       REM **Instructions for OL,OW** | Exercise **15** |
| 140       INPUT OL,OW | Example 2 flowchart |
| 150       REM **Input tests for OL, OW** | Exercise **14** |
| 160       LET AO = OL*OW | Example 3 flowchart |
| 105     LET OT = 0 | Example 3 flowchart |
| 170       LET OT = OT+AO | Example 3 flowchart |
| 180     NEXT NO | Example 3 flowchart |
| 190     LET WA = OA−OT | Example 3 flowchart |
| 110    IF OP = 0 THEN 190 | **(This line can now be completed.)** |
| 19 LET TA = 0 | Example 4 flowchart |
| 200    LET TA = TA+WA | Example 4 flowchart |
| 210 NEXT NW | Example 4 flowchart |
| 220 REM **Instructions for G1** | Exercise **15** |
| 230 INPUT G1 | Example 4 flowchart |
| 240 REM **Input test for G1** | Exercise **19** |
| 250 REM **Instructions for NC** | Exercise **15** |
| 260 INPUT NC | Example 4 flowchart |
| 270 REM **Input test for NC** | Exercise **19** |
| 280 LET GC = G1/NC | Example 5 flowchart |
| 290 LET GP = TA/GC | Example 5 flowchart |
| 410 END | |

Notice that lines 105 and 19 are entered when mentioned in the flowchart, but they are numbered to come before the loops in which OT and TA change value. Lines 105, 19, and 110 show the advantages of being able to enter lines out of order and of leaving gaps between line numbers so lines can be added.

It would be worthwhile to enter and debug the program through line 210 before going any further. However, output values are needed to check the execution of the program. The output could include the following four values for one room.

1. Overall wall area of each wall (from line 70).
2. Total area of openings in each wall (from line 160).
3. For each wall, area to be painted (from line 190).
4. For the room, total wall area to be painted (from line 200).

Lines added to the program to print these values may be removed later, or they may be left in the finished program if the output would be helpful to the user. The next example shows the lines that can be added to give the output suggested in 1 and 2 above. You will be asked in the exercises to write the lines to give the output suggested by 3 and 4 above.

## EXAMPLE 2

75 PRINT "OVERALL WALL AREA: ";OA;" SQUARE UNITS"
165 PRINT "OPENING AREA: ";AO;" SQUARE UNITS"

The square units are square feet, square meters, or other square units corresponding to the units used in measuring the rooms.

After this much of the program is debugged, the program can be finished. Finishing the program includes adding REM and PRINT statements for documentation and to space output lines, adding a statement at the beginning to clear the screen, and adding a quit or rerun option before the END statement. After the program is finished, the entire program should be debugged again.

# Exercises

1. Complete the program in Example 1 by replacing each line reserved by REM with the BASIC statement that should be there.
2. Why can line 110 not be completely written until after line 190 is written?
3. What kind of statements must be added when just part of a program is to be tested and debugged?

4. Write output statements for the area to be painted on each wall and for the total wall area of the room. Add the statements to your program.

5. What additional information could be given in output after line 190? Write the output statements and add them to your program.

6. Play computer with your room-painting program, using the input values given below. (The wall area of the room is 542 square units.)

    wall 1:  10 by 10, one 2 by 5 opening
    wall 2:  10 by 20, two 3 by 5 openings
    wall 3:  10 by 10, one 3 by 6 opening
    wall 4:  10 by 20, no openings

7. Why is OT not initialized at the beginning of the program? Why is it not initialized in line 115?

8. What happens if you enter dimensions of 3 and 4 for a wall and 4 and 5 for the opening in that wall? Since this would indicate an error these values should be rejected. Insert lines after line 160 that give a message and then return program control to line 130 if OA < AO.

9. Write a statement to round a fraction of a cent to the nearest cent. (See Exercise **14,** page 148.)

# Laboratory Activities

1. Enter the room-painting program as you have written it so far. Run and debug it. Test the program by using input values to test all branches. (You should use input values for which you can easily find the correct output values. Then compare the computer output with the correct values.)

2. Check your answer to Exercise **6** by using the data given there as input for your room-painting program.

3. Using your analysis and flowchart from Exercise **23** on page 158, complete the room-painting program. Be sure to include appropriate output statements. (Use the statement you wrote for Exercise **9** to round the sales tax to the nearest cent.) Enter, run, and debug the completed room-painting program. Test it with input values that give a known output. Save the program as PAINTER.

4. Use your flowchart from Exercise **24** on page 158 to write a program to help solve the problem. Run and debug the program.

5. Use your flowchart from Exercise **25** on page 158 to write a program to help solve the problem. Run and debug the program.

# 5.5  THE WHOLE THING

A painter, who gives estimates and computes final costs for billing, would find the room-painting program very useful, especially if it was extended to include any number of rooms and to consider labor and equipment costs. Similar programs can be written for many other trades and professions.

The interest program developed earlier and the checking account program from Activity **5** on page 162 are examples of types of programs that many people can use. The exercises below suggest additional problems for you to analyze.

# Exercises

1. The problem is to find how many bundles of shingles are needed to reroof a house. The roof consists of two rectangular surfaces, and three bundles of shingles cover 100 square feet. You cannot buy part of a bundle, so the output should be a whole number. Analyze the problem and write a program to help solve it.

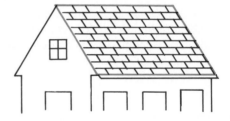

2. Change the shingle program to find the cost of the shingles.

3. Suppose a roofer charges by the bundle to put on a new roof. Change the shingle program to find the cost of reroofing.

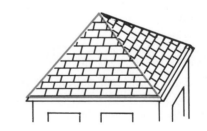

4. Change the shingle program for a roof that consists of four triangular surfaces.

5. Change the shingle program above so it can be used for a roof that consists of two triangles and two trapezoids.
(The area of a trapezoid is .5*H*(B1+B2), where H is the height and B1 and B2 are the lengths of the parallel sides.)

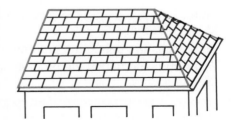

6. The Perry family plans to use their present car for six years. At the end of that time, they want to have $5,000 saved toward the price of a new car. The problem is to find how much money they must save monthly (if they save the same amount every month) to have the necessary amount at the end of six years. They expect to earn 8% interest, compounded monthly, on the money they save. If SM is the amount they must save monthly, then

$$SM = (5000/((1 + IR/12) \uparrow (YR*12)))/(YR*12)$$

where 12 is the number of times a year interest is compounded, IR is the interest rate, and YR is the number of years until the money is needed. Analyze the problem and write a program to help solve it.

7. Change the monthly savings program so that the number of times a year interest is compounded is supplied as input. Use CP for the variable.

8. Change the monthly savings program so that the total amount needed is supplied as input. Use TA for the variable.

9. In a school diving competition, there are eight divers and three judges. Each judge scores each dive with a number (not necessarily an integer) from 0 to 10. The score for each dive is found by adding the three scores given by the judges and multiplying the sum by a number based on how difficult the dive is. (The divers do not all have to do the same dives.) The problem is to find each diver's total score. A diver's total score is the sum of that diver's scores for the individual dives. Analyze the problem and write a program to help solve it.

10. Change the diving program so the number of judges is supplied as input.

---

# Laboratory Activities ▬▬▬▬▬

1. Enter, run, and debug the program in Exercise **3**. Save the program as RECTANGULAR ROOF.

2. Enter, run, and debug the program in Exercise **4**. Save the program as TRIANGULAR ROOF.

3. Enter, run, and debug the program in Exercise **5**. Save the program as TRIANGULAR TRAPEZOIDAL ROOF.

4. Enter, run, and debug the program in Exercise **8**. Save the program as MONTHLY SAVINGS.

5. Enter, run, and debug the program in Exercise **9**.

6. Enter, run, and debug the program in Exercise **10**. Save the program as DIVING.

# Vocabulary

SQR (147)

# Summary

1. Playing computer shows what will happen when a program is run. It involves going through a program line by line, writing down the effect of executing each line.
2. When playing computer, you should choose input values to check every line, branch, and subroutine.
3. If any bugs are found and corrected while playing computer, every line that might be affected should be retested.
4. Program-related tasks can be separated into human tasks and tasks suitable for a computer.
5. Some program-related computer tasks are printing strings, accepting and storing input, testing input, performing arithmetic operations, displaying output, and checking for some errors in the use of BASIC.
6. Some program-related tasks that the computer cannot do include gathering data, deciding input requirements, judging the value of results, understanding the reasons for doing things, and, in general, doing anything it has not been told how to do.
7. SQR(X) is the principal square root of X, where X is a nonnegative number.
8. Any problem that a computer will help solve must first be broken down into human tasks and computer tasks by making repeated analyses, each one more detailed than the last.
9. The computer tasks must be analyzed in enough detail that a program can be written. The analysis may be in list form or in a flowchart.
10. Analyzing a problem successfully involves much thought, some trial and error, and some changing and revising.
11. Variables should be chosen during the final analysis, before the program is written, and a variable list should be kept.
12. The final analysis of the computer tasks should be detailed, use BASIC keywords, and include reminders for such things as input instructions, input tests, and where a variable should be initialized.

13. After the final analysis is made, the program can be written by following the analysis.
14. Part of a program can be debugged by adding output statements that may or may not be left in the final program.
15. A program is finished by adding documentation, a clearscreen statement, a quit option if desired, and any other helpful statements. The entire program should then be debugged again.

## Chapter Test

1. Which of the following can be done by playing computer?
   a. Show what will happen when the program is run
   b. Determine output as quickly as the computer would
   c. Locate program bugs
2. How should input be chosen when you play computer?
3. If you correct a bug while playing computer, what else must you do?
4. Why must the tasks be clearly separated into two groups when a problem is analyzed?

**Tell whether each of the following is a computer task or a human task.**

5. Deciding what input to allow
6. Testing input
7. Displaying output
8. Gathering data
9. Doing arithmetic operations
10. Making flowcharts
11. Checking for BASIC syntax errors
12. Analyzing a problem

**Give the output or error message for each command below. (Do not consider computer error.)**

13. PRINT SQR(9)
14. PRINT SQR(1)
15. PRINT SQR(36)
16. PRINT SQR(81)
17. PRINT −SQR(49)
18. PRINT SQR(−16)
19. PRINT SQR(.25)
20. PRINT SQR(.01)

**Use the following information in problems 21-50.**

The problem is to find the cost of making insulation kits for cylindrical hot water tanks. The outside of the tank will be wrapped with insulation, but the top and bottom will be left uncovered. Each kit will have the same amount of packaging and contain the same amount of fastening material (tape or clips) and the same instructions, but the amount of insulating material will depend on the size of the tank to be covered.

The following is a first analysis of the problem.
  I. Choose the fastening materials (tape or clips) to be used.
  II. Calculate the fixed costs for each kit (the costs that do not depend on tank size).
  III. Decide what tank sizes to make the kits for.
  IV. Calculate the amount of insulation needed for each tank size.
  V. Find out the cost of a square unit of insulation.
  VI. Calculate the cost of insulation for each tank size.
  VII. Decide on the packaging to be used (a fixed cost).
  VIII. Decide whether to make and sell the kits.

**21.** With which tasks in the analysis do you think a computer can help?

The following is a flowchart of some of the tasks in the first analysis and a list of the variables used.

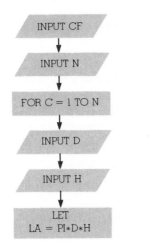

**CF represents fixed costs per kit.**

**N represents number of tank sizes.**

**D represents diameter of tank.**

**H represents height of tank.**

**LA represents area to be covered for tank size entered.**
**Set PI=3.14 before loop.**

**22.** Which step in the flowchart indicates that what follows may change for each tank size?
**23.** Why should the value for PI be assigned before the loop?
**24.** Should CU, the cost per square unit of insulation, be entered before the beginning of the loop or after? Why?
**25.** Which quantities must be measured in the same units? Does it matter what units are used?
**26.** In what units is the value of LA found?
**27.** In what units must the value for CU be given?

**Give the necessary restrictions on the values of each variable listed below.**
**28.** CF        **29.** N        **30.** D        **31.** H        **32.** CU

**The flowchart and variable list for the problem are continued below. Complete them.**

**33.**

LET CI = LA*CU

CI represents

LET CK =

CK represents the total cost for one kit for tank size entered.

PRINT
D,H,LA,CK

Print

Close the loop.

PRINT CF

Label and print on last two lines.

PRINT CU

**34.** Which flowchart step in problem **33** indicates that what follows does not change for each tank size?

**35.** Complete the following program statements that correspond to steps in the flowchart. Refer to your answers for problems **22-32**. (You may use more lines than indicated.)

```
100 PRINT "ENTER FIXED COSTS FOR EACH KIT"
110 INPUT CF
120 IF CF
130
150 INPUT N
160 IF N = INT(N) AND N > 0 THEN 200
170 IF N = 0 THEN 400
180 GOTO 130
200 FOR C = 1 TO N
400 END
```

**36.** Why should additional lines not be inserted between line 160 and line 200?

**Assign suitable line numbers to the statements below.**

**37.**      PRINT "ENTER COST PER SQUARE UNIT OF INSULATION"
             INPUT CU

**Write the statements described below. Give them suitable line numbers.**

**38.** The statement assigning the value to PI

**39.** An input test for CU

**40.** An input instruction and input statement for D

**41.** An input instruction and input statement for H

**42.** Any necessary input tests for D and H

**43.** Assign a line number to each statement below.

```
REM FIND AREA TO BE COVERED
LET LA = PI*D*H
REM FIND COST OF INSULATION
LET CI = LA*CU
REM FIND TOTAL COST FOR KIT
LET CK = CI+CF
PRINT "TANK DIAMETER: ";D
PRINT "TANK HEIGHT: ";H
PRINT "SQUARE UNITS INSULATION: ";LA
PRINT "COST OF KIT THIS SIZE: ";CK
PRINT "FIXED COSTS FOR EACH KIT ARE $";CF
PRINT "INSULATION COST PER SQUARE UNIT IS $";CU
REM ROUND CALCULATED COST TO NEAREST CENT
LET CI = INT(100*CI+.5)/100
NEXT C
```

**44.** What kinds of statements are still missing from the beginning of the program?

**Can a statement to clear the screen be inserted so the final display will include only the output described below, as far as it will fit on the screen? If so, what line number should be used?**

**45.** All output from any one run (any number of tank sizes)

**46.** Only the output from all six PRINT statements in problem **43** (for all tank sizes entered)

**47.** What line numbers could be used for the quit option?

**48.** Suppose the kits will be sold for 150% of what they cost to make (CK). Add statements to have the computer compute the selling price (SP) for the tank size entered. The amount should be labeled and printed on the last line before the fixed-costs output line.

**Use the following information in problems 49 and 50.**

Fixed costs include advertising (CA), packaging (CP), fasteners (CC), instructions (CB), and the cost of doing business (CO).

**49.** Write input instructions, input statements, and input tests so these five costs can be entered into the computer one at a time. Give the statements suitable line numbers.

**50.** Write a statement to have the computer calculate CF from the values entered as input.

# COMPUTER LITERACY

Today, computers are a part of everyday life. To determine the impact of computers on society, we can look at the advantages and disadvantages they offer.

Society has received many benefits from computers. They have enabled banks, supermarkets, and department stores to provide faster service to customers and process data more efficiently. In fact, many of today's institutions could not handle their current volume of paperwork without the aid of computers.

Computers are used to help control crime. Law enforcement agencies use computers to provide services that are faster and more protective than before computers were used. Many people use computerized alarm systems in their homes and cars.

**A computer being used by law enforcers.**

# IMPACT ON SOCIETY

Communications have been improved by computers. Many telephone services are controlled by computers and could not be provided without them. Communication satellites are controlled by computers and help people who are far away from one another keep in touch. Satellites also make it possible for an event in one part of the world to be seen at the same time in another part of the world.

New jobs have been created by the computer industry. Also, thousands of new businesses have developed as a result of the widespread use of computers.

Many jobs that are repetitious and tedious for people can be performed by computers. Some examples of such jobs are data processing, filing, and performing calculations.

Federal, state, and local governments use computers for many purposes. For example, computers are used to store information for government services such as welfare and licensing. This results in greater efficiency and better services in these areas.

Along with the benefits mentioned, there are some shortcomings of computers. For example, people sometimes use computers to steal money from banks and businesses. Information about individuals or businesses can be stolen from a computer's data file and used illegally.

Many office and factory workers have been replaced by computers. These people need to be trained in other areas, possibly even areas involving computers, if they are to continue working.

People can become too dependent upon computers and even lose their ability to do the work themselves. People may also feel threatened by a lack of knowledge about computers.

The widespread use of computers by federal, state, and local governments has its drawbacks. One of the most widely publicized disadvantages is the invasion of the privacy of individual citizens.

The use of computers has both positive and negative impacts on society. We should be aware of both. We must understand what computers are able to do. At the same time, we must realize that people are always in control.

The Nacerino family uses a computer to help them plan and update their budget. The program they use tells the computer to store, process, and print lists and tables of data.

# VARIABLES, ARRAYS, AND MATRICES

A computer can process many forms of data in many ways. It can process data containing numbers, letters, and other symbols. Lists or tables of data can be processed. In this chapter, you will learn how to program a computer to carry out such tasks.

## 6.1 STRING VARIABLES

In earlier chapters you used the computer to process only numeric data. However, the computer can also process data that contain strings (which may contain letters, numbers, or symbols). Data that contain both numbers and strings are called **alphanumeric data.**

Just as a numeric variable is used to name a memory location in which a numeric value is stored, a **string variable** is used to name a memory location in which a string is stored. A string variable may be a letter followed by a dollar sign ($). For example, A$, G$, and X$ are string variables. Many BASICs allow a string variable to be any valid numeric variable followed by a dollar sign.

In PRINT statements, strings are always enclosed in quotation marks, even if they are null strings being used to print blank spaces. However, some BASICs do not require that strings entered as input and in DATA statements be enclosed in quotation marks. The following programs test whether quotation marks are allowed or needed with strings entered as input. (Notice that string variables are not enclosed in quotation marks.)

---

**TEST 1**

```
10 PRINT "TEST FOR QUOTATION MARKS"
20 PRINT "ENTER YOUR NAME IN QUOTATION MARKS"
30 REM ERROR MESSAGE MEANS TEST FAILED
40 INPUT N$
50 PRINT N$
60 END
```

### TEST 2

Change line 20 in Test 1 to the following line.

20 PRINT "ENTER YOUR NAME WITHOUT QUOTATION MARKS"

---

The use of quotation marks in DATA statements can be tested the same way.

---

### TEST 3

Change lines 20 and 40 in Test 1 to the following lines.

20 DATA "EIGHT"
40 READ N$

### TEST 4

Change line 20 in Test 3 to the following line.

20 DATA EIGHT

---

*Note:* Attempting to use a numeric variable to read string data produces an error message.

Some additional characteristics of string variables are listed below.

1. If strings are not enclosed in quotation marks, they cannot contain commas. This is because the computer assumes the comma is there to separate data.
2. Spaces after characters in a string are read as part of the string.
3. The shortest possible string, of course, is a null string.
4. The maximum and minimum number of characters that can be used in a string depends on the BASIC.
5. The rules for string variables in LET statements are the same as those for numeric variables.

---

### EXAMPLE 1

10 PRINT "STRINGS IN LET STATEMENTS"
20 LET C$ = "MINDY HUMPHREY"
30 LET D$ = "123-4567"
40 PRINT C$,D$
50 END

Lines 20 and 30 show string variables on the left-hand sides of the equals signs and strings on the right-hand sides of the equals signs.

## EXAMPLE 2

```
10 PRINT "STRING VARIABLES IN LET STATEMENTS"
20 READ G$,H$
30 DATA "COME VISIT WITH US. "
40 DATA "I THINK YOU WILL LIKE IT."
50 LET J$ = H$
60 PRINT J$
70 PRINT G$;H$
80 END
```

Line 50 shows string variables on both the left-hand and right-hand sides of the equals sign.

In line 50 of Example 2, J$ is set equal to H$. Two strings are equal only if they have exactly the same characters and spaces. (Numeric data and alphanumeric data cannot be equal to each other.) Equality of strings can be used as a condition in an IF - THEN statement, as shown in the example below.

## EXAMPLE 3

```
10 PRINT "ENTER YES OR NO"
20 INPUT A$
30 IF A$ = "YES" THEN 60
40 IF A$ = "NO" THEN 80
50 PRINT "ENTER YES OR NO PLEASE"
55 GOTO 20
60 PRINT "YOU ENTERED YES"
70 GOTO 90
80 PRINT "YOU ENTERED NO"
90 END
```

# Exercises

1. What are data called that are a mixture of numbers, letters, or symbols?
2. What is a string variable?
3. When can strings contain commas?
4. What is the shortest string possible?
5. When is the statement A$ = B$ true?
6. When is the statement A$ = B true?

**Tell whether each string variable is valid or invalid in your BASIC. If invalid, tell why.**

| | | | | |
|---|---|---|---|---|
| **7.** A1 | **8.** $A | **9.** "A$" | **10.** Y$ | **11.** AO$ |
| **12.** 1A$ | **13.** $$ | **14.** XX$ | **15.** $X$ | **16.** ?$ |

**Write a READ statement for the DATA statements in each exercise below. Be sure to use the right types of variables in each case.**

**17.** 10 DATA "JANE SHARFIN", "123-45-6789"

**18.** 10 DATA "SHARFIN, JANE", 40,"$3.65"

**19.** 10 DATA "REGGIE HERMANN",350

**20.** 10 DATA "MILES JONES"
20 DATA "15 E. 1ST STREET"
30 DATA "MINNEAPOLIS, MN",55440

**21.** 10 DATA "MARY MILLS"
20 DATA "PHS"
30 DATA "NATIONAL HONOR SOCIETY"

**Find and correct the errors in the following statements.**

**22.** 10 LET "APPLE" = A$

**23.** 10 READ X,Y,Z$
20 DATA "RIGHT",10,50

**24.** 10 LET A = A$

**25.** 10 IF "A$" = "AIM" THEN 100

**26.** 10 LET D$ = DOLLARS

**If N$ = "ABC DEF GH", tell whether each of the following is true or false.**

**27.** If R$ = "ABC DEF GH" then R$ = N$.

**28.** If S$ = "ABCDEF GH" then S$ = N$.

**29.** N$ = "ABCDEFGH".

**30.** If T$ = "CBA FED HG" then T$ = N$.

**31.** If W$ = " ABC DEF GH " then W$ = N$.

# Laboratory Activities

**1.** Enter and run Tests 1 and 2. Follow the instructions for entering the input. In your BASIC, must a string entered as input be enclosed in quotation marks? May it be enclosed in quotation marks?

**2.** Enter and run Tests 3 and 4. In your BASIC, must a string in a DATA statement be enclosed in quotation marks? May it be enclosed in quotation marks?

**3.** Replace the string variable in line 40 of Test 3 with a numeric variable and run the test again. What error message is printed?

**4.** If your BASIC allows strings both with and without quotation marks, replace line 20 in Test 3 with each line below. Run the program in each case and compare the outputs.

> 20 DATA "EIGHT, TEN"
> 20 DATA EIGHT, TEN

**5.** Change lines 40 and 50 in the program in Activity **4** to read two strings and print them close together. Then use each line 20 shown below and compare the outputs.

> 20 DATA EIGHT, ∧TEN
> 20 DATA EIGHT,TEN
> 20 DATA EIGHT∧,∧TEN

**6.** Enter and run the program in Example 1.

**7.** Enter and run the program in Example 2.

**8.** Enter and run the program in Example 3.

**9.** Write a quit option in which the user can enter "YES" to use the program again or "NO" to quit. (Be sure to include input instructions.)

**10.** Write and run a program to find the average score for each of five students for five tests. Have the output show each student's name and average score. Use the following READ statement and DATA statements (suitably numbered) in the program. Save the program as TEST SCORES.

> READ N$,S1,S2,S3,S4,S5
> DATA "JIM CUNNINGHAM",89,78,75,80,92
> DATA "ANN PALMER",93,97,91,86,88
> DATA "SUSAN EASTERDAY",90,89,91,87,93
> DATA "JUDY CAPONE",75,80,85,90,95
> DATA "ANDRE JACKSON",80,80,78,75,70

**11.** Load BATTING AVERAGE. Change the program so the name of the batter is entered as input and is included with the output from the original program. Run the program. Replace BATTING AVERAGE with the revised program.

**12.** Load SALES TAX. Change the program so the name of the item to which the tax applies is entered as input and is included in the output. Also, have the computer round the sales tax to the nearest cent. Include a quit option. Run the program. Replace SALES TAX with the revised program.

**13.** Write and run a program that will ask for a date, a name, and an amount to be entered as input, and will then print a check such as the one shown below.

```
┌─────────────────────────────────────────────────────────┐
│ ┌─────────────────────────────────────────────────────┐ │
│ │                                 DATE 27 JULY 1982   │ │
│ │  PAY TO THE ORDER OF:                               │ │
│ │  CARLOS SMITH                          $150.31      │ │
│ │  ONE HUNDRED FIFTY AND 31/100 DOLLARS               │ │
│ │           SIGNED  _____  │ │
│ └─────────────────────────────────────────────────────┘ │
└─────────────────────────────────────────────────────────┘
```

**14.** Write and run a program to compute the weekly wages of each employee whose name, number, hours worked, and hourly wage are entered as input. The output should include all information given as input, as well as the weekly wage. All output should be clearly labeled and there should be a quit option. Use the data given below. Save the program as WEEKLY WAGES.

| Number | Name | Hours Worked | Hourly Wage |
|--------|------|--------------|-------------|
| 40369 | Johnson, James | 38 | $7.75 |
| 37521 | Bailey, Cliff | 40 | $8.75 |
| 50651 | Keane, Betty | 35 | $9.80 |
| 65432 | Saco, Tony | 37 | $8.00 |

**15.** Write and run a program to compute winning percentages of baseball teams if the name of the team, number of games won, and number of games lost are either entered as input or supplied in DATA statements. Have the computer print the name of the team, number of games won, number of games lost, and winning percentage. Use the following data.

| Team | Won | Lost |
|------|-----|------|
| St. Louis | 56 | 50 |
| Cincinnati | 50 | 56 |
| Pittsburg | 43 | 62 |
| New York | 40 | 65 |
| Philadelphia | 32 | 73 |

# PASCAL                         READING

The format of a READLN statement in *Pascal* is similar to that of the WRITELN statement.

READLN variable names;

The variable names are separated by commas. Each variable name must have been defined in the declaration statement. A READLN statement is similar to an INPUT statement in BASIC. This statement tells the computer to stop executing the program and ask for data to be entered. Spaces are used to separate the data entered. A WRITELN statement should be used with a READLN statement to give input instructions.

```
PROGRAM RECTANGLEPERIMETER;
VAR LENGTH, WIDTH, PERIMETER: REAL;
BEGIN
      WRITELN ('ENTER LENGTH AND WIDTH');
      WRITELN ('LEAVE A SPACE BETWEEN THE NUMBERS');
      READLN (LENGTH, WIDTH);
      PERIMETER :=2.0*(LENGTH+WIDTH);
      WRITELN ('LENGTH ','WIDTH ','PERIMETER');
      WRITELN (LENGTH : 6:1, WIDTH :6:1, PERIMETER :10:1)
END.
```

If the input for the program above is 3.2 6.8, then the output will appear as shown below.

| LENGTH | WIDTH | PERIMETER |
|--------|-------|-----------|
| 3.2 | 6.8 | 20.0 |

## Exercises

Write programs in *Pascal* for each of the following. Use **READLN** statements to input data. Give input instructions using **WRITELN** statements.

1. Exercise **22,** page 80
2. Exercise **23,** page 80
3. Exercise **24,** page 80
4. Exercise **25,** page 80
5. Activity **13,** page 81
6. Activity **14,** page 81
7. Activity **15,** page 81

# 6.2 SUBSCRIPTED VARIABLES AND ARRAYS

In the algebraic equations $a_1x + b_1y = c_1$ and $a_2x + b_2y = c_2$ the variables *a, b,* and *c* have *subscripts.*(The same letter with a different subscript is, in fact, a different variable.) In the first equation, *a* has a subscript of 1 and $a_1$ is read "*a* sub 1." Variables in BASIC can also be subscripted, though the notation is different.

| Algebraic Notation | BASIC Notation |
|:---:|:---:|
| $a_1$ | A(1) |
| $b_i$ | B(I) |
| $x_{j+1}$ | X(J+1) |
| $y_{2j+3}$ | Y(2*J+3) |
| $h_0$ | H(∅) |

In many BASICs, a **subscripted variable** may be any valid variable followed by a nonnegative integer, or a variable or expression whose value is a nonnegative integer. The integer, variable, or expression must be in parentheses.

The number of different subscripts that can be used with the same variable depends on the BASIC. Some BASICs allow 10, some 11, and some have no limit. In this book, a limit of 10 will be used. Later in this chapter you will learn how to extend the limit if there is one.

Some BASICs start numbering subscripts with 0, and others start with 1. In this book, we will start with 1. (If your system starts with 0, subtract 1 from each subscript shown.)

---

**TEST 1**

```
10 PRINT "TEST FOR LIMIT ON SUBSCRIPTS"
15 REM ERROR MESSAGE MEANS SUBSCRIPT IS TOO GREAT
20 PRINT "ENTER TEST INTEGER"
30 INPUT MX
40 FOR I = 1 TO MX          FOR I = 0 TO MX in some BASICs
50     LET A(I) = I
60     PRINT "A(";I;") IS ALLOWED"
70 NEXT I
80 END
```

---

In some BASICs, A and A(I) cannot both be used in the same program or they are considered the same variable. However most BASICs allow both and consider them to be different variables.

## TEST 2

```
10 PRINT "TEST FOR USE OF A AND A(I)"
15 REM ERROR MESSAGE MEANS ONLY ONE CAN BE USED
20 READ A,A(I)
30 DATA 10,20
40 PRINT A,A(I)
50 PRINT "IF 20 IS PRINTED TWICE, A AND A(I) ARE"
60 PRINT "CONSIDERED THE SAME VARIABLE IN YOUR BASIC"
70 END
```

Subscripted variables are useful when numbers, such as those generated in a loop, are to be saved for later use in a program.

## EXAMPLE 1

```
10 PRINT "SAVING NUMBERS GENERATED IN A LOOP"
15 DATA 25,45,65,86,105,125,145,185
20 FOR I = 1 TO 8
30     READ A(I)
40 NEXT I
50 FOR I = 1 TO 8
60     PRINT "A(";I;")",A(I)
70 NEXT I
80 END
```

```
SAVING NUMBERS GENERATED IN A LOOP
A(1)            25
A(2)            45
A(3)            65
A(4)            86
A(5)            105
A(6)            125
A(7)            145
A(8)            185
```

The first FOR/NEXT loop assigns each number in the DATA statement to a different variable from A(1) to A(8), as shown in the output.

If A is used in place of A(I) in line 30 of the program in Example 1, each time the READ statement is executed the last value assigned to A will be replaced by a new one.

A set of data stored in memory locations named by a variable is called an **array.** For example, the set of data in A(1) to A(8) is called array A. The memory locations are also sometimes called array A. Each value or variable is an *element* of the array.

In most BASICs, string variables can also be subscripted.

---

## TEST 3

For this test, lines 30 and 60 in Example 1 should be replaced with the lines below. The numbers in the DATA statement should each be enclosed in quotation marks if necessary.

```
30 READ A$(I)
60 PRINT "A$(";I;")",A$(I)
```

If subscripted string variables are allowed, the output in the right-hand column appears as it does in Example 1. The set of data in A$(1) to A$(8) ,or the set of memory locations themselves, is called *string array* (or array) A$.

---

The following program shows how strings can be read into an array and printed.

---

## EXAMPLE 2

```
10 REM READ AND WRITE ALPHANUMERIC DATA
20 DATA "PETERKA","TOM ",95,"DEDIC","MIKE ",96
22 DATA "ROMANELLI","RENEE ",91,"CHIU","SHERMAN ",86
24 DATA "ROMAN","MARIA ",88
30 REM LINES 40-60 READ LAST NAMES, FIRST NAMES, AND SCORES
40 FOR I = 1 TO 5
50    READ L$(I),F$(I),S(I)
60 NEXT I
270 REM LINES 280-320 PRINT FIRST NAME, LAST NAME, AND SCORE
280 FOR I = 1 TO 5
300    PRINT F$(I);L$(I),S(I)
320 NEXT I
330 END
RUN
```

```
TOM PETERKA        95
MIKE DEDIC         96
RENEE ROMANELLI    91
SHERMAN CHIU       86
MARIA ROMAN        88
```

Sometimes it is necessary to combine strings. The next example shows one way to combine them in output.

---

**EXAMPLE 3**

```
10 REM COMBINING STRINGS IN OUTPUT
20 DATA "SAYS","POPPINS  ","MARY  ","SUPER"
30 DATA "CALI","FRAGI","LISTIC"
40 DATA "EXPIALI","DOCIOUS"
50 FOR I = 1 TO 9
60     READ A$(I)
70 NEXT I
80 PRINT A$(3);A$(2);A$(1)
90 FOR J = 4 TO 9
100    PRINT A$(J);
110 NEXT J
120 END
RUN
```

MARY  POPPINS  SAYS
SUPERCALIFRAGILISTICEXPIALIDOCIOUS

Notice that if strings are to be printed out of order, the variables are listed separately, as in line 80.

---

The next example shows how to combine strings to form new strings that are assigned to their own variables.

---

**EXAMPLE 4**

Change lines 80-110 in Example 3 to the following lines.

```
80 LET A$ = A$(3)+A$(2)+A$(1)
90 LET B$ = A$(4)+A$(5)+A$(6)+A$(7)+A$(8)+A$(9)
100 PRINT A$
110 PRINT B$
```

The output appears as it does in Example 3.

---

# Exercises

1. How can the same letter be used to write different variables?
2. What numbers may be used as subscripts?
3. What two sets are called array X?
4. What two sets are called string array (or array) N$?

**5.** How are strings combined in output only?

**6.** How are strings combined to form new strings?

**Tell whether each variable is valid or invalid in your BASIC. If invalid, tell why.**

| | | | |
|---|---|---|---|
| **7.** A(0) | **8.** 1A(2) | **9.** X∗(1) | **10.** C(I+1) |
| **11.** E(2J+3) | **12.** XY(5) | **13.** D(−1) | **14.** Z(%) |
| **15.** B(INT(X/Y)) | **16.** F(2.5) | **17.** K$(0) | **18.** A$(−5) |
| **19.** A6$(6) | **20.** KL$(50) | **21.** $$(4) | **22.** A$(#) |
| **23.** X$(2∗I) | **24.** Y$(Y) | **25.** DAN$(10) | **26.** B($) |

**Write each subscripted variable in BASIC.**

**27.** $a_2$      **28.** $x_i$      **29.** $b_{i+j}$      **30.** $d_{2j+1}$      **31.** $x_0$

**Use the READ/DATA statements below to determine the value of each subscripted variable in Exercises 32-36.**

```
10 READ X(1),X(3),X(2),X(5),X(4)
20 DATA −5,0,3,257,3.56
```

**32.** X(1)      **33.** X(2)      **34.** X(3)      **35.** X(4)      **36.** X(5)

**Combine the statements in Exercises 37-41 with the statements below. Give the output, showing all spaces.**

```
10 FOR I = 1 TO 5
20    READ X(I)
30 NEXT I
50 DATA −1,1,−2,2,0
60 END
```

**37.** 40 PRINT X(5),X(3),X(1),X(4),X(2)

**38.** 40 PRINT X(1),X(2),X(5)

**39.** 40 FOR I = 1 TO 5
42    PRINT X(I)
44 NEXT I

**40.** 40 FOR I = 1 TO 5
42    PRINT X(I),
44 NEXT I

**41.** 40 FOR I = 5 TO 1 STEP −1
42    PRINT X(I)
44 NEXT I

**For each set of statements, list the elements in array N.**

**42.** 10 FOR I = 7 TO 10
20    LET N(I) = I
30 NEXT I

**43.** 40 FOR I = 6 TO 1 STEP −1
50    LET N(I) = I
60 NEXT I

**Give the string stored in each of the following.**
**44.** A$(2) in Example 3          **45.** A$(7) in Example 3
**46.** A$ in Example 4          **47.** B$ in Example 4

# Laboratory Activities

1. Enter and run Test 1. Use a value of 5 for MX. Then change line 40 to the line shown to its right. Does your BASIC use 0 or 1 as the first subscript?

2. Enter and run Test 1, using the correct form for line 40 for your BASIC. What is the greatest subscript allowed in your BASIC? What error message is displayed if the subscript is too great? How many subscripts are allowed?

3. Experiment to find out whether or not an error message is displayed
   a) if a negative subscript is used
   b) if a noninteger subscript is used

4. Enter and run Test 2. In your BASIC, are A and A(I) both allowed? Are they considered different variables?

5. Enter and run the program in Example 1. Is the output the same as shown in the example?

6. In the program for Activity **5,** replace A(I) in lines 30 and 60 with A. Run the program. Compare the output with the output in Activity **5.**

7. Enter and run Test 3. Does your BASIC allow subscripted string variables?

8. If your BASIC allows subscripted string variables, the output in the right-hand column in Test 3 appears the same as the output in the right-hand column in Example 1, but it is not the same. What is the difference?

9. Enter and run the program in Example 2.

10. Enter and run the program in Example 3. Compare your output to the output shown in the example.

11. Make the changes described in Example 4. Run the program. Compare the output to that in Activity **10.**

12. Enter and run the programs from Exercises **37-41.** Use the output to check your answers to the exercises.

13. Add a print loop, as shown in Example 1, to each set of statements in Exercises **42** and **43.** Run the resulting program and use the output to check your answers to the exercises.

**14.** Load PAINTER. Replace the following variables with subscripted variables: OA (overall area of wall NW), OT (total area of the openings in wall NW), and WA (net area of wall NW). Delete the PRINT statements that give the values of those variables, and add PRINT statements to make a table showing the overall area, opening area, and net area of each wall. The table should come before the total wall area of the room is given. (Use line 211 to print the words "overall," "opening," and "net" in zones on one line. Print "area" in each zone on the next line. Then use a loop to print the values for each wall in the proper columns.) Run the program.

**15.** Load TRIANGLE PERIMETER. Change the program so the lengths are entered into array S. (Be sure to change the input tests and perimeter calculation also.) Also change the quit option to use "YES" and "NO" instead of numbers. Run the program.

**16.** Three positive numbers cannot be the lengths of sides of a triangle unless the sum of any two of them is greater than the third. The following lines can be used in the program in Activity **15** to test whether the perimeter is actually that of a triangle. They should be added after the perimeter is computed and before the perimeter is printed.

LET F=0
FOR I = 1 TO 3
LET D(I) = P−S(I)
IF D(I) > S(I) THEN (next I)
LET F = 1
NEXT I
IF F = 0 THEN (print perimeter)
PRINT "NOT A TRIANGLE"
GOTO (quit option)

Correctly number and complete these statements and add them to your program. Run the program. Replace TRIANGLE PERIMETER with the revised program.

**Use the data given below in Activities 17-24.**

$$22, -15, 0, 50, 100, 127, -143, -1, 3.4, 10.7$$

**17.** Write and run a program that uses subscripted variables to read the given numbers. Have the computer print the numbers in the given order on one line.

**18.** Change the program you wrote for Activity **17** to print the numbers in the reverse order in which they were read. Run the program.

**19.** Change the program you wrote for Activity **17** to print each number on a different line. Run the program.

**20.** Change the program you wrote for Activity **17** to print only the positive numbers. Run the program.

21. Change the program you wrote for Activity **17** to find and print the greatest number. Run the program.
22. Change the program you wrote for Activity **17** to find and print the sum of the ten numbers. Run the program.
23. Change the program you wrote for Activity **22** to find and print the average of the ten numbers. Run the program.
24. Change the program you wrote for Activity **23** to subtract each number from the average of the numbers and to print the differences. Run the program.

# 6.3  DIMENSIONED VARIABLES

In most BASICs, a **DIM** (short for dimension) **statement** is used to increase the number of subscripts allowed for an array. In other words, it extends the limit on the number of subscripts allowed with the same variable. A $\mathrm{DIM}$ statement has the following format.

$$\mathrm{DIM}\ X(N)$$

variable ⟶⟵ **index** of the $\mathrm{DIM}$ statement (a positive integer or, in some BASICs, a variable or expression whose value is a positive integer)

When it is executed, the $\mathrm{DIM}$ statement assigns each subscripted variable in the array to a location in memory. This statement must be executed before any of the subscripted variables in the array are used in the program.

The statement $10\ \mathrm{DIM}\ B(15)$ means that 15 is the greatest subscript that can be used with B. In a BASIC in which 1 is the least subscript allowed, 15 memory locations are assigned (for B(1) to B(15)) when the $\mathrm{DIM}$ statement is executed. In a BASIC in which 0 is the least subscript allowed, 16 locations (for B(0) to B(15)) are assigned. While these locations do not all have to be used, they cannot be used for any other data, so it is important not to use an unnecessarily great index in a $\mathrm{DIM}$ statement. However, an error message is displayed if a subscript is used that is greater than the index of the $\mathrm{DIM}$ statement.

In most BASICs, there is a limit to the size of an array (that is, to the index in a DIM statement). There is also a limit to the amount of computer memory available for arrays.

---

### TEST 1

Change Test 1 on page 180 by adding the following line.

35 DIM A(MX)

This statement should allow any integer up to a limit that varies with the BASIC to be entered as input without causing an error message to be printed.

---

A DIM statement is said to *declare an array.* When an array is declared using a variable, as shown in Test 1, its size cannot be changed easily in most BASICs without rerunning the program. If a quit option is to be included, the DIM statement should declare an array of the greatest size likely to be needed. If this is not practical, a quit option should not be used.

More than one array may be declared in the same DIM statement.

---

### EXAMPLE 1

10 DIM A(50),B(25),C(100)

---

# Exercises

1. What statement is used to increase the size allowed for an array?
2. What is the format of a DIM statement?
3. Where in a program should a DIM statement appear?

**For your system, tell how many elements could be in each array declared in the DIM statements in Exercises 4-10.**

**4.** 10 DIM A(16)  **5.** 10 DIM S(28)  **6.** 10 DIM V(120)

**7.** 10 DIM N$(35)  **8.** 10 DIM T$(12)  **9.** 10 DIM L$(33)

**10.** 10 DIM F(46),M$(67),P(100),C$(93)

**Write a DIM statement to declare the size of each array in Exercises 11-16.**

**11.** 20 FOR C = 1 TO 36  **12.** 10 FOR N = 1 TO 26
    30    LET A(C) = C      20    READ L$(N)
    40 NEXT C      30 NEXT N

**13.** 40 DATA 1,1,2,4,3,9,4,16,5,25,6,36,7,49,8,64,9,81,10,100
    50 FOR I = 1 TO 15
    55    READ N(I),S(I)
    60 NEXT I

**14.** 10 FOR T = 1 TO 99 STEP 2
    20    LET B(T) = T
    30 NEXT T

**15.** 30 FOR D = 5 TO 20
    40    LET R(D) = SQR(D)
    50 NEXT D

**16.** 10 FOR N = 1 TO 30
    20    LET A(N) = N+1
    30    FOR C = 0 TO 13
    40      LET B(C+1) = 2*N
    50    NEXT C
    60 NEXT N

# Laboratory Activities

**1.** Enter and run Test 1. Use various input values to find, if possible, the greatest array size your BASIC allows.

**2.** Add a quit option to Test 1. What happens when you choose to use the program again and use a different value for MX?

**Add the necessary statements to the statements in the exercises listed below so you can check your answers to the exercises.**

**3.** Exercise **11**

**4.** Exercise **12**

**5.** Exercise **13**

**6.** Exercise **14**

**7.** Exercise **15**

**8.** Exercise **16**

**9.** Enter and run the following program.
```
10 PRINT "ENTER THE NUMBER OF COLUMNS ON YOUR SCREEN"
20 INPUT C
30 DIM A$(C)
40 FOR I = 1 TO C
50    LET A$(I) ="*"
60    PRINT A$(I);
70 NEXT I
80 END
```

10. Experiment with the program in Activity **9,** to use other symbols, to make stripes of different widths across the screen, and to make stripes across the screen with different symbols in each stripe.

11. Load AVERAGE. Change the program so up to 100 numbers are loaded into an array and listed in the output before their average is given. Run the program.

12. Load TEST SCORES. Change the program so the students' names are read into an array and each student's scores are read into array S. Have the program print each student's name, scores, and average. Run the program.

13. Write and run a program that can be used to average up to 20 scores for up to 50 students. Put the names of the students in the class in the DATA statements, and have the scores for each student entered as input. Be sure the input instructions print the name of the student whose scores should be entered. Save the program as TEST SCORES FOR 50.

14. Load BASKETBALL PERCENTAGE. Change the program so the names of up to 16 teams and their won/lost records are entered as input and stored in arrays. The output should be a table listing teams, their records, and percentages. Run the program and save it as BASKETBALL PERCENTAGE 16.

15. Load DIVING. Use arrays to make the program usable for up to 60 divers and 6 judges. The output should show the scores for each diver from each judge, as well as the total score for each diver. Run the program and save it as DIVING 60.

# 6.4 DATA SORTING AND RANDOM NUMBERS

One of the most useful tasks a computer can perform is to rapidly *sort* large amounts of data into an order specified by the program or user. The program in Example 1 sorts numerical data.

## EXAMPLE 1

```
10 REM PUT NUMBERS IN ORDER FROM GREATEST TO LEAST
20 DATA 10,18,21,5,27
30 REM READ THE NUMBERS INTO AN ARRAY
40 FOR I = 1 TO 5
50    READ A(I)
60 NEXT I
```

```
90 REM INITIALIZE A FLAG
100 LET FL = 0
110 REM COMPARE EACH NUMBER TO THE NEXT
115 REM EXCHANGE IF NEXT NUMBER IS GREATER
120 FOR I = 1 TO 4
130     IF A(I) >= A(I+1) THEN 190
140     REM EXCHANGE A(I) AND A(I+1)
150     LET H = A(I+1)
160     LET A(I+1) = A(I)
170     LET A(I) = H
180     REM IF EXCHANGE MADE, SET FLAG TO 1
185     LET FL = 1
190 NEXT I
200 REM IF FLAG SET, RESET TO 0 AND MAKE ANOTHER PASS
210 IF FL = 1 THEN 100
250 REM PRINT NUMBERS IN ORDER
260 FOR I = 1 TO 5
270     PRINT A(I);" ";
280 NEXT I
290 END
RUN
27   21   18   10   5
```

The effect of the first two passes through the *sorting loop* in lines 120-190 is shown below.

| | I | I+1 | A(1) | A(2) | A(3) | A(4) | A(5) | Exchange? |
|---|---|---|---|---|---|---|---|---|
| **Pass 1** | 1 | 2 | 10 | 18 | 21 | 5 | 27 | yes |
| | 2 | 3 | 18 | 10 | 21 | 5 | 27 | yes |
| | 3 | 4 | 18 | 21 | 10 | 5 | 27 | no |
| | 4 | 5 | 18 | 21 | 10 | 5 | 27 | yes |
| **At end of first pass** | | | 18 | 21 | 10 | 27 | 5 | |
| | | | | | | | | |
| **Pass 2** | 1 | 2 | 18 | 21 | 10 | 27 | 5 | yes |
| | 2 | 3 | 21 | 18 | 10 | 27 | 5 | no |
| | 3 | 4 | 21 | 18 | 10 | 27 | 5 | yes |
| | 4 | 5 | 21 | 18 | 27 | 10 | 5 | no |
| **At end of second pass** | | | 21 | 18 | 27 | 10 | 5 | |

Notice that, on each pass through the sorting loop, a *flag* keeps track of whether any exchanges are made. If an exchange is made, the sorting loop is executed again. If no exchange is made, the data is completely sorted.

A general rule or process used to solve a problem is called an **algorithm.** The algorithm used in Example 1 is called a **bubble sort.** There are many other sorting algorithms in use, such as shell sort, Shell-Metzger sort, and quicksort.

Strings can also be sorted. They are compared using the same symbols used to compare numerical data, but these symbols have special meanings when they are used with strings.

| Comparison | Meaning |
|---|---|
| A$ < B$ | A$ comes alphabetically before B$. |
| A$ = "END" | A$ contains the same characters in the same order as the string on the right. |
| A$ > "LONG" | A$ comes alphabetically after the string on the right. |
| A$ < =B$ | A$ comes alphabetically before B$, or it contains the same characters as B$ in the same order. |
| "YES" >= "YE" | The string on the left comes alphabetically after the string on the right, or it contains the same characters in the same order. |
| A$ <> B$ | A$ and B$ do not contain the same characters in the same order. |

The program below sorts strings alphabetically. The process is the same as for sorting numbers, except alphabetical order is similar to numerical order from least to greatest.

---

## EXAMPLE 2

The following lines can be used in the program in Example 1.

```
10 REM PUT STRINGS IN ALPHABETICAL ORDER
20 DATA "PETERKA","DEDIC","ROMANELLI"
22 DATA "CHIU","ROMAN"
30 REM READ THE NAMES INTO AN ARRAY
50    READ L$(I)
110 REM COMPARE EACH NAME TO THE NEXT
115 REM EXCHANGE IF NEXT NAME COMES FIRST ALPHABETICALLY
130    IF L$(I) <=L$(I+1) THEN 190
140    REM EXCHANGE L$(I) AND L$(I+1)
150    LET H$ = L$(I+1)
160    LET L$(I+1) = L$(I)
170    LET L$(I) = H$
250 REM PRINT NAMES IN ORDER
270    PRINT L$(I)
```

RUN
CHIU
DEDIC
PETERKA
ROMAN
ROMANELLI

If first names are included in the program, they will also have to be exchanged each time the corresponding last names are exchanged.

---

Many events that are important in science, industry, social science, business, and almost any other field occur without an observable pattern. They are said to occur *randomly,* or to be *random events.*

Numbers can also occur randomly. A computer can produce a set of random numbers using a *random number generator.*

Random number generators operate differently in different computers. The most common methods of operation are described below.

| **Function** | **Effect** |
|---|---|
| RND | 1. Generates a random number greater than 0 and less than 1. If used again, it generates another random number unrelated to the first one. |
| RND(∅) | 2. Same as RND.<br>3. Same as RND, but if used again, it generates the same random number. |
| RND(N)<br>where<br>N>O | 4. Same as RND.<br>5. Generates a random integer between 1 and N. |

In this book, **RND** will be used as the random number generator. We will assume it has the effect described in Effect 1 above. (You should replace RND with the function used in your BASIC.)

A loop can be used to generate a set of random numbers.

---

**EXAMPLE 3**

```
10 PRINT "TO FILL AN ARRAY WITH RANDOM NUMBERS"
15 DIM R(20)
20 FOR N = 1 TO 20
30    LET R(N) = RND
35    PRINT R(N)
40 NEXT N
50 END
```

In some systems, rerunning the program in Example 3 generates a new set of random numbers. Other systems give the same set each time. This is because some random number generators are *seeded,* or reset, each time and others are not.

Some random number generators can be seeded by using a keyword such as RANDOMIZE or RANDOM, before the statement or loop in which RND is used. Others are seeded by using a negative value of X in RND(X), while still others are seeded unless a negative value for X is used. In this book we will assume the random number generator is seeded each time a RND statement is executed.

Although the RND function generates a random number between 0 and 1, it can be used to find a random number between any two integers or to find a random integer between any two integers.

---

**EXAMPLE 4**

To fill an array with random numbers between 2 and 3, replace line 30 in the program in Example 3 with the line below.
30 LET R(N) = RND+2

To fill an array with random numbers between 0 and 100, use this line.
30 LET R(N) = 100*RND

To fill an array with random integers from 0 to 49, use this line.
30 LET R(N) = INT(50*RND)

---

# Exercises

1. In a bubble sort, what numbers are compared?
2. If the numbers compared are in the wrong order, what is done?
3. What is the flag used for?
4. What does it mean if the flag is not set to 1 on a pass through the sorting loop?
5. Complete the chart for the first pass through the sorting loop in Example 1. What is the effect of executing lines 150-170?

| after line | H | A(I) | A(I+1) |
|---|---|---|---|
| 130 | | | |
| 150 | | | |
| 160 | | | |
| 170 | | | |

6. What is a general rule or process used to solve a problem called?

**Use the following strings to tell whether the statement given is true or false.**

A\$ = "DOG", B\$ = "CAT", C\$ = "DOGS", D\$ = "DO GS"

**7.** A\$ < B\$        **8.** B\$ < C\$        **9.** C\$ = D\$        **10.** D\$ <= A\$

**11.** C\$ = A\$        **12.** D\$ >= C\$        **13.** B\$ <= D\$        **14.** A\$ > D\$

**15.** What are events called that occur without an observable pattern?

**16.** Find out from your manual or your teacher how to generate a set of random numbers using your computer.

**Write statements for your system that will generate the random numbers described in Exercises 17-24.**

**17.** Between 0 and 5                    **18.** Between 0 and 10

**19.** Between 1 and 2                    **20.** Between 1 and 6

**21.** Integers from 0 to 50              **22.** Integers from 1 to 6

**23.** Integers from 5 to 10             **24.** Even integers from 0 to 20

# Laboratory Activities

**1.** Enter and run Example 1.

**2.** Change the program in Example 1 to sort and print 10 numbers supplied in a DATA statement. Run the program.

**3.** Change the program in Example 1 to sort up to 20 numbers entered as input. Run the program.

**4.** Change the program in Example 1 to sort the numbers from least to greatest. Run the program.

**5.** Enter and run the program in Example 2.

**6.** Add first names to the DATA statements in Example 2. Change the program so it will sort the last names alphabetically and print each last name followed by the correct first name. Run the program.

**7.** Put the strings for Exercises **7-14** into DATA statements in the program in Example 2. Run the program to check your answers to the exercises.

**8.** Enter and run the program in Example 3.

**9.** Make the changes described in Example 4. Run each program.

**Write and run a program that will generate and fill an array with 20 numbers from the set described in the exercise named. Have the computer print the array.**

**10.** Exercise **17**                    **11.** Exercise **18**

**12.** Exercise **19**                    **13.** Exercise **20**

**Write and run a program that will generate and fill an array with the numbers described in the exercise named. Have the computer print the array.**

**14.** Exercise **21**                    **15.** Exercise **22**

**16.** Exercise **23**                    **17.** Exercise **24**

**18.** Change the program in Example 2 to sort the last names of the students in your class alphabetically. Have the output show the last name and first name of each student in that order. Run the program.

**19.** The median of an array of numbers is the middle number when the numbers are arranged in order. (If there is no middle number, the median is the average of the two middle numbers.) Write and run a program that will find the median of any 13 numbers entered as input.

**20.** Change the program you wrote for Activity **19** to find the median of any 14 numbers entered as input. Run the program.

**21.** Change the program you wrote for Activity **20** to accept up to 20 numbers as input. Test to determine whether an odd or even quantity of numbers has been entered. Then use the correct formula to find the median. (*Hint:* If a number N is even then N/2 = INT(N/2).) Run the program.

**22.** Change the program in Activity **21** to accept up to 30 numbers as input. Run the program.

**23.** When a die is tossed, random integers from 1 to 6 are generated. Write and run a program to simulate tossing a die 100 times.

**24.** Change the program in Activity **23** to count how many times each integer occurs and to show, in order from 1 to 6, the integer and the number of times that integer occurred. Run the program.

**25.** Write and run a program to simulate up to 100 tosses of a coin and to display the total numbers of heads and tails that occur.

# 6.5  MATRICES

The arrays you have worked with so far have been lists, or one-dimensional arrays, in which each variable has one subscript. The following table of baseball standings is a *two-dimensional array,* or **matrix** (plural: matrices).

| Team | W | L | PCT | GB |
|------|------|------|------|------|
| Los Angeles | 36 | 21 | .632 | 0 |
| Cincinnati | 35 | 21 | .625 | .5 |
| Houston | 28 | 29 | .419 | 8 |

The headings W, L, PCT, and GB stand for wins, losses, percentage of games won, and games behind the first-place team.

While the entire table forms a matrix, the numerical values alone form a matrix with 3 rows and 4 columns, or a 3×4 (read "3 by 4") matrix. Each element in the matrix is assigned to a variable with two subscripts.

---

**EXAMPLE 1**

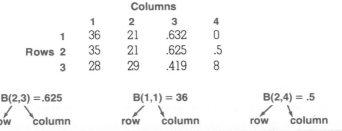

A computer can read values entered as input or from DATA statements and store or display a matrix of those values. In the example below, the values from the table in Example 1 are listed by rows in DATA statements. The subscripts for the variables are generated using nested loops.

---

**EXAMPLE 2**

```
20 DATA 36,21,.632,0
30 DATA 35,21,.625,.5
40 DATA 28,29,.419,8
50 DIM B(3,4)
60 FOR I = 1 TO 3
70    FOR J = 1 TO 4
80       READ B(I,J)
90    NEXT J
100 NEXT I
```

The matrix is dimensioned in line 50. The outer loop generates the row numbers, or first subscripts. For each row number, the inner loop generates the column numbers, or second subscripts.

---

The DIM statement in line 50 in Example 2 means that 3 and 4 are the greatest subscripts that can be used with B. That is, 3 is the greatest first subscript and 4 is the greatest second subscript. In a BASIC in which 1 is the least subscript allowed, 3×4, or 12, memory locations are assigned to the variables. This is exactly the number of elements in the matrix. In a BASIC in which 0 is the least subscript allowed, 4×5, or 20, memory locations are assigned to the variables.

For the baseball matrix, the column and row headings can be added using PRINT statements or they can be read from DATA statements and then printed. The matrix of values can be printed as shown in the next example. Notice that the PRINT statement in line 240 is needed to move the cursor to the next line before printing the next row.

**EXAMPLE 3**

```
200 FOR I = 1 TO 3
210    FOR J = 1 TO 4
220       PRINT B(I,J);" ";
230    NEXT J
240    PRINT
250 NEXT I
```

# Exercises

1. In a one-dimensional array, how many subscripts do the variables have?
2. In a two-dimensional array or matrix, how many subscripts do the variables have?
3. How many subscripts would you expect the variables to have in a three-dimensional array? In a six-dimensional array? In a twelve-dimensional array?

**Tell how many rows and columns there are in the matrix described by each expression.**

4. 4×5        5. 8×7        6. 6×6        7. 1×12

**Tell from which row and column of its matrix each element comes.**

8. B(3,4)        9. A(8,8)        10. D(1,5)        11. T(6,1)

**Tell how many memory locations would be assigned in your system by each DIM statement.**

12. DIM(2,7)        13. DIM(4,5)        14. DIM(6,3)        15. DIM(1,12)

**16.** Draw a chart like the one below. Use it to show the values of the variables generated by the nested loops.

| I | J | A(I,J) | |
|---|---|--------|---|
| | | | 10 DIM A(3,3) |
| 1 | 1 | | 20 FOR I = 1 TO 3 |
| 1 | 2 | | 30    FOR J = 1 TO 3 |
| 1 | 3 | | 40       READ A(I,J) |
| 2 | 1 | | 50    NEXT J |
| 2 | 2 | | 60 NEXT I |
| 2 | 3 | | 70 DATA 20,40,60 |
| 3 | 1 | | 75 DATA 80,10,25 |
| 3 | 2 | | 80 DATA 45,15,35 |
| 3 | 3 | | 100 END |

**17.** Use a chart like the one in Exercise **16** to show the values of the variables generated by the nested loops in Example 2.

# Laboratory Activities

**1.** Enter and run the statements in Examples 2 and 3. (Add an END statement if necessary.)

**2.** Add statements to the program in Activity **1** to print the team name at the left of each row. If necessary change line 220 to make room. Run the program.

**3.** Add statements to the program in Activity **2** to print the column heads. Run the program.

**4.** Complete the program in Activity **3**. Run the program and save it as BASEBALL MATRIX 1.

**5.** Enter and run the following program.

```
10 DIM A$(6,6)
30 FOR I = 1 TO 6
40    FOR J = 1 TO 6
50       LET A$(I,J)="*"
60       PRINT A$(I,J);
70    NEXT J
80    PRINT
90 NEXT I
100 END
```

**6.** Change the program in Activity **5** to print your initials in a 6×6 matrix. Run the program.

**7.** Load BASEBALL MATRIX 1. Change the program so the team records are entered into the matrix as input. Also have the team names (but not the column heads) entered as input. Run the program and save it as BASEBALL MATRIX 2.

**8.** Write and run a program using a matrix to read and print the values in the following wind-chill index chart. Add the headings to complete the chart.

| WIND-CHILL INDEX CHART | | | | | | | |
|---|---|---|---|---|---|---|---|
| Wind Speed | Temperature | | | | | | |
| | 30 | 20 | 10 | 0 | −10 | −20 | −30 |
| 10 mph | 16 | 2 | −9 | −22 | −31 | −45 | −58 |
| 15 mph | 11 | −6 | −18 | −33 | −45 | −60 | −70 |
| 20 mph | 3 | −9 | −24 | −40 | −52 | −68 | −81 |
| 25 mph | 0 | −15 | −29 | −45 | −58 | −75 | −89 |
| 30 mph | −2 | −18 | −33 | −49 | −63 | −78 | −94 |
| 35 mph | −4 | −20 | −35 | −52 | −67 | −83 | −98 |
| 40 mph | −4 | −22 | −36 | −54 | −69 | −87 | −101 |

**9.** The table below shows the amount in a savings account after *n* years if the principal is $1 and interest is compounded annually at the rate shown. Write and run a program to print the table from values in DATA statements.

| n | 1% | 2% | 3% | 4% | 5% |
|---|---|---|---|---|---|
| 1 | 1.0100 | 1.0200 | 1.0300 | 1.0400 | 1.0500 |
| 2 | 1.0201 | 1.0404 | 1.0609 | 1.0816 | 1.1025 |
| 3 | 1.0303 | 1.0612 | 1.0927 | 1.1249 | 1.1576 |
| 4 | 1.0406 | 1.0824 | 1.1255 | 1.1699 | 1.2155 |
| 5 | 1.0510 | 1.1041 | 1.1593 | 1.2167 | 1.2763 |

**10.** The formula $I=(1+R) \uparrow N$, where R is the interest rate as a decimal, is used to find each value in the table above. Change the program you wrote for Activity **9** to compute the values instead of reading them from DATA statements. Have the values rounded to the nearest ten thousandth. Run the program.

**11.** Change the program you wrote for Activity **10** to print a table for 25 years and interest rates from 5% to 12%. Run the program and save it as COMPOUND INTEREST TABLE.

**12.** To use a compound interest table for any principal, the value given in the table is multiplied by the principal. For example $500 invested at 5% compounded annually for 5 years increases to 500×1.2763 or $638.15 Change COMPOUND INTEREST TABLE to print a table for any principal entered as input. Run the program.

**13.** Two dice can be thrown at the same time to generate two independent sets of random integers from 1 to 6. All possible combinations of these integers can be shown in a 6×6 matrix by letting the row number represent the integers generated by one die and the column number represent the integers generated by the other die. For example, the element in row 4 and column 5 represents a combination of 4 spots on one die and 5 on the other. That is A(4,5) = (4,5). Write and run a program to print the matrix.

**14.** When two dice are thrown as described in Activity **13,** the sum of the spots on the dice is a random integer from 2 to 12. Change the program you wrote for Activity **13** to print a 6×6 matrix whose elements are the sums of the row and column numbers. Run the program.

**15.** Write and run a program to simulate the throwing of two dice 500 times. Use a 6×6 matrix to store a running total for each possible sum of the spots on the dice. The output should show a matrix like the one in Activity **14** with each sum replaced by the total number of times it occurred.

**16.** When three dice are thrown as described in Activity **13,** the sum of the spots on the dice is a random integer from 3 to 18. Write and run a program to print a 6 × 11 matrix to show all possible sums. (The rows represent the number represented when one die is thrown. The columns represent the sum when two dice are thrown.)

**Use any 4×4 matrix for Activities 17-22.**

**17.** Write and run a program to print the greatest number in the matrix.

**18.** Write and run a program to print the least number in the matrix.

**19.** Write and run a program to find the sum of the numbers in each row. Have the sum of each row printed in a 1×4 matrix.

**20.** Write and run a program to find the sum of the numbers in each column. Have the sum of each column printed in a 4×1 matrix.

**21.** Write and run a program to find the average of the numbers in each row. Have the averages printed in a 1×4 matrix.

**22.** Write and run a program to find the average of the numbers in each column. Have the averages printed in a 4×1 matrix.

# 6.6 ADDING AND SUBTRACTING MATRICES

The manager of a grocery store keeps a daily record of the sales of certain produce items. These records are used to find the average sales of each item for each day of the week so the manager can plan purchases to more closely match the demand. The records for two weeks are shown in matrix form below.

| Week 1 | M | T | W | R | F | S |
|---|---|---|---|---|---|---|
| Lettuce | 25 | 10 | 12 | 20 | 35 | 15 |
| Apples | 50 | 40 | 30 | 40 | 50 | 60 |
| Pineapples | 15 | 7 | 3 | 0 | 6 | 12 |
| **Week 2** | | | | | | |
| Lettuce | 20 | 20 | 12 | 30 | 16 | 18 |
| Apples | 40 | 30 | 20 | 30 | 40 | 60 |
| Pineapples | 7 | 16 | 2 | 5 | 15 | 10 |

To find the average sales, the sales for both weeks must first be added. In other words, corresponding elements of the two matrices must be added. The sums also form a matrix.

| Sum | M | T | W | R | F | S |
|---|---|---|---|---|---|---|
| Lettuce | 45 | 30 | 24 | 50 | 51 | 33 |
| Apples | 90 | 70 | 50 | 70 | 90 | 120 |
| Pineapples | 22 | 23 | 5 | 5 | 21 | 22 |

Matrices are added by adding their corresponding elements. To be added, matrices must have the same number of columns and the same number of rows.

A program can be written that will read the two matrices from DATA statements, add them, and print the sum. The first part, reading the matrices, is shown in Example 1.

---

**EXAMPLE 1**

```
 5 REM DECLARE THE ARRAYS
10 DIM W1(3,6),W2(3,6),S(3,6),A(3,6)
20 REM READ MATRIX FOR WEEK 1
30 FOR I = 1 TO 3
40    FOR J = 1 TO 6
50       READ W1(I,J)
60    NEXT J
70 NEXT I
80 DATA 25,10,12,20,35,15
85 DATA 50,40,30,40,50,60
90 DATA 15,7,3,0,6,12
```

```
100 REM READ MATRIX FOR WEEK 2
110 FOR I = 1 TO 3
120    FOR J = 1 TO 6
130        READ W2(I,J)
140    NEXT J
150 NEXT I
160 DATA 20,20,12,30,16,18
165 DATA 40,30,20,30,40,60
170 DATA 7,16,2,5,15,10
```

The second part of the program adds the matrices.

## EXAMPLE 2

```
200 REM ADD CORRESPONDING ELEMENTS
210 FOR I = 1 TO 3
220    FOR J = 1 TO 6
230        LET S(I,J) = W1(I,J)+W2(I,J)
240    NEXT J
250 NEXT I
```

The third part of the program prints the matrix for week 1, the matrix for week 2, and the matrix for the sum.

## EXAMPLE 3

```
300 FOR I = 1 TO 3
310    FOR J = 1 TO 6
320        PRINT W1(I,J);TAB(J*4);
330    NEXT J
340    PRINT
350 NEXT I
355 PRINT
360 FOR I = 1 TO 3
370    FOR J = 1 TO 6
380        PRINT W2(I,J);TAB(J*4);
390    NEXT J
400    PRINT
410 NEXT I
415 PRINT
420 FOR I = 1 TO 3
430    FOR J = 1 TO 6
440        PRINT S(I,J);TAB(J*4);
450    NEXT J
460    PRINT
470 NEXT I
480 END
```

The sales data for two weeks were added. To find the average for each produce item for each day of the week, each sum must be divided by 2(or multiplied by .5). The .5 is a constant by which the matrix is multiplied, and is called a *scalar.* The process of multiplying matrix S(I,J) by .5 is called *scalar multiplication.* The lines in the example below multiply the matrix S by .5 and print the product.

---

**EXAMPLE 4**

```
480 FOR I = 1 TO 3
490    FOR J = 1 TO 6
500       LET A(I,J) = .5*S(I,J)
510    NEXT J
520 NEXT I
530 FOR I = 1 TO 3
540    FOR J = 1 TO 6
550       PRINT A(I,J);TAB(J*6);
560    NEXT J
570 NEXT I
580 END
```

---

The manager also wants to know the difference between the numbers of items sold in the two weeks. To find the difference, subtract the sales for week 2 from the sales for week 1.

| Difference | M | T | W | R | F | S |
|---|---|---|---|---|---|---|
| Lettuce | 5 | −10 | 0 | −10 | 19 | −3 |
| Apples | 10 | 10 | 10 | 10 | 10 | 0 |
| Pineapples | 8 | −9 | 1 | −5 | −9 | 2 |

Positive numbers indicate that more items were sold during week 1. Negative numbers indicate that more items were sold during week 2. Zeros indicate that the same number of items was sold each week.

Matrices are subtracted by subtracting their corresponding elements. To be subtracted, matrices must have the same number of columns and the same number of rows.

The program in the following example subtracts the matrices and prints all three matrices.

---

**EXAMPLE 5**

Use the following lines in the program in Examples 1, 2, and 3.

```
10 DIM W1(3,6),W2(3,6),D(3,6)
200 REM SUBTRACT CORRESPONDING ELEMENTS
230    LET D(I,J) = W1(I,J)−W2(I,J)
440       PRINT D(I,J);TAB(J*4);
```

---

# Exercises ═══════════════════════

1. For two matrices to be added or subtracted, what must be true of their rows and columns?
2. How are two matrices added? Subtracted?
3. What is the result of adding or subtracting two matrices?
4. In Example 1, how many array elements are read each time the first inner loop is executed? Each time the second inner loop is executed?
5. In Example 1, how many DATA statements are read each time the first outer loop is executed? Each time the second outer loop is executed?
6. In Example 2, what is added to W1(3,4) when line 230 is executed? What is added to W2(2,6)?
7. In Example 3, what is the purpose of lines 340 and 410?
8. In Example 3, what is the purpose of lines 360-400?
9. If two matrices that have 7 rows and 4 columns each are added, how many rows and columns does the matrix containing the sum have?
10. What is a scalar?
11. What is scalar multiplication?
12. If a matrix with 5 rows and 8 columns is multiplied by the scalar 18, how many rows and columns does the matrix containing the products have?

# Laboratory Activities ═══════════════

1. Enter and run the program in Examples 1, 2, and 3. Compare the output to the matrices on page 202.
2. Use the lines in Example 4 in the program in Activity **1**. Run the program.
3. Use the lines in Example 5 as described. Run the program.
4. Change the program in Activity **1** to print row and column labels as in the original matrices. Run the program.

**The following matrix shows the inventory of pairs of brand name shoes at an athletic shop. Use it for Activities 5 and 6.**

|  | Athlete | Sport | Health | Sneaker |
|---|---|---|---|---|
| **Jogging** | 15 | 20 | 25 | 18 |
| **Basketball** | 10 | 18 | 25 | 23 |

5. The matrix below shows the numbers of pairs of shoes received in an order by the athletic shop. Write and run a program to update the inventory. Have all three matrices printed with the rows and columns correctly labeled.

|  | Athlete | Sport | Health | Sneaker |
|---|---|---|---|---|
| **Jogging** | 5 | 8 | 7 | 4 |
| **Basketball** | 5 | 8 | 7 | 4 |

6. The matrix below shows the sales of shoes during one month. Write and run a program to subtract the sales from the updated inventory from Activity **5**. Have all three matrices printed with all the rows and columns correctly labeled.

|  | Athlete | Sport | Health | Sneaker |
|---|---|---|---|---|
| **Jogging** | 10 | 19 | 28 | 16 |
| **Basketball** | 11 | 23 | 20 | 25 |

**To create a table for interest compounded semiannually from the table on page 200, use two times the number of years and one-half the interest rate. For example, the entry for 2 years at 4% compounded semiannually is the same as the entry for 4 years at 2% compounded annually (1.0824). Use this information in Activities 7 and 8.**

7. Write and run a program to print a 12 year interest table for a principal of $1 at interest rates from 2% to 10% in steps of 2% compounded semiannually. Have the values rounded to the nearest thousandth, and all rows and columns correctly labeled.

8. Change the program you wrote for Activity **7** to compute the amount accumulated when the principal, interest rate (as a decimal), and number of years are entered as input. Tell the user to enter only those values in the table. Run the program.

# Vocabulary

alphanumeric data (173)

string variable (173)

subscripted variable (180)

array (182)

DIM (187)

index (187)

algorithm (192)

bubble sort (192)

RND (193)

RANDOM (194)

matrix (196)

# Summary

1. A string variable is used to name a memory location in which a string is stored. In many BASICs, a string variable may be any valid numeric variable followed by a dollar sign ($).
2. Some BASICs do not require that strings entered as input and in DATA statements be enclosed in quotation marks.
3. The rules for string variables in LET statements are the same as those for numeric variables.
4. Two strings are equal only if they have exactly the same characters, including spaces.
5. Strings can be combined in output. They also can be combined to form new strings that are assigned to their own variables.
6. In many BASICs, any valid variable may be subscripted. A subscript is a nonnegative integer, or a variable or expression whose value is a nonnegative integer.
7. The number of different subscripts that can be used with the same variable depends on the BASIC. Some BASICs allow 10, some 11, and some have no limit.
8. In most BASICs, a DIM statement is used to increase the number of subscripts allowed for an array. A DIM statement has the format DIM X(index).
9. DIM statements must be executed before any of the subscripted variables in the array are used in the program.
10. One useful task a computer can perform is to rapidly sort large amounts of data into an order specified in the program or by the person using the program. One algorithm used to do this is called a bubble sort.

11. Logical symbols are used to compare strings. A$ = B$ means A$ contains the same characters in the same order as B$. A$ < B$ means A$ comes before B$ alphabetically. A$ > B$ means A$ comes after B$ alphabetically. A$ <> B$ means A$ and B$ do not contain the same characters in the same order. A$ <= B$ means A$ comes alphabetically before B$ or it contains the same characters as B$ in the same order. A$ >= B$ means A$ comes alphabetically after B$ or it contains the same characters as B$ in the same order.

12. Many events occur without an observable pattern, or randomly. A computer can produce a set of random numbers using a random number generator.

13. A matrix is a two-dimensional array. Each element of a matrix is represented by a variable with two subscripts, one for the row and one for the column in which the element is found. A DIM statement is used to indicate the greatest subscripts to be used with each variable.

14. Two matrices can be added or subtracted by finding the sum or difference of their corresponding elements. The sums and differences also form matrices. To be added or subtracted, matrices must have the same number of rows and the same number of columns.

15. A scalar is a constant. The product of a scalar and a matrix can be found by multiplying each element of the matrix by the scalar.

## Chapter Test

**Tell whether each of the following variables is valid or invalid in your BASIC. If invalid, tell why.**

| | | | | |
|---|---|---|---|---|
| **1.** X$ | **2.** A∗$ | **3.** CC$ | **4.** $B | **5.** Y4$ |
| **6.** D$4 | **7.** #$ | **8.** K$(1) | **9.** XX$(3) | **10.** F(2)$ |
| **11.** $$(1) | **12.** A$(3∗I) | **13.** Z($) | **14.** A(IH,2) | **15.** MN$(4,5) |

**If X$ =''JOEL'', tell whether each of the following is true or false.**

**16.** If Y$ = ''∧JOEL∧'', then X$ = Y$.

**17.** If Y$ = ''∧MIKE∧'', then X$ <= Y$.

**18.** If Y$ = ''LEOJ'', then X$ = Y$.

**19.** If Y$ = ''JEAN'', then X$ < Y$.

**20.** If Y$ = ''JOEL∧'', then X$ <> Y$.

**21.** If Y$ = ''SHANE'', then X$ > Y$.

**22.** If Y$ = ''CARL'', then X$ >= Y$.

**Find and correct the errors in the following statements.**

**23.** 10 DATA "NUMBER",1,2
20 READ N,X,Y

**24.** 10 LET R$ = R

**25.** 20 LET "APRIL" = M$

**Use the program below in problems 26-28.**

```
10 READ A$,B$,C$
20 DATA "LION","BEAR","TIGER"
30 IF A$ <= B$ THEN 60
40 PRINT C$
50 GOTO 80
60 LET B$ = A$
70 PRINT B$
80 END
```

**26.** What is the output of the program?

**27.** Change line 30 to the following line.

```
30 IF A$ > B$ THEN 60
```

What is the output?

**28.** Change line 30 to the following line.

```
30 IF B$ <> A$ THEN 70
```

What is the output?

**Use the program below in problems 29-32.**

```
10 DATA −2,1,−3,4,6,3
20 FOR I = 1 TO 6
30     READ X(I)
40 NEXT I
50 FOR I = 2 TO 6 STEP 2
60     PRINT X(I)
70 NEXT I
80 END
```

**29.** What is the output of the program?

**30.** What is the value of X(I) in line 30 when I = 3?

**31.** Change line 50 so all the data will be printed in the opposite order from which they are read.

**32.** Change the program to sort the data from least to greatest and print the sorted data all on one line.

**33.** What is the purpose of a DIM statement?

**34.** Find and correct the error in the following program.

```
10 FOR I = 1 TO 20
20     READ B(I)
30 NEXT I
32 DATA −2,3,4,10,1,−5,7,22,20,16
34 DATA 6,−9,−12,−30,−3,15,−21,−66,−60,−48
40 DIM B(25)
50 FOR I = 2 TO 20 STEP 2
60     PRINT B(I)
70 NEXT I
80 END
```

**35.** What is the output for the program in problem **34?**

**36.** What is the output for the corrected program in problem **34?**

**37.** Write a DIM statement to declare the size of the array in the lines below.

```
10 FOR A = 0 TO 50 STEP 5
20     READ X$(A)
30 NEXT A
```

**38.** Write and run a program to sort and print the following names in alphabetical order according to the last names. Have the correct first name printed before each last name.

| | |
|---|---|
| Karen Rhodes | Justin Humphrey |
| Tom Rice | Curtis Banbury |
| Darlene Morris | Cindy Bauer |
| Phil Zengler | Jennifer May |
| Eva Crowell | Ben Croson |

**Write statements for your system that will generate the random numbers described below.**

**39.** Between 0 and 1

**40.** Between 1 and 25

**41.** Integers from 0 to 10

**42.** Integers from 15 to 49

**43.** Write a program that uses the statement you wrote for problem **42** to generate and fill an array with 30 numbers from the set described in the problem. Include statements to print the array.

**44.** Write a program that asks the person using the program to enter any integer from 1 to 50. Then have the computer generate a random integer from 1 to 50 and print a message telling the user whether the two integers are the same. Include a quit option.

**45.** Write nested FOR/NEXT loops to read the DATA statements below into a 3 × 3 matrix. Include an appropriate DIM statement.

```
10 DATA 10,20,30
20 DATA 5,15,25
30 DATA 1,2,3
```

**46.** Write nested FOR/NEXT loops to print the data from problem **45** so the data in line 10 are printed on the first line, the data in line 20 are printed on the second line, and the data in line 30 are printed on the third line.

**47.** Change the lines you wrote for problem **46** to print the data in line 30 on the first line, the data in line 20 on the second line, and the data in line 10 on the third line.

### Use the following matrices in problems 48-50.

#### Sock Inventory Week 1 (in pairs of socks)

| Brand | Black | Brown | Blue |
|---|---|---|---|
| Flatfoot | 25 | 29 | 33 |
| Control Top | 15 | 23 | 19 |
| Fuzzy | 54 | 43 | 27 |

#### Sock Inventory Week 2 (in pairs of socks)

| Brand | Black | Brown | Blue |
|---|---|---|---|
| Flatfoot | 12 | 15 | 10 |
| Control Top | 3 | 8 | 7 |
| Fuzzy | 25 | 20 | 15 |

**48.** Write a program to find the amount of money tied up in inventory for each week if each pair of socks costs the store $2.00. Have all four matrices printed with all rows and columns correctly labeled.

**49.** Write a program to find the number of pairs of socks sold during week 1. (Subtract the inventory for week 2 from the inventory for week 1.) Have all three matrices printed with all rows and columns correctly labeled.

**50.** The following matrix shows the number of pairs of socks sold during week 2. Write a program to find the total number of pairs of socks sold during weeks 1 and 2. Have all three matrices printed with all rows and columns correctly labeled.

#### Socks Sold Week 2 (in pairs of socks)

| Brand | Black | Brown | Blue |
|---|---|---|---|
| Flatfoot | 12 | 13 | 8 |
| Control Top | 1 | 6 | 5 |
| Fuzzy | 15 | 19 | 14 |

# COMPUTER LITERACY

It is impossible to predict exactly how computers will be used in the future. However, in the past few decades there have been rapid changes in computers and their use has increased. These facts can help us get an idea of what might happen to computers in the coming years.

The supercomputers of the future might be able to execute 100 million to 1 billion operations per second. It would probably take you about 266 years working eight hours a day to add as many four-digit numbers as the future supercomputers might add in one second. If this great speed is achieved, it will help scientists, engineers, business persons, and other computer users in their work.

In contrast, microcomputers might be used by many people at home, at school, in small businesses, and so on. The availability of such inexpensive microcomputer systems may affect society more than any other future change in computers.

Many homes already rely on computers in many ways. For example, the security in some homes is controlled by computers. Energy conservation through temperature control and lighting control is a benefit of using computers. Other uses for computers in our homes include information storage, recreation, hobbies, and education. In the near future, there will be an increase in the number of homes in which computers are used.

A microcomputer being used to control the security of a home.

# FUTURE
# OF COMPUTERS

Computers are already at work in many areas of entertainment. For example, computer games are very popular, and the number of different games will probably increase in the future. Entertainment parks, such as Disney World in Orlando, Florida, use computers to control rides and to move the parts of their animated characters. In the future, parks similar to these might experience an increase in the use of computers.

With the increase in the use of computers, more people will need to learn computer languages. BASIC and other languages are already taught in secondary and elementary schools. For the distant future, we might see the development and use of natural languages (such as English) to program computers, as well as languages designed for use in specific areas (such as medicine, education, and engineering).

In the future, it is likely that more and more people will use computers. As a result people working together with computers might be able to solve many of the problems facing the world.

**A computerized elephant used in an entertainment park.**

Computers play a major role in America's space program. Many different computer programs are used to tell the computers how to perform the necessary tasks.

# EXTENDING BASIC

There are usually several different ways—all of them correct—to program a computer in BASIC to perform any given task. There are many advantages to knowing different ways to achieve a result. One advantage is that you can choose the method that best fits the program you are writing and the system you are using. In this chapter you will learn some new BASIC commands and some new ways to use commands you already know. You will also learn how to use some of the mathematical functions that are a part of BASIC.

## 7.1 SOME NEW IDEAS

In many BASICs, a program does not need an END statement. However, since leaving the statement out does not save much typing or memory, you may want to continue using an END statement as documentation within the program.

Some typing and memory are saved by leaving out the keyword LET. This is allowed in many BASICs.

---

**EXAMPLE 1**

Each set of statements below has the same effect in BASICs that do not require the keyword LET.

| | | |
|---|---|---|
| 10 LET X = 0 | 10 LET X = 0 | 10 X = 0 |
| 20 LET N = 1 | 20    N = 1 | 20 N = 1 |
| 30 LET P = 5 | 30    P = 5 | 30 P = 5 |
| 40 LET Q = 25 | 40    Q = 25 | 40 Q = 25 |

Using at least one LET may make a program easier to read.

---

Many BASICs allow more than one statement on a line, with a separator (: in some BASICs and / in others) between statements. Keep in mind that while this saves some memory and typing, it makes editing more difficult and makes insertion of additional statements much more difficult.

---

**EXAMPLE 2**

In BASICs that allow multiple statements on a line, the three sets of statements in Example 1 can be written on one line, as follows.

10 LET X = 0:LET N = 1:LET P = 5:LET Q = 25

10 LET X = 0:N = 1: P = 5: Q = 25

10 X = 0:N = 1:P = 5:Q = 25

---

Another work and memory saver used in many BASICs is the combined PRINT and INPUT statement.

---

**EXAMPLE 3**

In BASICs that allow PRINT and INPUT statements to be combined, lines 30 and 35 on the left below can be replaced by line 30 on the right.

30 PRINT "ENTER YOUR NAME";      30 INPUT "ENTER YOUR NAME"; NM$
35 INPUT NM$

---

A number can be tested to see if it is negative by comparing it to zero. There are other ways to test for a negative number. One way is to use the SGN function. (A few BASICs may not have this function.)

**SGN**(X) indicates the sign (+ or −) of X. If X < 0, then SGN(X) = −1. If X = 0, then SGN(X) = 0. If X > 0, then SGN(X) = 1.

$$SGN(-6) = -1 \qquad SGN(-2) = -1$$
$$SGN(0) = 0 \qquad SGN(9) = 1$$
$$SGN(15) = 1 \qquad SGN(2-6) = -1$$

Statements using the SGN function can often replace statements that compare a number to 0.

---

**EXAMPLE 4**

The statements below          The statements below
mean X is negative.           mean X is nonnegative.

X < 0                         X >= 0
SGN(X) = −1                   SGN(X) <> −1
SGN(X) < 0                    SGN(X) > −1
SGN(X) <> 1 AND SGN(X) <> 0   SGN(X) = 0 OR SGN(X) = 1

---

Another way to test for a negative number is to use the ABS function.

**ABS**(X) is the absolute value of X. If $X < 0$ then ABS(X) $= -X$.
If $X >= 0$, then ABS(X) $= X$.

| | |
|---|---|
| ABS($-6$) = 6 | ABS($-2$) = 2 |
| ABS(0) = 0 | ABS(9) = 9 |
| ABS(3+5) = 8 | ABS(6$-$3 ↑ 2) = 3 |

---

**EXAMPLE 5**

| The statements below mean X is negative. | The statements below mean X is nonnegative. |
|---|---|
| $X < 0$ | $X >= 0$ |
| $X <>$ ABS(X) | $X =$ ABS(X) |
| $X <$ ABS(X) | |

---

In many cases, statements using the ABS function can replace statements that compare a number to 0. However, the ABS function is more useful when the sign of a number does not matter, as in finding the distance between two points on a number line.

---

**EXAMPLE 6**

```
10 PRINT "THIS PROGRAM FINDS THE DISTANCE BETWEEN"
15 PRINT "TWO POINTS ON A NUMBER LINE"
20 PRINT "ENTER THE COORDINATES OF THE POINTS";
30 INPUT P,Q
40 LET D = ABS(P-Q)
50 PRINT "THE POINTS ARE ";D;" UNITS APART"
60 END
```

Instead of asking for the greater number first, this program lets the numbers be entered in any order. The absolute value of the difference of two numbers is the same, no matter which number is subtracted from the other.

---

Suppose there is one set of data that is needed in two or more places in a program, and the data will be used differently each time. How can the computer be supplied with the original unchanged data each time? Any of the following three methods can be used.

1. Repeat the DATA statements the number of times they are needed. (Of course, if there are many data and they are used several times, typing them is tiresome and gives many opportunities for errors. Also, repeating the data uses up a great amount of computer memory.)

2. Enter one complete set of data in several DATA statements, read the data into an array, and copy the array each time the data are needed.

**EXAMPLE 7**

70 PRINT "HOW MANY DATA ARE THERE?"
80 INPUT N
90 DIM A(N),B(N)
100 FOR C = 1 TO N
110     READ A(C)
120 NEXT C
130 DATA . . .          Use as many DATA statements as need-
135 DATA . . .          ed to contain the data.
150 FOR C = 1 TO N
160     B(C) = A(C)     The array of values in B is a copy of the
170 NEXT C             array of values in A.

This method should work, but again it may use a large amount of memory to store the extra copy of the original data.

3. Since there is already one unchanged copy of the data in memory (in the DATA statements), tell the computer to go back to the beginning of the data. This can be done using a **RESTORE statement.**

**EXAMPLE 8**

To use a RESTORE statement with the set of statements in Example 7, the following changes can be made.

140 RESTORE              The computer returns to the first value in
160     READ B(C)        the first DATA statement.

# Exercises

1. What is the advantage of using END or LET even if it is not required?
2. What are some advantages of putting more than one statement on a line? What are some disadvantages?
3. What are the advantages of combining PRINT and INPUT statements?

**Give the value of each function in Exercises 4-15.**

4. SGN(−10)        5. SGN(48)        6. SGN(−1)
7. SGN(3−5)        8. SGN(4−2↑2)     9. SGN(4−(−2))

**10.** ABS(−10)      **11.** ABS(48)      **12.** ABS(−1)

**13.** ABS(3−5)      **14.** ABS(4−2↑2)      **15.** ABS(4−(−2))

**16.** For what two values of X does SGN(X) = ABS(X)?

**17.** If N does not equal zero, what is the value of SGN(ABS(N))?

**18.** If A does not equal zero, what is the value of ABS(SGN(A))?

**19.** What is the purpose of a RESTORE statement?

# Laboratory Activities

**1.** Test your BASIC to find out if an END statement is required. (Use any program and leave out the END statement.)

**2.** Test your BASIC to find out if the keyword LET is required. (Use the second and third sets of statements in Example 1 and add a PRINT statement in each case.)

**3.** Test your BASIC to find out if more than one statement is allowed on one line. (Use the first line in Example 2 and add a PRINT statement.) If more than one statement does not seem to be allowed on one line, check your manual to find out if you used the right separator.

**4.** Test your BASIC to find out if combined PRINT and INPUT statements are allowed. (Use the line on the right in Example 3 and add a PRINT statement. If necessary check your manual for the right separator.)

**5.** Test your BASIC to find out if it has a SGN function. If it does, use your computer in calculator mode to check your answers to Exercises **4-9.**

**6.** Test your BASIC to find out if it has an ABS function. If it does, use your computer in calculator mode to check your answers to Exercises **10-15.**

**7.** Write and run a short program that requires a nonnegative number as input. Include an input test. If your BASIC has a SGN function, use each statement in the left-hand column of Example 4 one at a time in your input test. Compare the results of using each of the four statements.

**Write and run a short program that requires the input described below. If your BASIC permits, combine the input instructions with the INPUT statement. If your BASIC has the SGN function, use it in the input test for each program.**

  **8.** A negative number          **9.** A positive number

**10.** A nonpositive number      **11.** A nonzero number

**If your BASIC has the ABS function, do the following activities.**

12. Change the program you wrote for Activity **7** to use the ABS function to test the input. Use each statement in the left-hand column of Example 5 one at a time. Run the program.

13. Change each program you wrote for Activities **8-11** to use the ABS function to test the input. Run each program.

14. Enter the program in Example 6. Run the program using positive numbers, negative numbers, and zero as input. Are there any numbers that should be rejected?

15. Enter the set of statements in Example 7. Put at least 15 values in the DATA statements. Add a print loop to print arrays A and B. Run the program. Do the arrays contain the same data?

16. Make the changes described in Example 8. Use the same data you used for Activity **15**. Add a print loop to see whether the arrays contain the same data. Run the program.

17. Using the data below, write and run a program to find and print the sum of the data (read into array D), to find and print the product of the sum and each datum in turn (store the products in array D), and to add each product to the corresponding datum and print the result. Use RESTORE at least once in your program.

DATA 1,5,4,3,9,8,15,5,25,11,2,9,3

# 7.2 MORE ABOUT CONDITIONAL BRANCHES

A program may give a list of choices called a **menu,** and ask the person using the program to indicate a choice by number. If there are only a few choices, IF-THEN statements can be used to cause a branch depending on the input. However, the more choices there are, the more branches that are needed. Fortunately, many branches can be combined in one **ON-GOTO statement.** The lines in Examples 1 and 2 have the same effect.

## EXAMPLE 1

40 PRINT "ENTER 1,2,3,OR 4";

A menu would tell what 1, 2, 3, and 4 stand for.

50 INPUT N
60 IF N = 2 THEN 150
62 IF N = 3 THEN 200

If N is 2, 3, or 4, the program branches as directed.

64 IF N = 4 THEN 250
70 IF N <> 1 THEN 40

If N is not 1, 2, 3, or 4, input is rejected.

100 (If the input is 1, this line is executed.)

**EXAMPLE 2**

```
40 PRINT "ENTER 1,2,3,OR 4";
50 INPUT N
60 ON N GOTO 100, 150, 200, 250
70 GOTO 40
```

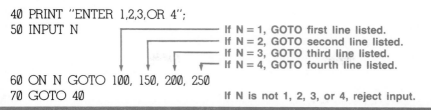

If N = 1, GOTO first line listed.
If N = 2, GOTO second line listed.
If N = 3, GOTO third line listed.
If N = 4, GOTO fourth line listed.

If N is not 1, 2, 3, or 4, reject input.

**ON-GOSUB statements** are used to combine many GOSUB statements into one statement. Each subroutine to which the program might branch must end with RETURN.

**EXAMPLE 3**

```
10 PRINT "THIS IS A QUIZ ABOUT GEOMETRIC FIGURES"
20 PRINT "TELL HOW MANY SIDES THE FIGURE NAMED HAS"
30 LET T = 1
40 LET F = INT(RND*4)+1         F is a random integer from 1 to 4.
50 ON F GOSUB 200,250,300,350   Branch to one of four lines.
60 INPUT S
70 IF S = N THEN 120
80 LET T = T+1                  Count tries for this question.
85 IF T = 4 THEN 110            Allow three tries.
90 PRINT "TRY AGAIN!"
100 GOTO 60
110 PRINT "NO, IT HAS ";N;" SIDES"      After three tries give answer.
120 PRINT "TRY ANOTHER? (Y OR N) ";
130 INPUT Q$
140 IF Q$ = "N" THEN 400    ⎤——→ Quit option
160 GOTO 30                 ⎦
200 PRINT "QUADRILATERAL" ⎤
210 LET N = 4             ⎬—→ First subroutine
220 RETURN                ⎦
250 PRINT "PENTAGON" ⎤
260 LET N = 5        ⎬———→ Second subroutine
270 RETURN           ⎦
300 PRINT "HEXAGON" ⎤
310 LET N = 6       ⎬———→ Third subroutine
320 RETURN          ⎦
350 PRINT "OCTAGON" ⎤
360 LET N = 8       ⎬———→ Fourth subroutine
370 RETURN          ⎦
400 END
```

In either an ON-GOTO or ON-GOSUB statement, the word ON may be followed by a variable, as in the examples, or by any expression that can be evaluated.

Some BASICs do not allow ON-GOTO and ON-GOSUB statements. However, branching statements can still be combined if the BASIC allows computed line numbers in a GOTO or GOSUB statement, as shown in Example 4 below.

---

**EXAMPLE 4**

In BASICs that allow computed branches, line 60 in Example 2 can be written as follows.

60 GOTO (N+1)*50

---

In many BASICs, the word THEN in an IF-THEN statement may be followed by a statement rather than a line number. In such BASICs, IF-THEN statements may be used not only for conditional branching, but to make other statements conditional also.

---

**EXAMPLE 5**

Each set of statements below has the same effect in BASICs that allow statements after THEN.

```
20 INPUT N                    20 INPUT N
30 IF N > 0 THEN 50           30 IF N <= 0 THEN N = ABS(N)
40 LET N = ABS(N)
50 LET A = N−1                50 LET A = N−1
```

---

Some BASICs allow **IF-THEN-ELSE statements.**

---

**EXAMPLE 6**

In the program in Example 3, lines 85 and 90 can be combined in one IF-THEN-ELSE statement.

90 IF T = 4 THEN 110 ELSE PRINT "TRY AGAIN!"

or

90 IF T < 4 THEN PRINT "TRY AGAIN!" ELSE 110

In the same program lines 140 and 160 can also be combined the same way.

140 IF Q$ = "N" THEN 400 ELSE 30

or

140 IF Q$ = "Y" THEN 30 ELSE 400

---

# Exercises

**1.** What is a menu in a computer program?

**2.** How are ON-GOTO statements used?

3. How are ON-GOSUB statements used?
4. What must follow the word ON in an ON-GOTO or ON-GOSUB statement?
5. In an ON-GOTO or ON-GOSUB statement, how many line numbers should be listed?
6. How are computed branches used?
7. In a BASIC that allows computed branches, which of the following statements can replace line 50 in Example 3?
   **a.** 50 GOSUB 50*(F+3)
   **b.** 50 GOSUB 50+50*F
8. Write an IF-THEN statement that sets X equal to 5 if A is negative.
9. Write an IF-THEN-ELSE statement that is equivalent to the lines below.

```
50 IF N <= 0 THEN 80
60 PRINT "N IS POSITIVE"
70 GOTO 90
80 PRINT "N IS NOT POSITIVE"
90 END
```

# Laboratory Activities

1. Test your BASIC to find out if it allows ON-GOTO statements. (Use the lines in Example 2 and add PRINT statements and any other necessary statements.)
2. Test your BASIC to find out if it allows ON-GOSUB statements. (Use the lines in Example 2 and add PRINT statements and any other necessary statements.)
3. Test your BASIC to find out if it allows computed line numbers in GOTO or GOSUB statements. (Use the line in Example 4 as described and add PRINT statements and any other necessary statements. Change the test as needed for GOSUB.)
4. Enter and run the program in Example 3. (Change line 40 if necessary.)
5. If your BASIC allows computed branches, change the program in Example 3 to use computed branches. Run the program.
6. Enter and run both sets of statements in Example 5. (Add PRINT statements so you can compare the outputs.) Is the output in each case the same?
7. If your BASIC allows IF-THEN-ELSE statements, add an INPUT and a GOTO statement to the statements you wrote for Exercise 9 and run the program. Does the program give the expected output?

8. If your BASIC allows IF-THEN-ELSE statements, use each statement in Example 6 in the program in Example 3. Enter and run each program to be sure it gives the same output as the original program.

9. The quiz in Example 3 may ask the same questions more than once and leave others unasked. The following lines change the program to use all subroutines once in random order, as long as the person using the program does not choose to quit. Make the changes, debug the program, and check the results.

| | |
|---|---|
| 25 LET C = 1 | Initialize a counter. |
| 42 IF FL(F) <> 1 THEN 46 | If flag for this F is not set to 1, take branch to line 46. |
| 44 GOTO 40 | If flag is set, pick another F. |
| 46 LET FL(F) = 1 | Set flag to 1 before taking branch to subroutine. |
| 70 IF S = N THEN 112 | |
| 112 LET C = C+1 | Add 1 to counter before continuing. |
| 114 IF C = 5 THEN 400 | If all subroutines were used, quit. |

10. Add five more subroutines to the program in Activity **9.** Run the program.

11. In the program you wrote for Activity **10,** initialize a variable R in line 26. Add a line to count the number (R) of times the person using the program gives a correct answer. Then add lines to print the total number of correct answers after the person quits or all subroutines are used. Run the program.

12. Using the program you wrote for Activity **11** as a guide, write and run a quiz program with 20 questions. Use sports scores, historic dates, or any other topic for which numerical answers can be given.

# 7.3 THE LOGICAL COMPUTER

A computer cannot use "common sense," since it does not have any. However, a computer does follow formal and strict *rules of logic.* A digital computer uses two **logical values,** true and false, but it uses numbers instead of the words true and false. The number 0 is used for false and 1 or −1 (depending on the computer) is used for true.

When a computer reads an IF-THEN statement, it first decides whether the condition following IF is true or false. Control is transferred to the line listed after THEN on true and continues to the next line (or to the next statement on some computers) on false.

## EXAMPLE 1

```
10 IF 1+1 = 3 THEN 60
20 PRINT "CONDITION FALSE"
30 IF 1+1 = 2 THEN 60
40 PRINT "OOPS! LOOK FOR A BUG"
50 GOTO 70
60 PRINT "CONDITION TRUE"
70 END
```

**Condition is false so branch is not taken.**

**Condition is true so branch to line 60.**

In many BASICs, the condition following IF may be made up of two or more parts joined by AND or OR. The logical value of a compound statement depends on the logical value of each of its parts. A compound statement using AND is true only if all of its parts are true.

## EXAMPLE 2

```
10 INPUT X,Y,Z
20 IF X = 2 AND Y = 3 AND Z = 4     ←──────┌  20 IF X <> 2 THEN 30
     THEN 50                                │  22 IF Y <> 3 THEN 30
                                            └  24 IF Z = 4 THEN 50
30 PRINT "CONDITION FALSE"
40 GOTO 60
50 PRINT "CONDITION TRUE"
60 END
```

Lines 20, 22, and 24 on the right have the same effect as line 20 on the left.

A compound statement using OR is true unless all of its parts are false.

## EXAMPLE 3

Change line 20 in Example 2 to the following.
```
20 IF X = 2 OR Y = 3 OR Z = 4 THEN 50   ←─┌  20 IF X = 2 THEN 50
                                          │  22 IF Y = 3 THEN 50
                                          └  24 IF Z = 4 THEN 50
```

Because the symbols $+$, $-$, $*$, and $/$ are used for arithmetic operations, they are called **arithmetic operators.** Since AND and OR are used for logical operations, they are called **logical operators.** Another useful logical operator allowed in some BASICs is **NOT**.

If X = 4 is true, then NOT(X = 4) is false.
If X = 4 is false, then NOT(X = 4) is true.

### EXAMPLE 4

In BASICs that allow NOT, the statements in each pair below have the same effect.

IF X >= 2 THEN 60                IF X < 2 THEN 60
IF NOT(X < 2) THEN 60            IF NOT(X >= 2) THEN 60

In many BASICs, the computer can be instructed to print the logical values of statements as output.

### EXAMPLE 5

A computer prints characters that are in quotation marks and the values of expressions that are not in quotation marks.

PRINT "2 = 2"
2 = 2
PRINT "2+2 = ";3+1
2+2 = 4
PRINT "3+2 = ";4
3+2 =4
PRINT "NOT(2+2 = 4)"
NOT (2+2 =4)

A computer prints 1(−1 in some BASICs) if the statement is true, and 0 if it is false.

PRINT 2 = 2
1(or −1)
PRINT 2+2 = 3+1
1(or −1)
PRINT 3+2 = 4
0
PRINT NOT(2+2 = 4)
0

In most BASICs, logical values of statements can be used in computations.

### EXAMPLE 6

10 INPUT N
20 LET A = (N < 2)*3+1
30 PRINT A

Line 20 above has the same effect as each of the following sets of statements.

20 IF N < 2 THEN 26              20 IF N >= 2 THEN 26
22 A = 1                        22 A = 4
24 GOTO 30                      24 GOTO 30
26 A = 4                        26 A = 1

20 IF N < 2 THEN A = 4 ELSE A = 1

Just as every statement has a logical value, every variable has a logical value. If the arithmetic value of a variable is 0, its logical value is also 0. If the arithmetic value is not 0, the logical value is 1 or −1.

## EXAMPLE 7

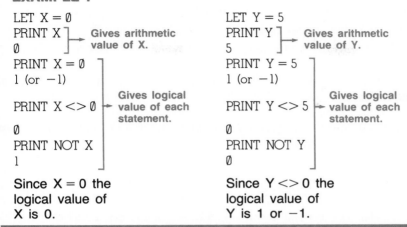

LET X = 0
PRINT X ⎤→ Gives arithmetic
0          ⎦   value of X.

PRINT X = 0 ⎤
1 (or −1)    ⎥
             ⎥  Gives logical
PRINT X <> 0 ⎥→ value of each
             ⎥  statement.
0            ⎥
PRINT NOT X  ⎥
1            ⎦

Since X = 0 the
logical value of
X is 0.

LET Y = 5
PRINT Y ⎤→ Gives arithmetic
5          ⎦   value of Y.

PRINT Y = 5 ⎤
1 (or −1)    ⎥
             ⎥  Gives logical
PRINT Y <> 5 ⎥→ value of each
             ⎥  statement.
0            ⎥
PRINT NOT Y  ⎥
0            ⎦

Since Y <> 0 the
logical value of
Y is 1 or −1.

In most BASICs, the logical value of a variable can be used in an IF-THEN statement or as part of a compound condition. In each program in Examples 8-10, IF X is equivalent to IF X <> 0.

## EXAMPLE 8

```
10 FOR X = 0 TO 3
20    IF X THEN 50
30    PRINT "X = 0"
40    GOTO 55
50    PRINT "X = ";X
55 NEXT X
60 END
```

## EXAMPLE 9

Replace lines 20 and 30 in Example 8 with the following.

```
20 IF X THEN 50 ELSE PRINT "X = 0"
```

## EXAMPLE 10

```
10 FOR X = 0 TO 2
20    FOR N = 1 TO 3
30       IF X AND N = 2 THEN 50
40       PRINT "X = ";X;" AND  N = ";N    Line 40 is executed when
                                          either X or N = 2 is false.
50    NEXT N
60 NEXT X
70 END
```

# Exercises

1. Name (in words) the logical values a digital computer uses.
2. How are logical values used in an IF-THEN statement?
3. What is the logical value of a compound statement using AND? Using OR?
4. What is the difference between an arithmetic operator and a logical operator?

**If A = 2, B = 3, and C = 5, give the logical value (true or false) of each of the following statements.**

5. A = 2                             6. C = 3
7. B = 2 + 1                         8. C = A + B
9. A = 3 AND B = 3                  10. A = 3 OR B = 3
11. A = 2 AND B = 3 AND C = 5      12. A = 2 OR B = 2 OR C = 2
13. A = 2 AND B = 2 AND C = 5      14. A = 1 OR B = 2 OR C = 3
15. A = 2 AND B > 2 AND C < 6      16. A = 3 OR B > 2 OR C = 3
17. NOT(A =2)       18. NOT(B = 2)          19. NOT(A > B)

20. If a computer can be instructed to print the logical value of a statement, how is the instruction written?
21. Give the output of the program below when 1 is entered as input and when any other number is entered as input.

```
10 INPUT N
20 LET V = 6*(N = 1)+2
30 PRINT V
40 END
```

22. Write an IF-THEN statement (and whatever other lines are needed) to replace line 20 in Exercise **21**. (Use 1 for true.)
23. Write an IF-THEN-ELSE statement to replace line 20 in Exercise **21**. (Use 1 for true.)
24. What is the logical value of a variable?
25. If X = 3, what is the logical value of X? Of NOT X?

**Write a statement using NOT that is equivalent to each of the following.**

26. X <> 5              27. N > 15              28. R <= 0

**For each of the following statements, write yes or no to tell if program control will be transferred to line 40 if N = 0.**

29. 10 IF N THEN 40                    30. 10 IF NOT N THEN 40
31. 10 IF N+1 AND NOT N THEN 40        32. 10 IF N OR N+1 THEN 40

# Laboratory Activities ▬▬▬▬

1. Enter and run the program in Example 1.
2. Enter and run the program in Example 2. Then replace line 20 with the equivalent statements using IF-THEN and run the program again. Compare the outputs.
3. Change line 20 in the program in Example 2 to the line given in Example 3. Run the program. Then replace line 20 with the equivalent statements using IF-THEN and run the program again. Compare the outputs.
4. If your BASIC includes NOT, write and run a program to show that the statements in each pair in Example 4 give the same results.

**With your computer in calculator mode, do each activity below that can be done on your computer.**

5. Enter each command listed in Example 5 and compare your results with those shown.
6. Enter each command in Example 7. Does your computer give the logical values of statements as output? Does your BASIC include the operator NOT? (If you answer "no" to either question, check with your teacher or your manual to be sure you are correct.) If your computer gives logical values as output, how does it represent false? True?
7. Enter LET commands to set A = 2, B = 3, and C = 5. Then enter PRINT commands to check your answers to each of Exercises **5-19**.
8. Use PRINT commands to check your answers to Exercises **25-28**. (Use LET commands for Exercises **26-28**.)
9. Enter and run the first set of statements shown in Example 6. Then replace line 20 as described in the example and run the set of statements. Do you get the same results in each case?
10. Follow the instructions in Activity **9** for Exercises **21-23**.
11. Enter and run the program given in Example 8.
12. If your BASIC has IF-THEN-ELSE statements, change the program from Activity **11** using the line shown in Example 9. Run the program and compare the output with that for Activity **11**.
13. Enter and run the program in Example 10. Record the output.
14. Write and run a program to print the arithmetic values of the variables whose logical values are true. Use array A to store the arithmetic values read from a DATA statement.
15. Change the program in Activity **14** to print the arithmetic values of the variables whose logical values are true and whose arithmetic values are negative.

# PASCAL                              LOOPS

REPEAT/UNTIL statements in *Pascal* are similar to FOR/NEXT statements in BASIC.

PROGRAM COUNTSTO10;
VAR COUNTER: REAL;
BEGIN
    WRITELN('THIS PROGRAM COUNTS TO 10');
    COUNTER : = 1.0;
    REPEAT
        WRITELN(COUNTER);
        COUNTER : = COUNTER + 1.0    **There is not a semicolon**
    UNTIL COUNTER > 10.0          **after 1.0 since it is in the**
END.                            **last statement before END.**

The initial value of the REPEAT/UNTIL loop in the program above is assigned in the statement COUNTER: = 1.0;. When COUNTER becomes 10.0, the loop is completed and control is transferred to the statement that follows the UNTIL statement (in this case, END.).

A READLN statement can be used in a loop.

       .
       .
       .

REPEAT
    READLN (RADIUS);        **A READLN statement is similar to an**
    AREA : = 3.14*RADIUS*RADIUS;    **INPUT statement in BASIC.**
    WRITELN(RADIUS:10:2, AREA:10:2);
UNTIL RADIUS = 0
       .
       .

A 0 is used as a dummy datum and indicates the end of the loop.

## Exercises   Write a program in *Pascal* for each of the following. Use REPEAT/UNTIL statements in the programs.

**1.** Exercise **13,** page 126      **2.** Exercise **14,** page 126
**3.** Exercise **15,** page 126      **4.** Exercise **16,** page 126

Write a program in *Pascal* for each of the following. Use a READLN statement in a REPEAT/UNTIL loop and use a dummy datum to indicate the end of the loop.

**5.** Activity **15,** page 81      **6.** Activity **16,** page 81

# 7.4  ALPHAS AND NUMERICS

When a key on a computer keyboard is pressed, it sends a unique signal to the computer. The computer "decodes" the signal to determine which key was pressed. The signal is represented by a number, so each character has a unique code number. There are several different codes in use, but the most common one is the **ASCII** (**A**merican **S**tandard **C**ode for **I**nformation **I**nter-change) code. ASCII not only includes character codes, but also some codes for controlling I/O devices.

There are 256 numbers in ASCII, from 0 to 255. The codes from 0 to 31 are used to send signals to control the screen and other output devices. The codes from 32 to 90 are character codes, including codes for the capital letters. (Not all computers use the control codes the same way.) Consult your manual to find out the way your system uses the codes from 91 to 255.

In many BASICs, **ASC**(X$) gives the ASCII code for any string character X$. (If there is more than one character in X$, the computer returns only the code for the first character.)

PRINT ASC("A")         PRINT ASC("#")
65                     35
PRINT ASC("ABCD")      PRINT ASC(" ∧")
65                     32

Many characters have more than one code, so the computer may give responses different from the ones shown above.

In most BASICs, **CHR$**(N) gives the character that has ASCII code N.

PRINT CHR$(75)         PRINT CHR$(34)
K                      ''
PRINT CHR$(57)         PRINT CHR$(36)
9                      $

Statements containing CHR$ can often be used to get characters into output that are not shown on the keyboard or that are not even coded by any of the keys.

A string cannot be used in computations even if it consists entirely of numeric characters (for example "12"). Only numbers and numeric variables can be used in computations. In some BASICs, **VAL**(X$) can be used to change a string to a number.

---

**EXAMPLE 1**

```
10 PRINT "VAL(X$) IS THE NUMBER NAMED BY X$"
20 PRINT "ENTER ANY NUMBER";
30 INPUT X$                     The input is assigned to a string varia-
                                ble.
40 PRINT VAL(X$)        ⎤       VAL (X$) is a number. It can be used in
50 PRINT 2+VAL(X$)      ⎦ ────→ computations.
60 PRINT X$             ⎤       X$ is a string. Trying to use it in compu-
70 PRINT 2+X$           ⎦ ────→ tations produces an error message.
80 END
```

---

Many BASICs use **STR$**(X) to change a number to a string.

---

**EXAMPLE 2**

```
10 PRINT "STR$(N) IS THE STRING THAT NAMES THE NUMBER N"
20 PRINT "ENTER ANY NUMBER ";
30 INPUT N                      The input must be a number.
40 PRINT N              ⎤       Since N is a number, it can be used in
50 PRINT 3*N            ⎦ ────→ computations.
60 PRINT STR$(N)        ⎤       STR$(N) is a string. Trying to use it in
70 PRINT 3*STR$(N)      ⎦ ────→ computations produces an error mes-
80 END                          sage.
```

---

Most BASICs allow **LEN**(X$), which gives the number of characters in X$.

---

**EXAMPLE 3**

```
10 PRINT "LEN(X$) GIVES THE NUMBER OF CHARACTERS IN X$"
20 PRINT "ENTER YOUR NAME";
30 INPUT X$
40 LET LN = LEN(X$)
50 PRINT "YOUR NAME HAS ";LN;" CHARACTERS, INCLUDING SPACES"
60 END
```

---

The LEN function can be used to align characters in output. For example, decimal points can be aligned using this function.

---

**EXAMPLE 4**

The method for aligning decimal points used in steps 50-100 can be used in any program.

```
5 PRINT "THIS PROGRAM USES LEN TO ALIGN DECIMAL POINTS"
20 DATA 1.234,12.34,.1234,1234
```

```
30 FOR N = 1 TO 4
40    READ DP
50    LET DI = INT(DP)
60    LET LD = LEN(STR$(DI))
70    LET TB = 20−LD          Decimal points will be in column 20.
80    PRINT TAB(TB);DI;       Print part of number to left of decimal
                              point.
90    IF DP = DI THEN PRINT ".";   Add decimal point if integer.
100   PRINT DP−DI             Print part of number to right of decimal
                              point (0 for integers).
110 NEXT N
120 END
```

Many BASICs provide an easier way to align decimal points with **PRINT USING statements.**

**EXAMPLE 5**

In some BASICs that allow PRINT USING statements, lines 50-100 can be replaced with the lines below.

```
50 LET A$ = "XXXX.XXXX"
60 PRINT TAB(16);
70 PRINT USING A$;DP
```

# Exercises

1. What character and control code is most commonly used for computers?
2. How many ASCII codes are there?
3. Write a statement to print the ASCII code for C.
4. Write a statement to print the ASCII code for the comma.
5. Write a statement to print the character with ASCII code 80.
6. How can a character that has an ASCII code but no corresponding key on a keyboard be printed?
7. If A$ = "3.14159", how can A$ be used to supply the number 3.14159?
8. If C = 1.713, how can C be used to supply the string "1.713"?
9. Can a string be used in an arithmetic operation?
10. Write a statement to print the number of characters in D$.

# Laboratory Activities

**Do all of the activities for which your BASIC has the necessary commands.**

1. Using the computer in calculator mode, enter the ASC commands on page 231 and compare your results with those given.

2. Enter and run the following program. Use each character shown on the keyboard and record the result. For which characters do you get an error message rather than an ASCII code?

```
10 PRINT "THIS PROGRAM GIVES ASCII CODES"
20 INPUT K$
30 PRINT "FOR KEY ";K$;" THE ASCII CODE IS ";ASC(K$)
40 GOTO 20
50 END
```

3. Using the computer in calculator mode, enter the CHR$ commands on page 231 and compare your results with those given.

4. Enter and run the following program. Notice whether or not there are characters printed that are not marked on the keyboard.

```
10 PRINT "THIS PROGRAM PRINTS EACH CHARACTER"
12 PRINT "AND ASCII CODE"
20 PRINT "ASCII CODE ","CHARACTER"
30 FOR N = 32 TO 122
40     PRINT N,CHR$(N)
50 NEXT N
60 END
```

5. Change lines 30 and 50 in the program in Activity **4** to the following, and delete line 20.

```
30 INPUT N
50 GOTO 30
```

Check your manual to find the ASCII codes for some output controls such as bell, line feed, return, and back space. Then run the program and enter each output control code you found as input. Record the results.

6. Enter and run the program in Example 1. Do you get the output described? Enter a letter as input. What is VAL(X$) if X$ is a letter?

**Delete lines 50 and 70 from the program in Example 1. Run the program using the following input and record your results.**

7. BASIC          8. 1692AMERICA          9. 40 ACRES

10. Enter and run the program in Example 2. Do you get the output described? What happens if you experiment with input as you did for the program in Example 1?

**11.** Enter and run the program from Example 3. Experiment using input other than your name.

**12.** Enter and run the program in Example 4. Then change the program to print the decimal point in column 28.

**13.** Change the program in Example 4 to use an INPUT statement rather than READ/DATA statements. In your program, have the person using the program enter four numbers into an array and also choose the column in which the decimal point is to be printed. Run the program.

**14.** Change the program in Activity **13** so the person using the program can enter up to 20 numbers. Run the program.

**15.** Change the program in Activity **14** to find the sum of the numbers entered and to print the sum with the decimal point aligned under the other decimal points. Run the program.

**16.** Change the program you wrote for Activity **14** to use any set of data in which each item has the same number of digits to the left of the decimal point. Have this number entered as input. Run the program.

**If your BASIC allows PRINT USING statements, do the following activities.**

**17.** Change the program in Example 4 as described in Example 5. Enter and run the program. (If it does not run correctly, consult your teacher or your manual to see how your BASIC uses PRINT USING statements.)

**18.** Do Activities **12-15** using PRINT USING statements wherever possible.

# 7.5 THE COMPUTER AND MATHEMATICS

You have seen how easily a computer can evaluate expressions. It can be used to make short work of even the most difficult computations.

Polynomials can be used to mathematically describe such things as the behavior of bridges, the sound of music, and the hills and valleys of landscapes. There are many ways to use a computer in working with polynomials. For example, a computer can find a *zero of a polynomial* (a value of the variable for which the polynomial equals zero) or solve a polynomial equation by substitution much more quickly than a person can.

## EXAMPLE 1

```
10 FOR X = 0 TO 5
20    LET Y = X↑3+11*X↑2−6*X−50
30    PRINT X,Y
40 NEXT X
50 END
RUN
```

| 0 | −50 |
|---|---|
| 1 | −44 |
| 2 | −10 |
| 3 | 58 |
| 4 | 166 |
| 5 | 320 |

For X = 2 and 3 rows: **−10<0<58, so Y = 0 for some value of X between 2 and 3.**

Replace line 10 with the following line.

```
10 FOR X = 2 TO 3 STEP .2
RUN
```

| 2 | −10 |
|---|---|
| 2.2 | .688000083 |
| 2.4 | 12.784 |
| 2.6 | 26.3360002 |
| 2.8 | 41.3920001 |

For rows 2 and 2.2: **−10<0<.688000083, so Y = 0 for some value of X between 2 and 2.2.**

Replace line 10 as many times as necessary to find the zero to the desired accuracy.

Many BASICs have a **DEF statement** that can be used to define functions not already programmed into the computer. The format of this statement is DEF FN A(X) (or DEF A(X) in some BASICs), where A is any letter and X is the variable in the function.

## EXAMPLE 2

Each of the following programs gives the same output.

```
10 LET X = 5
20 LET Y = 4*X↑3
30 LET X = 7
40 LET Z = 12*X↑2
50 PRINT Y,Z
60 END
```

```
10 DEF FN A(X) = 4*X↑3
20 DEF FN B(X) = 12*X↑2
30 PRINT FN A(5),FN B(7)
40 END
```

Formulas can be used to solve some polynomial equations.

| Equation | Formula |
|----------|---------|
| $ax + b = c$ | $x = (c - b)/a$ |
| $ax + b = cx + d$ | $x = (d - b)/(a - c)$ |
| $x^n = b$ | $x = b^{(1/n)}$ |
| $ax^2 + bx + c = 0$ | $x = (-b + \sqrt{b^2 - 4ac})/2a$ |
| | or |
| | $x = (-b - \sqrt{b^2 - 4ac})/2a$ |

When one of these formulas is used in a program, the input should be tested to avoid division by zero.

---

**EXAMPLE 3**

```
10 PRINT "TO SOLVE AN EQUATION OF THE FORM AX+B = C"
20 PRINT "ENTER A,B,C IN THAT ORDER, SEPARATED BY COMMAS"
25 PRINT "A MUST NOT BE ZERO"
30 INPUT A,B,C
40 IF A = 0 THEN 25
50 LET X = (C−B)/A
60 PRINT "X = ";X
70 END
```

---

Computers can also be used when working with sequences, series, variations, means, permutations, combinations, and binomial expansions. Many of these topics involve factorials.

---

**EXAMPLE 4**

```
10 PRINT "THIS PROGRAM COMPUTES N! (N FACTORIAL)"
20 PRINT "ENTER A POSITIVE INTEGER ";
30 INPUT N
32 IF N <> INT(N) THEN 20
34 IF N <= 0 THEN 20
40 LET NF = 1
50 FOR M = 1 TO N
60    LET NF = M*NF
70 NEXT M
80 PRINT N;"! = ";NF
90 END
```

---

Pascal's triangle, which can be used when expanding binomials and working with permutations, can be printed by a computer.

## EXAMPLE 5

```
10 PRINT "THIS PROGRAM PRINTS THE FIRST 10 ROWS"
11 PRINT "OF PASCAL'S TRIANGLE"
20 FOR R = 1 TO 10
30     LET T = 1
40     FOR C = 1 TO R
50        LET P(R,C) = P(R−1,C)+P(R−1,C−1)
60        LET P(1,1) = 1
70        PRINT TAB(T);P(R,C);
80        LET T = T+4
90     NEXT C
100    PRINT
110    PRINT
120 NEXT R
130 END
```

# Exercises

1. What advantage is there to using a computer to do computations?
2. Suppose a polynomial function of $x$ has a value of 4 when $x = -10$ and a value of $-1$ when $x = -8$. What does this tell us about a zero of the polynomial?
3. What method was used to solve the equation in Example 3?
4. When a formula is used to solve an equation, what should the input be tested for?

# Laboratory Activities

1. Enter and run the program in Example 1. Find the zero to the nearest tenth.
2. If your BASIC allows a DEF statement, change the program in Example 1 by defining the polynomial as a function of $x$. Run the program.
3. The polynomial in the program in Example 1 has two more real zeros. Change the program to find them to the nearest tenth.
4. Enter and run the programs in Example 2. Compare the outputs.

**Enter the program in Example 3. Use it to solve each of the following equations.**

5. $4x + 9 = 1$
6. $5 = 3x - 4$
7. $1.2x + 3 = -9$
8. $6.25x - 3.25 = 9.5$

9. Rewrite the input test in line 40 of the program in Example 3, using NOT to express the condition following IF. Run the program.

10. Change the program in Example 3 to print the message "X MAY BE ANY REAL NUMBER" if 0 is entered for A and $B = C$. Run the program.

11. Change the program in Activity **10** to print the message "NO SOLUTIONS" if 0 is entered for A and $B \neq C$. Run the program.

12. Use the program you wrote for Activity **11** to solve the equations in Activities **5-8**.

13. Write and run a program to solve equations of the form $ax + b = cx + d$. If $a = c$ and $b = d$, the message given in Activity **10** should be printed. If $a = c$ and $b \neq d$, the message given in Activity **11** should be printed.

**Use the program you wrote for Activity 11 to solve each of the following equations.**

14. $3x + 4 = 7x - 8$

15. $5 - 3x = -3x + 2$

16. $1.5x - 2 = 6.5x$

17. $8 + 6x = 6x + 8$

18. Write and run a program to solve equations for the form $x^n = b$. (If $n = 0$, then $x^n = 1$.)

**Use the program you wrote for Activity 18 to solve each of the following equations.**

19. $x^2 = 16$

20. $x^0 = 30$

21. $18 = x^6$

22. $x^4 = 12$

23. Write and run a program to solve equations of the form $ax^2 + bx + c = 0$. (If $b^2 - 4ac < 0$, the message "NO REAL ROOTS" should be printed.)

**Use the program you wrote for Activity 23 to solve each of the following equations.**

24. $3x^2 + 8x + 3 = 0$

25. $2x^2 + 5x - 4 = 0$

26. $4x^2 - 4x + 1 = 0$

27. $4x^2 + 3x + 5 = 0$

**Enter the program in Example 4. Use it to find each of the following.**

28. 7!

29. 10!

30. 14!

31. 20!

32. Experiment to find the greatest number whose factorial you can find using your computer.

33. Enter and run the program in Example 5.

34. Pascal's triangle is often printed in the pattern produced by using the following lines in the program in Example 5.

```
12 PRINT "HOW MANY COLUMNS ON YOUR SCREEN? ";
14 INPUT CS
30 LET T = CS/2-2*(R-1)
```

Enter and run the program.

**35.** Change the program in Activity **34** to print a triangle using * in place of the numbers.

**36.** A power of a binomial is expanded by multiplying. For example, $(a + b)^3$ $= a^3 + 3a^2b + 3ab^2 + b^3$. The coefficients in this expansion can be read directly from Pascal's triangle. (Add one to the exponent to find the row.) Change the program in Activity **33** to find and print the coefficients for the expansions of $(a + b)^n$ for $n = 2$ to $n = 8$. Run the program.

**37.** Change the program you wrote for Activity **36** to find the coefficients for the expansion of $(a - b)^n$ for $n = 6$ to $n = 9$.

# 7.6 MATHEMATICAL FUNCTIONS

Two numbers that occur often in mathematics are $\pi$ and $e$.

The number $\pi$ is the ratio of the circumference and the measure of the diameter of any circle. There are several ways to supply the value of $\pi$ in a program. Two of them are shown below. (A few computers have a value for $\pi$ in read-only memory.)

PI = 3.14159265
PI = 355/113

Both values are correct to 7 digits.

The number $e$ is used in computations involving growth and decay. It has an approximate value of 2.718289. The **EXP function,** which raises $e$ to a power, can be used to supply the value of $e$ in a program.

EXP(1) gives the value of $e^1$ or $e$.
EXP(X) gives the value of $e^x$.

---

**EXAMPLE 1**

```
10 PRINT "THIS PROGRAM LISTS POWERS OF E"
20 FOR N = 0 TO 10
30     PRINT "E ↑ ";N;" = ";EXP(N)
40 NEXT N
50 END
```

Besides raising $e$ to a power, the computer can also find the exponent needed to make $e^x$ equal any given number $a$. This exponent is called the natural logarithm of $a$ and the exponent is written LOG(A). (In some BASICs, it is written LN(A).)

**LOG**(A) gives the natural logarithm (the log to base $e$) of A.

In some BASICs, logarithms to the base 10 can be found using CLOG. However, in most BASICs the logarithm to the base 10 of A is found using the fraction LOG(A)/LOG(10).

Remember that logarithms to any base are defined only for positive numbers. Whether A is entered as input or is the result of computation, it should be tested to see that it is positive before its logarithm is computed.

The tests below can be used to find which of the keywords LOG, LN, and CLOG are allowed. Using the wrong keyword usually does not cause an error message to be printed, but results in incorrect output.

**TEST 1**

```
10 PRINT "N","LOG(N)"
20 FOR N = 1 TO 5
30    PRINT N,LOG(N)
40 NEXT N
50 END
```

**TEST 2**

Change lines 10 and 30 in Test 1 to the following.

```
10 PRINT "N","LN(N)"
30    PRINT N,LN(N)
```

**TEST 3**

Change lines 10 and 30 in Test 1 to the following.

```
10 PRINT "N","CLOG(N)"
30    PRINT N,CLOG(N)
```

Trigonometric functions are used in many applications of mathematics. A computer can calculate values of trigonometric functions very rapidly. However, the values are found for angle measures in radians, not for angle measures in degrees. For an angle whose measure is R radians the measure in degrees is R·180/$\pi$.

Because of rounding errors, a computer can give rather strange values for trigonometric functions near critical points (for angles for which the function value is zero or is not defined). This should be taken into account when the computer is used to compute values of trigonometric functions.

Trigonometric functions usually available in BASIC include **SIN** (sine), **COS** (cosine), and **TAN** (tangent).

---

**EXAMPLE 2**

```
10 PRINT "THIS PROGRAM PRINTS A TABLE OF SINES"
20 PRINT "RADIANS","DEGREES","SINE"
30 LET PI = 355/113
40 FOR R = 0 TO 6.3 STEP .1
50    LET D = R*180/PI
60    PRINT R,D,SIN(R)
70 NEXT R
80 END
```

---

There is also a function in most BASICs that gives the measure of an angle in radians if the tangent of the angle is known. This function is the **ATN** (arctangent) function.

---

**EXAMPLE 3**

```
10 PRINT "THIS PROGRAM FINDS THE MEASURE OF AN ANGLE"
12 PRINT "GIVEN ITS TANGENT"
20 PRINT "TANGENT","RADIANS","DEGREES"
30 LET PI = 3.141592
40 FOR N = -100 TO 100 STEP 2
50    LET R = ATN(N)
60    LET D = R*180/PI
70    PRINT N,R,D
80 NEXT N
90 END
```

---

# Exercises

1. How can the value of $\pi$ be supplied in a program?
2. How can the value of $e$ be supplied in a program?
3. If $e^n = d$, what is $n$ called in terms of $d$?
4. What fraction will give the logarithm to the base 10 of 4?
5. In what units must the measure of G be given to find SIN(G)?
6. If the measure in radians of an angle is known, how can the measure in degrees be found?
7. What trigonometric functions are usually available in BASIC?
8. If the tangent of an angle is known, how can the measure of the angle be found? In what units will it be given?

# Laboratory Activities

1. Find out whether or not your computer has a value for $\pi$ stored in read-only memory.
2. Enter and run the program given in Example 1.
3. Enter and run Tests 1, 2, and 3. For each test compare the output with the values below to find which keywords your system uses.

| N | Natural Logarithm | Base 10 Logarithm |
|---|---|---|
| 1 | 0 | 0 |
| 2 | .693147181 | .301029996 |
| 3 | 1.09861229 | .477121255 |
| 4 | 1.38629436 | .602059991 |
| 5 | 1.60943791 | .698970004 |

4. Enter and run the program in Example 2.
5. Enter and run the program in Example 3.
6. Replace line 40 in the program in Example 3 with the line below. Run the program.

   40 FOR N = −2 TO 2 STEP .1

7. Enter and run the following program.

```
10 PRINT "THIS PROGRAM SHOWS THE EFFECT"
12 PRINT "OF ROUNDING ERROR"
20 FOR A = 0 TO 6.3 STEP .1
30     LET S2 = (SIN(A)) ↑ 2
40     LET C2 = (COS(A)) ↑ 2
50     LET SM = S2+C2        sin² a + cos² a = 1
60     LET ER = 1−ABS(SM)    Line 60 gives the size of the error.
70     PRINT SM,ER
80 NEXT A
90 END
```

8. Enter and run the following program.

```
10 PRINT "THIS PROGRAM PRINTS A GRAPH OF THE SINE"
20 LET P2 = 355/113
30 LET ST = .3
40 FOR A = 0 TO 4*P2 STEP ST
50     LET Y = SIN(A)
60     LET T = INT(19*Y+20)
70     PRINT TAB(T);
80     PRINT "*"
90 NEXT A
100 END
```

9. Change the program in Activity **8** by adding the following lines.

```
12 PRINT "HOW MANY COLUMNS WIDE SHOULD THE GRAPH BE?"
14 PRINT "(NOT MORE THAN THE NUMBER"
15 PRINT "OF COLUMNS ON THE SCREEN) ";
16 INPUT C
60 LET T = (C/2−1)*Y+C/2
```

Run the program several times, using a different value for C each time. Record the effect of these changes on the output.

10. Change the program in Activity **9** by changing the value of ST in line 30. Run the program and record the effect on the output.

11. Change the program in Activity **9** by replacing lines 30 and 40 with the following lines.

```
30 LET ST = −.3
40 FOR A = 0 TO −6.3 STEP ST
```

Run the program. Compare the output with the output for Activity **9**.

12. Add the following line to the program in Activity **9**. Run the program and notice the effect on the output.     `85 GOTO 40`

13. In the program in Activity **9**, use a value for C that is at least four less than the number of columns on the screen. Change the program so it prints SINE rather than *. Run the program.

14. Replace SIN(A) by COS(A) in line 50 of the program in Activity **9**. Run the program and compare the output with the output for Activity **9**. (Line 10 will also need to be changed.)

15. Write and run a program to find the measure of the diameter of any circle if its circumference is entered as input.

16. Write and run a program to print the natural logarithm and logarithm to the base 10 of any number entered as input. Make sure the output is correctly labeled.

17. Write and run a program to print a table of sines, cosines, and tangents for angles (in radians) of 0, $\pi/4$, $\pi/2$, $3\pi/4$, $\pi$, $5\pi/4$, $3\pi/2$, $7\pi/4$, and $2\pi$. Use 355/113 for $\pi$.

18. The formula for growth and decay is $y = ne^{kt}$, where $y$ is the final amount, $n$ is the starting amount, $t$ is time, and $k$ is a constant that is positive for growth and negative for decay. For certain bacteria, $k = 0.788$ when $t$ is measured in hours. Write and run a program to find $t$ if the number of bacteria at the start and the number of bacteria after $t$ hours are entered as input. (Since $k$ is positive, the number of bacteria increases.)

19. Radioactive elements decay according to the formula given in Activity **18**. The half-life of an element is the length of time it takes for half the initial atoms to disintegrate. Write a program to find $k$ if the half-life is entered as input. Run the program using the data below.

| Element | silicon 31 | hydrogen 3 | radon 219 |
|---|---|---|---|
| **Half-life** | 2.62 hours | 12.3 years | 4 seconds |

# Vocabulary

SGN (216)

ABS (217)

RESTORE (218)

menu (220)

ON-GOTO (220)

ON-GOSUB (221)

IF-THEN-ELSE (222)

logical values (224)

arithmetic operators (225)

logical operators (225)

NOT (225)

ASCII (231)

ASC (231)

CHR$ (231)

VAL (231)

STR$ (232)

LEN (232)

PRINT USING (233)

DEF (236)

EXP (240)

LOG (241)

SIN (242)

COS (242)

TAN (242)

ATN (242)

# Summary

1. In many BASICs, a program does not need an END statement.

2. In many BASICs, the word LET is not required in a statement assigning a value to a variable.

3. Many BASICs allow more than one statement on a line, with a separator between statements.

4. Many BASICs allow PRINT statements and INPUT statements to be combined.

5. SGN(X) indicates the sign (+ or −) of X. If $X < 0$, then $SGN(X) = -1$. If $X = 0$, then $SGN(X) = 0$. If $X > 0$, then $SGN(X) = 1$.

6. ABS(X) is the absolute value of X. If $X < 0$, then $ABS(X) = -X$. If $X > 0$, then $ABS(X) = X$.

7. A RESTORE statement sends the computer back to the beginning of the first DATA statement in a program.

8. A menu lets a user choose from a list of choices by entering the number of the choice.

9. An ON-GOTO statement combines many branch statements into one statement. The format for an ON-GOTO statement is ON X GOTO line numbers, where X is a variable or an expression that can be evaluated.

10. An ON-GOSUB statement combines many GOSUB statements into one statement. The format for an ON-GOSUB statement is ON X GOSUB line numbers, where X is a variable or an expression that can be evaluated.

11. Some BASICs allow computed line numbers in a GOTO or GOSUB statement. This allows GOTO and GOSUB to be used in place of ON-GOTO and ON-GOSUB.

12. In many BASICs, THEN may be followed by either a line number or a statement. Therefore, IF-THEN statements can be used to make either branches or statements conditional.

13. In some BASICs, conditional branches and statements can be combined using IF-THEN-ELSE statements.

14. A computer uses two logical values, true (1 or −1) and false (0).

15. The logical value of a compound statement using AND is true only if each part of the statement is true. The logical value of a compound statement using OR is true unless all parts of the statement are false.

16. AND, OR, and NOT are logical operators.

17. If a statement is true, then the same statement preceded by NOT is false.

18. In many BASICs, a PRINT statement gives the logical value of a statement that is not enclosed in quotation marks.

19. A variable has the logical value false if its value is 0, and the logical value true if its value is not 0.

20. The most commonly used keyboard coding system is ASCII (American Standard Code for Information Interchange). ASCII includes character codes and codes for controlling I/O devices.

21. In many BASICs, ASC(X$) gives the ASCII code for the first character in any character string X$.

22. In most BASICs, CHR$(N) gives the character that has ASCII code N. Statements using CHR$ can be used to print characters that are not represented by keys on the keyboard.

23. Numbers and numeric variables can be used in computations, but strings and string variables cannot.

24. If X$ contains only a numeral, some BASICs use VAL(X$) to change the string to a number.

25. Many BASICs use STR$(X) to change a number X to a string.

26. Most BASICs use LEN(X$) to give the number of characters in X$. The LEN function can be used to align output.

27. Many BASICs use PRINT USING statements for aligning output.

28. A computer can make short work of difficult computations, such as finding the zeros of a polynomial by substitution.

29. Many BASICs allow user-defined functions introduced by DEF FN A(X) or DEF A(X), where A is any letter and X is the variable in the function.

30. Computer programs can be written for use with many mathematical tasks, such as solving polynomial equations, finding factorials, and printing Pascal's triangle.

31. The value of $\pi$ can be supplied in several ways for use in computer programs. Some computers have a value for $\pi$ in read-only memory.

32. EXP(N) gives the value of $e^n$. EXP(1) gives the value of $e$.

**33.** LOG(A) gives the value of *n* if $e^n$=A. LOG(A) is the natural logarithm (the logarithm to the base *e*) of A.

**34.** In some BASICs, the logarithm to the base 10 of A is found using LOG(A)/LOG(10). In other BASICs, it is found using CLOG(A).

**35.** A computer gives the values of trigonometric functions for angle measures in radians. For an angle with a measure of R radians, the measure in degrees is R·180/π.

**36.** Rounding errors must be accounted for when using computer values of trigonometric functions.

**37.** Most BASICs include the trigonometric functions SIN, COS, and TAN. The trigonometric function ATN(T) gives the value in radians of the angle whose tangent is T.

## Chapter Test

**Name one advantage and one disadvantage of each of the following.**

**1.** Using END or LET, even if it is not required

**2.** Putting more than one statement on a line

**3.** Combining PRINT and INPUT statements

**Complete each sentence.**

**4.** In a computer program, a list of choices is called a _____.

**5.** ASCII stands for _____.

**6.** AND, OR, and NOT are called logical _____.

**7.** PRINT USING is used for aligning _____.

**8.** The word true or false, or the number standing for the word, is called the _____ of a statement or variable.

**Give the value of each of the following.**

**9.** SGN(16)

**10.** SGN(0)

**11.** SGN(−30.25)

**12.** SGN(6−2↑2)

**13.** SGN(5−2∗4)

**14.** SGN(−2−(−5))

**15.** −SGN(4.162)

**16.** −SGN(−3)

**17.** ABS(0)

**18.** ABS(−21)

**19.** ABS(14.62)

**20.** ABS(3↑2−10)

**21.** ABS(12−6∗2)

**22.** ABS(2∗8−5)

**23.** −ABS(14)

**24.** −ABS(−3.6)

**25.** ABS(SGN(−5))

**26.** SGN(ABS(−10))

**Write yes or no to tell whether each of the following can be used in computation.**

**27.** ASC(A$)

**28.** VAL(A$)

**29.** CHR$(125)

**30.** STR$(12)

**31.** LEN(A$)

**32.** VAL("340")

## Write a set of IF-THEN statements to replace each given statement.

**33.** 100 ON D GOTO 250,350,150,300,200

**34.** 200 ON ST GOSUB 500,600,700

## Use the statements below for problems 35 and 36.

    10 IF X = 2 THEN 30
    20 GOTO 60

**35.** Write a statement to replace the statements above using IF-THEN-ELSE 60.

**36.** Write a statement to replace the statements above using IF-THEN-ELSE 30.

## Give the logical value (as a word) for each statement below.

**37.** 7 = 4+3

**38.** 5 = 6

**39.** 6 > 5

**40.** 4 >= 3+1

**41.** 6 <= 7

**42.** 12 <> 7+3

**43.** 4+1 = 5 AND 9 = 1+8

**44.** 7 = 5+2 AND 5 < 0

**45.** 3+2 = 4 OR 3+2 = 6

**46.** 4 < 5 OR 5 < 6

**47.** −3 > 0 OR 3 > 0

**48.** NOT(2+1 <= 3)

**49.** NOT(2 = 3)OR 1 = 2

**50.** NOT (2+1 = 3) AND 0 < 3

## Give the output of each command.

**51.** PRINT "3+1 = 4"

**52.** PRINT "3+1 = ";3+1

**53.** PRINT "3+1 = ";4

**54.** PRINT 3+1 = 4

**55.** PRINT 3+1 = 3+1

**56.** PRINT 3+1 = 5

## Let N = 1. For each of the following statements, write yes or no to tell if program control will be transferred to line 40.

**57.** 10 IF ABS(N)=SGN(N) THEN 40

**58.** 10 IF N THEN 40

**59.** 10 IF ABS(SGN(N))=N THEN 40

**60.** 10 IF NOT N THEN 40

**61.** 10 IF SGN(N)=−1 THEN 40

**62.** 10 GOSUB 3*(13+N)

**63.** 10 IF NOT N THEN 60 ELSE 40

**64.** 10 IF SGN(N)<0 THEN 40

**65.** 10 IF N<>ABS(N) THEN 40

**66.** 10 GOTO 40*N

**67.** 10 IF N=ABS(N) THEN 40

**68.** 10 IF SGN(N)<>−1 THEN 40

**69.** 10 IF N AND NOT N THEN 40

**70.** 10 IF N OR NOT N THEN 40

**71.** 10 IF SGN(ABS(N))=N THEN 40

**72.** 10 IF N>0 THEN 40 ELSE 20

## Let A = 65, A$ = "65", and B$ = A$. The ASCII code for A is 65 and the ASCII code for B is 66. Give the output of each of the following.

**73.** ASC("B$")

**74.** CHR$(65)

**75.** VAL(A$)

**76.** STR$(A)

**77.** LEN(A$)

**78.** LEN(B$)

**79.** Write a statement to print the ASCII code for H.

**80.** Write a statement to print the character with ASCII code 38.

**In problems 81-84, let E\$ = "4.4953" and let N = 6.28.**

**81.** How can E\$ be used to supply the number 4.4953 in a program?

**82.** How can E\$ be used to supply the number 4 in a program?

**83.** What is LEN(E\$)?

**84.** How can N be used to supply the string "6.28" in a program?

**85.** Give the output of the program below.

```
10 DATA 1,2,3
15 DATA 4,5,6
20 FOR I = 1 TO 3
30     READ X(I)
40 NEXT I
50 RESTORE
60 FOR J = 1 TO 3
70     READ Y(J)
80     PRINT Y(J)
90 NEXT J
100 END
```

**Match each numbered item with the best lettered choice.**

| | |
|---|---|
| **86.** The value of $\pi$ | **a.** LOG(T) |
| **87.** EXP(1) | **b.** 180/$\pi$ |
| **88.** The measure of an angle whose tangent is T | **c.** LOG(T)/LOG(10) |
| **89.** The logarithm of T to the base $e$ | **d.** 2.7182818 |
| **90.** The cosine of an angle whose measure is T | **e.** 3.1415926 |
| **91.** The sine of an angle whose measure is T | **f.** ATN(T) |
| **92.** The tangent of an angle whose measure is T | **g.** TAN(T) |
| **93.** The logarithm of T to the base 10 | **h.** COS(T) |
| **94.** The measure of a 1-radian angle in degrees | **i.** SIN(T) |

**95.** Write and run a program to print a list of 10 names starting with the name with the least number of characters and ending with the name with the greatest number of characters. Have the names entered as input.

**96.** Write a program for solving equations of the form $a = nx - c$. Include input tests and messages for conditions under which $x$ may be any real number or there is no solution.

**97.** Write a program to find the zero of equations of the form $y = mx + b$ if $m$ and $b$ are entered as input.

# COMPUTER LITERACY

Artificial intelligence is the capability of a computer to perform functions, such as reasoning and learning, that are usually associated with human intelligence. Research in this field attempts to discover how much intelligence can be simulated by a computer.

Today's computers can play checkers, compose and play music, write poetry, and draw pictures. These activities seem to involve some thought. However, computers can do these things only because people have programmed them to do so.

A computer can be programmed to play a good game of chess, but it cannot be programmed to beat the best players. Computers still cannot be programmed to "think" on high enough level.

**A computerized chess game.**

# ARTIFICIAL INTELLIGENCE

Research in the area of pattern recognition illustrates some of the basic problems that have been encountered. Pattern recognition involves the ability to recognize letters, both handwritten and typewritten. It is very difficult for the computer to recognize differences in the ways letters are formed. Computers just do not have the capability to recognize all of the different forms for every letter. In contrast a human can recognize the letters with little trouble.

However, in some ways the computer is superior to the human brain. A person cannot even come close to the speed at which a computer performs computations. Also, the speed and accuracy of a computer's recall is much better than that of most humans.

In general, research in the field of artificial intelligence shows that very little is known about the complicated way humans think. Until more is known about human intelligence, true artificial intelligence will be difficult to create.

Computers can be used to draw pictures such as the one above. This is only one example of the many uses of computer graphic capabilities.

# APPENDIX:
# COMPUTER GRAPHICS

**Computer graphics** is the process of displaying output in the form of graphs, diagrams, or pictures. Many interesting graphic effects can be created using BASIC. In this appendix, some BASIC graphics will be explored.

## A.1 GRAPHICS IN BASIC

Shapes, such as letters of the alphabet, can be printed using PRINT statements and characters. A shape should be designed on a coding form or squared paper before writing a program to print the shape.

---

**EXAMPLE 1**

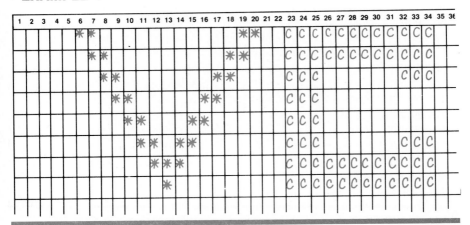

---

If the TAB function is available in a BASIC, it can be used in PRINT statements to position the characters that form the shape. Otherwise, blanks can be included in the strings with the characters. In the example below, the TAB function is used in a program to print the letters from Example 1.

---

**EXAMPLE 2**

```
10 REM PRINT LETTERS
20 PRINT TAB(6);"**";TAB(19);"**";TAB(23);"CCCCCCCCCCCC"
30 PRINT TAB(7);"**";TAB(18);"**";TAB(23);"CCCCCCCCCCCC"
40 PRINT TAB(8);"**";TAB(17);"**";TAB(23);"CCC";TAB(32);"CCC"
50 PRINT TAB(9);"**";TAB(16);"**";TAB(23);"CCC"
60 PRINT TAB(10);"**";TAB(15);"**";TAB(23);"CCC"
70 PRINT TAB(11);"**";TAB(14);"**";TAB(23);"CCC";TAB(32);"CCC"
80 PRINT TAB(12);"***";TAB(23);"CCCCCCCCCCCC"
90 PRINT TAB(13);"*";TAB(23);"CCCCCCCCCCCC"
100 END
```

---

The program below uses spaces in strings to position the symbols. The design in the program looks much like it would on the coding form used for designing it.

---

**EXAMPLE 3**

```
10   REM PRINT ARROW
20   PRINT "                              >"
30   PRINT "                             >>"
40   PRINT ">>>>                        >>>"
50   PRINT ">>>>                       >>>>"
60   PRINT ">>>>                      >>>>>"
70   PRINT ">>>>>>>>>>>>>>>>>>>>>>>>>>>>>>"
80   PRINT ">>>>>>>>>>>>>>>>>>>>>>>>>>>>>>>"
90   PRINT ">>>>>>>>>>>>>>>>>>>>>>>>>>>>>>>>"
100  PRINT ">>>>>>>>>>>>>>>>>>>>>>>>>>>>>>>"
110  PRINT ">>>>>>>>>>>>>>>>>>>>>>>>>>>>>>"
120  PRINT ">>>>                      >>>>>"
130  PRINT ">>>>                       >>>>"
140  PRINT ">>>>                        >>>"
150  PRINT "                             >>"
160  PRINT "                              >"
170  END
```

---

The appearance of certain designs can be improved by the characters used and by their positions. For example, the C in Example 1 can be designed to appear curved.

## EXAMPLE 4

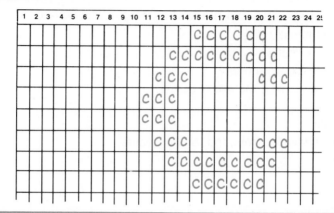

Letters and symbols can be combined to produce interesting effects.

## EXAMPLE 5

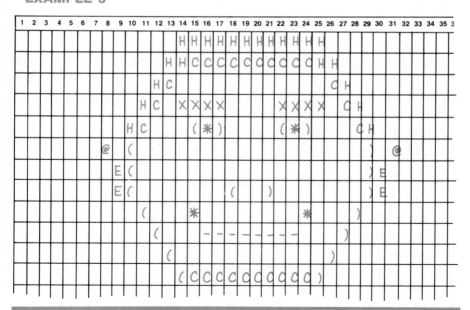

# Exercises

1. If your BASIC does not have the TAB function, rewrite the program in Example 2 to use spaces in the PRINT statements.

**Plan a design for each of the following on a coding form or squared paper. Use characters that make the designs interesting.**

2. Your first name
3. Your entire name
4. The numerals from 0 to 3
5. Your initials, using the entire screen
6. A square
7. A triangle
8. A cube (show the front, top, and one side)
9. A circle
10. An oval
11. A rocket
12. A smiling face
13. A cartoon character

# Laboratory Activities

1. Enter and run the program from Example 2 (or Exercise 1).
2. Enter and run the program in Example 3.
3. Write and run a program to print the C in Example 4.
4. Write and run a program to print the face in Example 5.

**Write and run a program to print your design for each exercise listed below.**

5. Exercise 2
6. Exercise 3
7. Exercise 4
8. Exercise 5
9. Exercise 6
10. Exercise 7
11. Exercise 8
12. Exercise 9
13. Exercise 10
14. Exercise 11
15. Exercise 12
16. Exercise 13

**17.** Write and run a program to print your initials in an oval.

**18.** Change the program you wrote for Activity **17** to print the initials of your school name in an oval. Run the program.

**19.** Find a logo that uses a design a computer can print. Write and run a program to print the logo.

# A.2  LOOPS AND MOTION

Loops and READ/DATA statements can be used to print repeating patterns, as shown in Example 1.

**EXAMPLE 1**

```
10 REM STRIPE
15 REM CLEAR SCREEN HERE
20 DATA "?","(","*","#","&"
30 REM READ THE SYMBOLS INTO AN ARRAY
40 FOR C = 1 TO 5
50    READ S$(C)
60 NEXT C
70 REM PRINT 5 IDENTICAL LINES
80 FOR G = 1 TO 5
90    FOR C = 1 TO 5
95       REM PRINT EACH SYMBOL 7 TIMES
100      FOR N = 1 TO 7
110         PRINT S$(C);
120      NEXT N
130   NEXT C
135   PRINT
140 NEXT G
160 END
RUN
```

```
???????(((((*******#######&&&&&&&
???????(((((*******#######&&&&&&&
???????(((((*******#######&&&&&&&
???????(((((*******#######&&&&&&&
???????(((((*******#######&&&&&&&
```

Many computer games depend on the fast-moving graphics that can be created using special graphics commands. BASIC graphics displayed on a monitor screen can also move, though not very fast. Example 2 shows how to create a moving design.

## EXAMPLE 2

```
6 REM THE CRAWLER
8 REM PRINT 10 BLANK LINES
10 FOR I = 1 TO 10
20     PRINT
30 NEXT I
35 REM PRINT THE CRAWLER
40 PRINT TAB(4);"***"
50 PRINT TAB(5);"*"
60 PRINT "**********"
70 PRINT TAB(3);"*";TAB(7);"*"
80 PRINT TAB(3);"*****"
90 PRINT TAB(2);"*";TAB(8);"*"
95 REM PRINT 16 BLANK LINES TO MOVE
97 REM CRAWLER UP THE SCREEN
100 FOR I = 1 TO 16
130     PRINT
140 NEXT I
150 END
```

The motion can sometimes be improved by controlling the speed and type of motion with a delay loop.

## EXAMPLE 3

These lines can be added to the program in Example 2 to slow down the motion.

```
110    FOR J = 1 TO 100
120    NEXT J
```

The program in Example 4 moves symbols from left to right in a straight line.

## EXAMPLE 4

```
5 REM INCHWORM
10 FOR N = 0 TO 36
15    REM PRINT WORM
20    PRINT ">>>>";
```

```
25    REM PAUSE
30    FOR C = 1 TO 100
40    NEXT C
45    REM BACKSPACE TO TAIL
50    FOR D = 1 TO 4
60        PRINT CHR$(8);
70    NEXT D
75    REM ERASE TAIL
80    PRINT " ";
85    REM PRINT NEW WORM
90 NEXT N
100 END
```

The random number generator can also be used to create unusual effects. In Example 5, it is used to choose random TAB settings. It can also be used to choose symbols randomly or to randomize any other data in a graphics program.

## EXAMPLE 5

```
10 FOR I = 1 TO 6
20    LET J = 40*RND+1
30       PRINT TAB(J);"*****";TAB(J+10);"***"
40 NEXT I
50 END
RUN
                                           **

  ***
          ***
       *****       ***
 *****        ***
                            *****
   ***
                 *****      ***
                 *****      ***
```

# Exercises

## Refer to the program in Example 1 for Exercises 1-6.

**1.** When would a DIM statement be needed for S$?

**2.** Which loop controls the number of columns of each symbol printed?

3. Which loop controls the number of different symbols printed on a line?

4. Which loop controls the number of lines printed?

5. For a screen 64 columns wide, how can the program be changed so the design almost fills the width of the screen?

6. How can the height of the stripe be increased? Decreased?

7. In Example 2, what is the purpose of the first loop in the program?

8. In Example 2, what is the purpose of the second loop in the program?

9. In Example 4, what happens each time line 60 in the program is executed?

**Design each of the following on a coding form or squared paper.**

10. A small rocket

11. A large pine tree

12. A billboard sign that fills most of the screen

# Laboratory Activities

1. Enter and run the program in Example 1.

2. Remove line 15 from the program in Activity **1** and run the program. Does this make a difference in the way the design appears on the screen?

3. Add three more DATA statements to the program in Activity **1,** using different symbols or the same symbols in a different order in each one. Then add the following lines.

```
35 FOR T = 1 TO 4
150 NEXT T
```

Run the program. If the pattern does not fill most of the screen or page, change the program so it does.

**If output from your computer is displayed on a monitor screen, do Activities 4-12.**

4. Enter and run the program in Example 2.

5. Use the lines in Example 3 as described and run the program. What is the effect of the delay loop?

6. Experiment with delay loops of different lengths in the program in Activity **4.**

7. Change the program in Activity **4** so the starting horizontal position of the crawler is chosen randomly. For a screen 64 columns wide, the line below can be used to compute the first TAB value (which will replace the 4 in line 40). Then replace TAB(5) with TAB(T+1), and so on. Run the program.

    37 LET T = 54*RND+3

8. Write and run a program to move the rocket you designed in Exercise **10** from the bottom of the screen to the top.

9. Enter and run the program in Example 4. If the inchworm does not crawl all the way across your screen, change the program so it does.

10. Replace the symbols that make up the inchworm in Activity **9** to make it a hairy caterpillar. Run the program.

11. Change the inchworm program to make the worm twice as long as it is in Example 4. Run the program.

12. Change the inchworm program in Activity **9** to have the worm crawl along for several lines, instead of just one. Run the program.

13. Enter and run the program in Example 5.

14. Enter and run the following program.

```
10 FOR T = 1 TO 10
20    PRINT TAB(16-T);"your name";TAB(41-T);"your name"
30 NEXT T
40 FOR T = 10 TO 1 STEP − 1
50    PRINT TAB(16-T);"your name";TAB(41-T);"your name"
60 NEXT T
70 GOTO 10
80 END
```

15. Enter and run the following program.

```
10 FOR R = 1 TO 2
20    FOR C = 1 TO 7
30       FOR N = 1 TO C
40          PRINT "your first name"
50       NEXT N
60       PRINT
70    NEXT C
80 NEXT R
90 END
```

16. The program below creates an optical illusion on a screen 40 columns wide. For a screen 64 columns wide, use a string with 21 symbols. (Be sure to include some spaces). Enter and run the program.

```
10 REM OPTICAL ILLUSION
20 FOR N = 1 TO 1000
30    PRINT "??? ??? ???";
40 NEXT N
50 END
```

**17.** Write and run a program to print the symbol * randomly on the screen.

**18.** Write and run a program to print the tree you designed in Exercise **11.**

**19.** Write and run a program to print the sign you designed in Exercise **12.** Have each line scroll off the top of the screen and immediately reappear at the bottom, making a continuously scrolling billboard.

# A.3 BAR GRAPHS

Someone once said "A picture is worth a thousand words." Maybe that is why *bar graphs* are frequently used to describe data. The horizontal bar graph shown below gives the results of a survey in which 50 high school students were asked to state their favorite food.

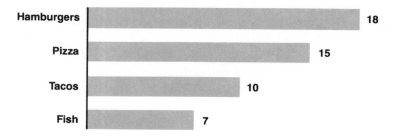

**Student Food Survey**

Computers can be programmed to print such bar graphs. The program in Example 1 will cause one horizontal bar to be printed.

**EXAMPLE 1**

```
10 REM THE BAR WILL BE 3 ROWS WIDE
20 FOR W = 1 TO 3
30    REM THE BAR WILL BE 20 COLUMNS LONG
40    FOR L = 1 TO 20
50       PRINT "*";
60    NEXT L
70    PRINT
80 NEXT W
```

```
90 END
RUN

********************
********************
********************
```

The width of the bar can vary. It should be chosen so the required
number of bars will fit on the page or screen.

The method used in Example 1 can be used to print the entire bar graph for
the student food survey.

## EXAMPLE 2

```
10   REM READ THE DATA INTO TWO ARRAYS
20   DATA "HAMBURGERS",18,"PIZZA",15,"TACOS",10,"FISH",7
30   FOR N = 1 TO 4
40       READ F$(N),S(N)
50   NEXT N
60   REM NUMBER OF BARS TO BE PRINTED
70   FOR N = 1 TO 4
80       REM SKIP TWO LINES BETWEEN BARS
90       FOR BL = 1 TO 2
100          PRINT
110      NEXT BL
120      REM W = WIDTH OF BAR
130      FOR W = 1 TO 3
140          REM PRINT FOOD NAME AT BEGINNING OF BAR
150          IF W <> 2 THEN 156
152          PRINT F$(N);TAB(12);
154          GOTO 170
156          PRINT TAB(12);
160          REM L = LENGTH OF BAR
170          FOR L = 1 TO S(N)
180              PRINT "*";
190          NEXT L
200          REM PRINT NUMBER AT END OF BAR
202          IF W <> 2 THEN 220
204          PRINT " ";S(N)
210          GOTO 230
220          PRINT
230      NEXT W
240  NEXT N
250  END
```

The bars in bar graphs are sometimes vertical instead of horizontal, as shown in the graph below.

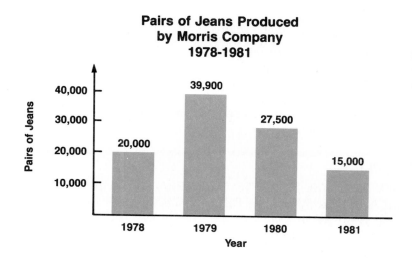

**Pairs of Jeans Produced
by Morris Company
1978-1981**

Using the data in the graph above in a program might produce bars that are too long for the screen or page. Therefore, the graph will have to be printed using a scale. To do this, first decide how many lines the longest bar will use. Then divide this number by the greatest datum. This gives the *scale factor*. Each datum is then multiplied by the scale factor. The program in Example 3 shows how a scale factor is used to print the bar graph above.

## EXAMPLE 3

```
10  REM READ DATA INTO AN ARRAY
20  DATA 20000, 39900, 27500, 15000
30  FOR D = 1 TO 4
40     READ N(D)
50  NEXT D
60  REM LET LONGEST BAR USE 15 LINES
65  REM SF = SCALE FACTOR
70  LET SF = 15/39900
80  REM MULTIPLY EACH DATUM BY SF
90  FOR D = 1 TO 4
100    LET NN(D) = INT(SF*N(D))
110 NEXT D
120 REM USE DATA IN ARRAY NN FOR GRAPH
125 REM L = TWO LESS THAN TOTAL LINES ON A PAGE
130 FOR L = 1 TO 22
140    REM NB = NUMBER OF BARS
```

```
150    FOR NB = 1 TO 4
160        REM IS CURSOR MORE THAN 1 LINE ABOVE TOP OF BAR?
170        IF 21−NN(NB) > L THEN 260
180        REM IS CURSOR AT TOP OR BELOW TOP OF BAR?
190        IF 21−NN(NB) < L THEN 230
200        PRINT TAB(8*NB);N(NB)
210        GOTO 260
220        REM PRINT BAR 3 LINES WIDE
230        FOR PR = 1 TO 3
240            PRINT TAB(8*NB);"*";
250        NEXT PR
260    NEXT NB
270    PRINT
280 NEXT L
290 REM PRINT DATE UNDER BAR
295 DATA 1978, 1979, 1980, 1981
300 FOR NB = 1 TO 4
310    READ DT(NB)
320    PRINT TAB(8*NB);DT(NB);
330 NEXT NB
340 END
```

To find the scale factor for a horizontal bar graph, decide how many columns the longest bar will use. Then divide this number by the greatest datum.

# Exercises

1. What should determine the width of the bars in a bar graph?
2. What is the purpose of lines 90-110 in Example 2?
3. What is the purpose of line 220 in Example 2?
4. When should a scale be used in printing a bar graph?
5. How is a scale factor computed?

**Compute the scale factor for Exercises 6 and 7.**

6. greatest datum = 40; lines to be used in longest bar = 20
7. greatest datum = 120; lines to be used in longest bar = 30

8. Use the following chart to record the attendance in your class for one week.

|       | Monday | Tuesday | Wednesday | Thursday | Friday |
|-------|--------|---------|-----------|----------|--------|
| Boys  |        |         |           |          |        |
| Girls |        |         |           |          |        |
| Total |        |         |           |          |        |

9. Use the chart from Exercise **8** to draw a vertical bar graph that shows the attendance record of the boys in your class.
10. Use the chart from Exercise **8** to draw a horizontal bar graph that shows the attendance record of the girls in your class.
11. Use the chart from Exercise **8** to draw a horizontal bar graph that shows the attendance of both boys and girls in your class.

# Laboratory Activities

1. Enter and run the program in Example 1.
2. Enter and run the program in Example 2.
3. Enter and run the program in Example 3.
4. Write and run a program to print the bar graph you drew for Exercise **9**.
5. Write and run a program to print the bar graph you drew for Exercise **10**.
6. Write and run a program to print the bar graph you drew for Exercise **11**. If necessary, use a scale factor.

**Write and run programs to print the bar graphs in Activities 7-10. If necessary use a scale factor.**

7. Percent of 12th grade students at Croson High School taking History, English, Science, and Mathematics classes

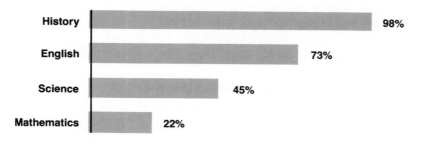

**8.** Amount of coal (in tons) mined by Soler Coal Company

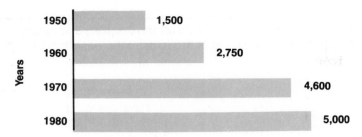

**9.** Students at Broadview High School

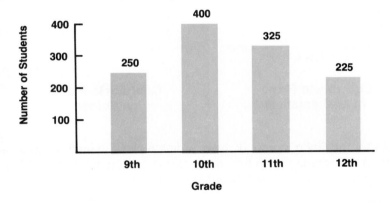

**10.** Refrigerator sales per week

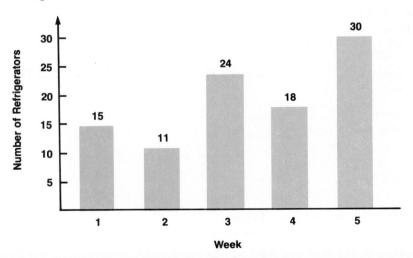

# A.4 COORDINATE GRAPHING

The monitor screen is a coordinate plane similar to the one used in mathematics. However, the numbering used for the columns and rows on the screen is different from the numbering of the axes in the coordinate plane in mathematics.

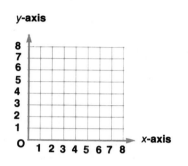

**Coordinate Plane
in Mathematics**

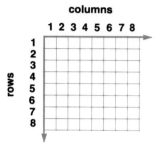

**Coordinate Plane
on Screen**

The axes for the first quadrant of the coordinate plane in mathematics can be printed on the screen. To do this, the y-axis is printed at the far left-hand side of the screen and the x-axis is printed at the bottom of the screen.

---

**EXAMPLE 1**

```
2 PRINT "ENTER NUMBER OF LINES ON SCREEN"
4 INPUT L
6 PRINT "ENTER NUMBER OF COLUMNS ON SCREEN"
8 INPUT C
10 REM PRINT VERTICAL LINE AT FAR LEFT-HAND SIDE OF SCREEN
20 FOR I = 1 TO L−1
30    PRINT "!"
40 NEXT I
50 REM PRINT HORIZONTAL LINE AT BOTTOM OF SCREEN
60 FOR I = 1 TO C
70    PRINT "−";
80 NEXT I
90 END
```

In this book, we will use 24 rows.

---

Plotting points on the screen can be more easily understood if the points are first marked on a coding form or squared paper. Example 2 shows the location of the point with coordinates (4, 5).

## EXAMPLE 2

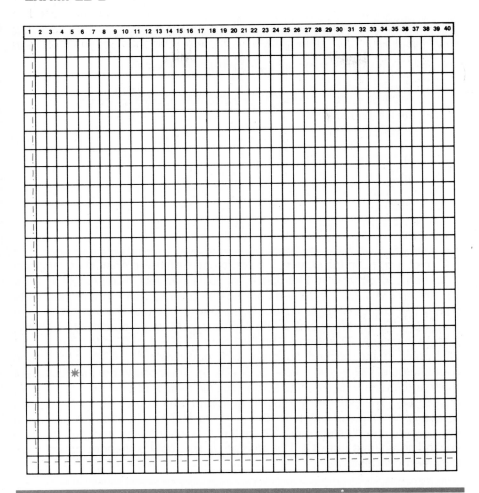

Notice that the point is in column 5 and row 19 on the coding form. The program to print this point is shown in Example 3.

## EXAMPLE 3

The following lines can be used in the program in Example 1.

```
25 IF I = L−5 THEN 38
34 GOTO 40
35 REM PRINTS PART OF VERTICAL LINE AND
36 REM * IN COLUMN 5 AND ROW 19
38 PRINT "!";"ᴧᴧᴧ*"
```

Only the first quadrant of the coordinate plane is used in Examples 1, 2, and 3. The program in Example 4 prints the x-axis and the y-axis, and shows all four quadrants. (This program is written for a 64 column screen.)

**EXAMPLE 4**

```
5 REM AXES INTERSECT NEAR CENTER OF SCREEN
10 FOR I = 1 TO 24
20    REM CHECK IF CURSOR IS HALFWAY DOWN SCREEN
30    IF I = 12 THEN 90
50    PRINT TAB(32);"!"
70    GOTO 120
80    REM PRINT X-AXIS
90    FOR J = 1 TO 64
100      PRINT "−";
110    NEXT J
120 NEXT I
130 END
```

To plot a point on the screen, the coordinates of the point must be changed to *screen coordinates.* In Example 4, the axes intersect in column 32 and row 12. (In other words, the screen coordinates are (32, 12).) In the coordinate plane, the coordinates assigned to the intersection of the x-axis and the y-axis are (0, 0). The point in the first quadrant with coordinates (5, 4) is located in column 37 and row 8 on the screen. (32 + 5 = 37 and 12 − 4 = 8.) The point in the second quadrant with coordinates (−4, 3) has screen coordinates of (32 + (−4), 12 − 3) or (28, 9). The point in the third quadrant with coordinates (−6, −5) has screen coordinates of (32 + (−6), 12 − (−5)) or (26, 17). The point in the fourth quadrant with coordinates (8, −2) has screen coordinates of (32 + 8, 12 − (−2)) or (40, 14). In other words, to find the screen coordinates, add 32 to the first coordinate and subtract the second coordinate from 12. The program in Example 5 changes coordinates to screen coordinates.

**EXAMPLE 5**

```
10 PRINT "ENTER THE COORDINATES"
15 INPUT X, Y
20 REM CHANGE FIRST COORDINATE
30 LET XS = X+32
40 REM CHANGE SECOND COORDINATE
50 LET YS = 12−Y
60 PRINT "THE SCREEN COORDINATES ARE"
70 PRINT "(";XS;",";YS;")"
80 END
```

The program above can be changed to find the screen coordinates for any point of intersection of the axes.

# Exercises

1. If only the first quadrant is to be shown on the screen where should the y-axis be printed? Where should the x-axis be printed?
2. What is the purpose of lines 25 and 38 in the program in Example 3?
3. Why was 32 used in the TAB function in line 50 in the program in Example 4?

**Compute the screen coordinates for the coordinates given below if the axes intersect at the point with screen coordinates (32, 12).**

4. (9, 1)                   5. (−15, 0)                   6. (6, −4)
7. (−3, −7)                 8. (0, −12)                   9. (−5, 2)

10. Compute the screen coordinates for the coordinates in Exercises **4-9** if the axes intersect at the point with screen coordinates (25, 25).

# Laboratory Activities

1. Enter and run the program in Example 1.
2. Use the lines in Example 3 as described. Run the program.
3. Replace line 38 in Activity **2** with the following line and run the program.

   38 PRINT "∧∧∧*"

   Is the output the same as in Activity **2**?
4. Change the program in Activity **2** to print a * in column 20 and row 20. Run the program.
5. Enter and run the program in Example 4. (If necessary, change the program to use the number of rows and columns on your screen.)
6. Change the program in Activity **5** to print the axes so they intersect in column 25 and row 20. Run the program.
7. Change the program in Activity **5** to print the Roman numerals I, II, III, and IV near the center of the quadrants they name. Run the program.
8. Change the program in Activity **5** to print the point with coordinates of (4, 5). Run the program.
9. Enter and run the program in Example 5.
10. Change the program in Activity **5** to print the points with the coordinates given in Exercises **4-9**. Run the programs.

# BASIC TERMS AND SYMBOLS

# TABLES

# GLOSSARY

# SELECTED ANSWERS

# INDEX

BASIC terms and symbols are listed below with the page number on which they are explained.

# BASIC TERMS

| | | |
|---|---|---|
| ABS (217) | IF-GOTO (111) | PRINT USING (233) |
| AND (112) | IF-THEN (110) | RANDOM (194) |
| ASC (231) | IF-THEN GOSUB (133) | RANDOMIZE (194) |
| ATN (242) | IF-THEN GOTO (111) | READ/DATA (73) |
| CHR$ (231) | INPUT (78) | REM (91) |
| CLOAD (84) | INT (116) | RESTORE (218) |
| CLOG (241) | LEN (232) | RETURN (132) |
| COS (242) | LET (48) | RND (193) |
| CSAVE (83) | LIST (59) | RUN (42) |
| DEF (236) | LN (241) | SAVE (83) |
| DIM (187) | LOAD (84) | SGN (216) |
| END (42) | LOG (241) | SIN (242) |
| EXP (240) | NEW (44) | SQR (147) |
| FOR/NEXT (124) | NOT (225) | STEP (124) |
| GOSUB (132) | ON-GOSUB (221) | STR$ (232) |
| GOTO (107) | ON-GOTO (220) | TAB (87) |
| IF-GOSUB (133) | OR (112) | TAN (242) |
| | PRINT (33) | VAL (231) |

# BASIC SYMBOLS

| | | | | |
|---|---|---|---|---|
| + | addition (31) | $>=$ | greater than or equal to (111) |
| , | comma (49) | $<$ | less than (111) |
| / | division (31) | $<=$ | less than or equal to (111) |
| = | equals sign (48) | * | multiplication (31) |
| ↑ | exponentiation (31) | $<>$ | not equal to (111) |
| ∧ | exponentiation (31) | " | quotation marks (41) |
| ** | exponentiation (31) | ; | semicolon (49) |
| $>$ | greater than (111) | – | subtraction (31) |

## Squares and Square Roots

| $n$ | $n^2$ | $\sqrt{n}$ | $\sqrt{10n}$ | $n$ | $n^2$ | $\sqrt{n}$ | $\sqrt{10n}$ |
|---|---|---|---|---|---|---|---|
| 1.0 | 1.00 | 1.000 | 3.162 | 5.5 | 30.25 | 2.345 | 7.416 |
| 1.1 | 1.21 | 1.049 | 3.317 | 5.6 | 31.36 | 2.366 | 7.483 |
| 1.2 | 1.44 | 1.095 | 3.464 | 5.7 | 32.49 | 2.387 | 7.550 |
| 1.3 | 1.69 | 1.140 | 3.606 | 5.8 | 33.64 | 2.408 | 7.616 |
| 1.4 | 1.96 | 1.183 | 3.742 | 5.9 | 34.81 | 2.429 | 7.681 |
| 1.5 | 2.25 | 1.225 | 3.873 | 6.0 | 36.00 | 2.449 | 7.746 |
| 1.6 | 2.56 | 1.265 | 4.000 | 6.1 | 37.21 | 2.470 | 7.810 |
| 1.7 | 2.89 | 1.304 | 4.123 | 6.2 | 38.44 | 2.490 | 7.874 |
| 1.8 | 3.24 | 1.342 | 4.243 | 6.3 | 39.69 | 2.510 | 7.937 |
| 1.9 | 3.61 | 1.378 | 4.359 | 6.4 | 40.96 | 2.530 | 8.000 |
| 2.0 | 4.00 | 1.414 | 4.472 | 6.5 | 42.25 | 2.550 | 8.062 |
| 2.1 | 4.41 | 1.449 | 4.583 | 6.6 | 43.56 | 2.569 | 8.124 |
| 2.2 | 4.84 | 1.483 | 4.690 | 6.7 | 44.89 | 2.588 | 8.185 |
| 2.3 | 5.29 | 1.517 | 4.796 | 6.8 | 46.24 | 2.608 | 8.246 |
| 2.4 | 5.76 | 1.549 | 4.899 | 6.9 | 47.61 | 2.627 | 8.307 |
| 2.5 | 6.25 | 1.581 | 5.000 | 7.0 | 49.00 | 2.646 | 8.367 |
| 2.6 | 6.76 | 1.612 | 5.099 | 7.1 | 50.41 | 2.665 | 8.426 |
| 2.7 | 7.29 | 1.643 | 5.196 | 7.2 | 51.84 | 2.683 | 8.485 |
| 2.8 | 7.84 | 1.673 | 5.292 | 7.3 | 53.29 | 2.702 | 8.544 |
| 2.9 | 8.41 | 1.703 | 5.385 | 7.4 | 54.76 | 2.720 | 8.602 |
| 3.0 | 9.00 | 1.732 | 5.477 | 7.5 | 56.25 | 2.739 | 8.660 |
| 3.1 | 9.61 | 1.761 | 5.568 | 7.6 | 57.76 | 2.757 | 8.718 |
| 3.2 | 10.24 | 1.789 | 5.657 | 7.7 | 59.29 | 2.775 | 8.775 |
| 3.3 | 10.89 | 1.817 | 5.745 | 7.8 | 60.84 | 2.793 | 8.832 |
| 3.4 | 11.56 | 1.844 | 5.831 | 7.9 | 62.41 | 2.811 | 8.888 |
| 3.5 | 12.25 | 1.871 | 5.916 | 8.0 | 64.00 | 2.828 | 8.944 |
| 3.6 | 12.96 | 1.897 | 6.000 | 8.1 | 65.61 | 2.846 | 9.000 |
| 3.7 | 13.69 | 1.924 | 6.083 | 8.2 | 67.24 | 2.864 | 9.055 |
| 3.8 | 14.44 | 1.949 | 6.164 | 8.3 | 68.89 | 2.881 | 9.110 |
| 3.9 | 15.21 | 1.975 | 6.245 | 8.4 | 70.56 | 2.898 | 9.165 |
| 4.0 | 16.00 | 2.000 | 6.325 | 8.5 | 72.25 | 2.915 | 9.220 |
| 4.1 | 16.81 | 2.025 | 6.403 | 8.6 | 73.96 | 2.933 | 9.274 |
| 4.2 | 17.64 | 2.049 | 6.481 | 8.7 | 75.69 | 2.950 | 9.327 |
| 4.3 | 18.49 | 2.074 | 6.557 | 8.8 | 77.44 | 2.966 | 9.381 |
| 4.4 | 19.36 | 2.098 | 6.633 | 8.9 | 79.21 | 2.983 | 9.434 |
| 4.5 | 20.25 | 2.121 | 6.708 | 9.0 | 81.00 | 3.000 | 9.487 |
| 4.6 | 21.16 | 2.145 | 6.782 | 9.1 | 82.81 | 3.017 | 9.539 |
| 4.7 | 22.09 | 2.168 | 6.856 | 9.2 | 84.64 | 3.033 | 9.592 |
| 4.8 | 23.04 | 2.191 | 6.928 | 9.3 | 86.49 | 3.050 | 9.644 |
| 4.9 | 24.01 | 2.214 | 7.000 | 9.4 | 88.36 | 3.066 | 9.695 |
| 5.0 | 25.00 | 2.236 | 7.071 | 9.5 | 90.25 | 3.082 | 9.747 |
| 5.1 | 26.01 | 2.258 | 7.141 | 9.6 | 92.16 | 3.098 | 9.798 |
| 5.2 | 27.04 | 2.280 | 7.211 | 9.7 | 94.09 | 3.114 | 9.849 |
| 5.3 | 28.09 | 2.302 | 7.280 | 9.8 | 96.04 | 3.130 | 9.899 |
| 5.4 | 29.16 | 2.324 | 7.348 | 9.9 | 98.01 | 3.146 | 9.950 |

# Cubes and Cube Roots

| $n$ | $n^3$ | $\sqrt[3]{n}$ | $\sqrt[3]{10n}$ | $\sqrt[3]{100n}$ | $n$ | $n^3$ | $\sqrt[3]{n}$ | $\sqrt[3]{10n}$ | $\sqrt[3]{100n}$ |
|-----|-------|--------------|----------------|-----------------|-----|-------|--------------|----------------|-----------------|
| 1.0 | 1.000 | 1.000 | 2.154 | 4.642 | 5.5 | 166.375 | 1.765 | 3.803 | 8.193 |
| 1.1 | 1.331 | 1.032 | 2.224 | 4.791 | 5.6 | 175.616 | 1.776 | 3.826 | 8.243 |
| 1.2 | 1.728 | 1.063 | 2.289 | 4.932 | 5.7 | 185.193 | 1.786 | 3.849 | 8.291 |
| 1.3 | 2.197 | 1.091 | 2.351 | 5.066 | 5.8 | 195.112 | 1.797 | 3.871 | 8.340 |
| 1.4 | 2.744 | 1.119 | 2.410 | 5.192 | 5.9 | 205.379 | 1.807 | 3.893 | 8.387 |
| 1.5 | 3.375 | 1.145 | 2.466 | 5.313 | 6.0 | 216.000 | 1.817 | 3.915 | 8.434 |
| 1.6 | 4.096 | 1.170 | 2.520 | 5.429 | 6.1 | 226.981 | 1.827 | 3.936 | 8.481 |
| 1.7 | 4.913 | 1.193 | 2.571 | 5.540 | 6.2 | 238.328 | 1.837 | 3.958 | 8.527 |
| 1.8 | 5.832 | 1.216 | 2.621 | 5.646 | 6.3 | 250.047 | 1.847 | 3.979 | 8.573 |
| 1.9 | 6.859 | 1.239 | 2.668 | 5.749 | 6.4 | 262.144 | 1.857 | 4.000 | 8.618 |
| 2.0 | 8.000 | 1.260 | 2.714 | 5.848 | 6.5 | 274.625 | 1.866 | 4.021 | 8.662 |
| 2.1 | 9.261 | 1.281 | 2.759 | 5.944 | 6.6 | 287.496 | 1.876 | 4.041 | 8.707 |
| 2.2 | 10.648 | 1.301 | 2.802 | 6.037 | 6.7 | 300.763 | 1.885 | 4.062 | 8.750 |
| 2.3 | 12.167 | 1.320 | 2.844 | 6.127 | 6.8 | 314.432 | 1.895 | 4.082 | 8.794 |
| 2.4 | 13.824 | 1.339 | 2.884 | 6.214 | 6.9 | 328.509 | 1.904 | 4.102 | 8.837 |
| 2.5 | 15.625 | 1.357 | 2.924 | 6.300 | 7.0 | 343.000 | 1.913 | 4.121 | 8.879 |
| 2.6 | 17.576 | 1.375 | 2.962 | 6.383 | 7.1 | 357.911 | 1.922 | 4.141 | 8.921 |
| 2.7 | 19.683 | 1.392 | 3.000 | 6.463 | 7.2 | 373.248 | 1.931 | 4.160 | 8.963 |
| 2.8 | 21.952 | 1.409 | 3.037 | 6.542 | 7.3 | 389.017 | 1.940 | 4.179 | 9.004 |
| 2.9 | 24.389 | 1.426 | 3.072 | 6.619 | 7.4 | 405.224 | 1.949 | 4.198 | 9.045 |
| 3.0 | 27.000 | 1.442 | 3.107 | 6.694 | 7.5 | 421.875 | 1.957 | 4.217 | 9.086 |
| 3.1 | 29.791 | 1.458 | 3.141 | 6.768 | 7.6 | 438.976 | 1.966 | 4.236 | 9.126 |
| 3.2 | 32.768 | 1.474 | 3.175 | 6.840 | 7.7 | 456.533 | 1.975 | 4.254 | 9.166 |
| 3.3 | 35.937 | 1.489 | 3.208 | 6.910 | 7.8 | 474.552 | 1.983 | 4.273 | 9.205 |
| 3.4 | 39.304 | 1.504 | 3.240 | 6.980 | 7.9 | 493.039 | 1.992 | 4.291 | 9.244 |
| 3.5 | 42.875 | 1.518 | 3.271 | 7.047 | 8.0 | 512.000 | 2.000 | 4.309 | 9.283 |
| 3.6 | 46.656 | 1.533 | 3.302 | 7.114 | 8.1 | 531.441 | 2.008 | 4.327 | 9.322 |
| 3.7 | 50.653 | 1.547 | 3.332 | 7.179 | 8.2 | 551.368 | 2.017 | 4.344 | 9.360 |
| 3.8 | 54.872 | 1.560 | 3.362 | 7.243 | 8.3 | 571.787 | 2.025 | 4.362 | 9.398 |
| 3.9 | 59.319 | 1.574 | 3.391 | 7.306 | 8.4 | 592.704 | 2.033 | 4.380 | 9.435 |
| 4.0 | 64.000 | 1.587 | 3.420 | 7.368 | 8.5 | 614.125 | 2.041 | 4.397 | 9.473 |
| 4.1 | 68.921 | 1.601 | 3.448 | 7.429 | 8.6 | 636.056 | 2.049 | 4.414 | 9.510 |
| 4.2 | 74.088 | 1.613 | 3.476 | 7.489 | 8.7 | 658.503 | 2.057 | 4.431 | 9.546 |
| 4.3 | 79.507 | 1.626 | 3.503 | 7.548 | 8.8 | 681.472 | 2.065 | 4.448 | 9.583 |
| 4.4 | 85.184 | 1.639 | 3.530 | 7.606 | 8.9 | 704.969 | 2.072 | 4.465 | 9.619 |
| 4.5 | 91.125 | 1.651 | 3.557 | 7.663 | 9.0 | 729.000 | 2.080 | 4.481 | 9.655 |
| 4.6 | 97.336 | 1.663 | 3.583 | 7.719 | 9.1 | 753.571 | 2.088 | 4.498 | 9.691 |
| 4.7 | 103.823 | 1.675 | 3.609 | 7.775 | 9.2 | 778.688 | 2.095 | 4.514 | 9.726 |
| 4.8 | 110.592 | 1.687 | 3.634 | 7.830 | 9.3 | 804.357 | 2.103 | 4.531 | 9.761 |
| 4.9 | 117.649 | 1.698 | 3.659 | 7.884 | 9.4 | 830.584 | 2.110 | 4.547 | 9.796 |
| 5.0 | 125.000 | 1.710 | 3.684 | 7.937 | 9.5 | 857.375 | 2.118 | 4.563 | 9.830 |
| 5.1 | 132.651 | 1.721 | 3.708 | 7.990 | 9.6 | 884.736 | 2.125 | 4.579 | 9.865 |
| 5.2 | 140.608 | 1.732 | 3.733 | 8.041 | 9.7 | 912.673 | 2.133 | 4.595 | 9.899 |
| 5.3 | 148.877 | 1.744 | 3.756 | 8.093 | 9.8 | 941.192 | 2.140 | 4.610 | 9.933 |
| 5.4 | 157.464 | 1.754 | 3.780 | 8.143 | 9.9 | 970.299 | 2.147 | 4.626 | 9.967 |

# Common Logarithms of Numbers

| n | 0 | 1 | 2 | 3 | 4 | 5 | 6 | 7 | 8 | 9 |
|---|---|---|---|---|---|---|---|---|---|---|
| 10 | 0000 | 0043 | 0086 | 0128 | 0170 | 0212 | 0253 | 0294 | 0334 | 0374 |
| 11 | 0414 | 0453 | 0492 | 0531 | 0569 | 0607 | 0645 | 0682 | 0719 | 0755 |
| 12 | 0792 | 0828 | 0864 | 0899 | 0934 | 0969 | 1004 | 1038 | 1072 | 1106 |
| 13 | 1139 | 1173 | 1206 | 1239 | 1271 | 1303 | 1335 | 1367 | 1399 | 1430 |
| 14 | 1461 | 1492 | 1523 | 1553 | 1584 | 1614 | 1644 | 1673 | 1703 | 1732 |
| 15 | 1761 | 1790 | 1818 | 1847 | 1875 | 1903 | 1931 | 1959 | 1987 | 2014 |
| 16 | 2041 | 2068 | 2095 | 2122 | 2148 | 2175 | 2201 | 2227 | 2253 | 2279 |
| 17 | 2304 | 2330 | 2355 | 2380 | 2405 | 2430 | 2455 | 2480 | 2504 | 2529 |
| 18 | 2553 | 2577 | 2601 | 2625 | 2648 | 2672 | 2695 | 2718 | 2742 | 2765 |
| 19 | 2788 | 2810 | 2833 | 2856 | 2878 | 2900 | 2923 | 2945 | 2967 | 2989 |
| 20 | 3010 | 3032 | 3054 | 3075 | 3096 | 3118 | 3139 | 3160 | 3181 | 3201 |
| 21 | 3222 | 3243 | 3263 | 3284 | 3304 | 3324 | 3345 | 3365 | 3385 | 3404 |
| 22 | 3424 | 3444 | 3464 | 3483 | 3502 | 3522 | 3541 | 3560 | 3579 | 3598 |
| 23 | 3617 | 3636 | 3655 | 3674 | 3692 | 3711 | 3729 | 3747 | 3766 | 3784 |
| 24 | 3802 | 3820 | 3838 | 3856 | 3874 | 3892 | 3909 | 3927 | 3945 | 3962 |
| 25 | 3979 | 3997 | 4014 | 4031 | 4048 | 4065 | 4082 | 4099 | 4116 | 4133 |
| 26 | 4150 | 4166 | 4183 | 4200 | 4216 | 4232 | 4249 | 4265 | 4281 | 4298 |
| 27 | 4314 | 4330 | 4346 | 4362 | 4378 | 4393 | 4409 | 4425 | 4440 | 4456 |
| 28 | 4472 | 4487 | 4502 | 4518 | 4533 | 4548 | 4564 | 4579 | 4594 | 4609 |
| 29 | 4624 | 4639 | 4654 | 4669 | 4683 | 4698 | 4713 | 4728 | 4742 | 4757 |
| 30 | 4771 | 4786 | 4800 | 4814 | 4829 | 4843 | 4857 | 4871 | 4886 | 4900 |
| 31 | 4914 | 4928 | 4942 | 4955 | 4969 | 4983 | 4997 | 5011 | 5024 | 5038 |
| 32 | 5051 | 5065 | 5079 | 5092 | 5105 | 5119 | 5132 | 5145 | 5159 | 5172 |
| 33 | 5185 | 5198 | 5211 | 5224 | 5237 | 5250 | 5263 | 5276 | 5289 | 5302 |
| 34 | 5315 | 5328 | 5340 | 5353 | 5366 | 5378 | 5391 | 5403 | 5416 | 5428 |
| 35 | 5441 | 5453 | 5465 | 5478 | 5490 | 5502 | 5514 | 5527 | 5539 | 5551 |
| 36 | 5563 | 5575 | 5587 | 5599 | 5611 | 5623 | 5635 | 5647 | 5658 | 5670 |
| 37 | 5682 | 5694 | 5705 | 5717 | 5729 | 5740 | 5752 | 5763 | 5775 | 5786 |
| 38 | 5798 | 5809 | 5821 | 5832 | 5843 | 5855 | 5866 | 5877 | 5888 | 5899 |
| 39 | 5911 | 5922 | 5933 | 5944 | 5955 | 5966 | 5977 | 5988 | 5999 | 6010 |
| 40 | 6021 | 6031 | 6042 | 6053 | 6064 | 6075 | 6085 | 6096 | 6107 | 6117 |
| 41 | 6128 | 6138 | 6149 | 6160 | 6170 | 6180 | 6191 | 6201 | 6212 | 6222 |
| 42 | 6232 | 6243 | 6253 | 6263 | 6274 | 6284 | 6294 | 6304 | 6314 | 6325 |
| 43 | 6335 | 6345 | 6355 | 6365 | 6375 | 6385 | 6395 | 6405 | 6415 | 6425 |
| 44 | 6435 | 6444 | 6454 | 6464 | 6474 | 6484 | 6493 | 6503 | 6513 | 6522 |
| 45 | 6532 | 6542 | 6551 | 6561 | 6571 | 6580 | 6590 | 6599 | 6609 | 6618 |
| 46 | 6628 | 6637 | 6646 | 6656 | 6665 | 6675 | 6684 | 6693 | 6702 | 6712 |
| 47 | 6721 | 6730 | 6739 | 6749 | 6758 | 6767 | 6776 | 6785 | 6794 | 6803 |
| 48 | 6812 | 6821 | 6830 | 6839 | 6848 | 6857 | 6866 | 6875 | 6884 | 6893 |
| 49 | 6902 | 6911 | 6920 | 6928 | 6937 | 6946 | 6955 | 6964 | 6972 | 6981 |
| 50 | 6990 | 6998 | 7007 | 7016 | 7024 | 7033 | 7042 | 7050 | 7059 | 7067 |
| 51 | 7076 | 7084 | 7093 | 7101 | 7110 | 7118 | 7126 | 7135 | 7143 | 7152 |
| 52 | 7160 | 7168 | 7177 | 7185 | 7193 | 7202 | 7210 | 7218 | 7226 | 7235 |
| 53 | 7243 | 7251 | 7259 | 7267 | 7275 | 7284 | 7292 | 7300 | 7308 | 7316 |
| 54 | 7324 | 7332 | 7340 | 7348 | 7356 | 7364 | 7372 | 7380 | 7388 | 7396 |

# Common Logarithms of Numbers

| n | 0 | 1 | 2 | 3 | 4 | 5 | 6 | 7 | 8 | 9 |
|---|---|---|---|---|---|---|---|---|---|---|
| 55 | 7404 | 7412 | 7419 | 7427 | 7435 | 7443 | 7451 | 7459 | 7466 | 7474 |
| 56 | 7482 | 7490 | 7497 | 7505 | 7513 | 7520 | 7528 | 7536 | 7543 | 7551 |
| 57 | 7559 | 7566 | 7574 | 7582 | 7589 | 7597 | 7604 | 7612 | 7619 | 7627 |
| 58 | 7634 | 7642 | 7649 | 7657 | 7664 | 7672 | 7679 | 7686 | 7694 | 7701 |
| 59 | 7709 | 7716 | 7723 | 7731 | 7738 | 7745 | 7752 | 7760 | 7767 | 7774 |
| 60 | 7782 | 7789 | 7796 | 7803 | 7810 | 7818 | 7825 | 7832 | 7839 | 7846 |
| 61 | 7853 | 7860 | 7868 | 7875 | 7882 | 7889 | 7896 | 7903 | 7910 | 7917 |
| 62 | 7924 | 7931 | 7938 | 7945 | 7952 | 7959 | 7966 | 7973 | 7980 | 7987 |
| 63 | 7993 | 8000 | 8007 | 8014 | 8021 | 8028 | 8035 | 8041 | 8048 | 8055 |
| 64 | 8062 | 8069 | 8075 | 8082 | 8089 | 8096 | 8102 | 8109 | 8116 | 8122 |
| 65 | 8129 | 8136 | 8142 | 8149 | 8156 | 8162 | 8169 | 8176 | 8182 | 8189 |
| 66 | 8195 | 8202 | 8209 | 8215 | 8222 | 8228 | 8235 | 8241 | 8248 | 8254 |
| 67 | 8261 | 8267 | 8274 | 8280 | 8287 | 8293 | 8299 | 8306 | 8312 | 8319 |
| 68 | 8325 | 8331 | 8338 | 8344 | 8351 | 8357 | 8363 | 8370 | 8376 | 8382 |
| 69 | 8388 | 8395 | 8401 | 8407 | 8414 | 8420 | 8426 | 8432 | 8439 | 8445 |
| 70 | 8451 | 8457 | 8463 | 8470 | 8476 | 8482 | 8488 | 8494 | 8500 | 8506 |
| 71 | 8513 | 8519 | 8525 | 8531 | 8537 | 8543 | 8549 | 8555 | 8561 | 8567 |
| 72 | 8573 | 8579 | 8585 | 8591 | 8597 | 8603 | 8609 | 8615 | 8621 | 8627 |
| 73 | 8633 | 8639 | 8645 | 8651 | 8657 | 8663 | 8669 | 8675 | 8681 | 8686 |
| 74 | 8692 | 8698 | 8704 | 8710 | 8716 | 8722 | 8727 | 8733 | 8739 | 8745 |
| 75 | 8751 | 8756 | 8762 | 8768 | 8774 | 8779 | 8785 | 8791 | 8797 | 8802 |
| 76 | 8808 | 8814 | 8820 | 8825 | 8831 | 8837 | 8842 | 8848 | 8854 | 8859 |
| 77 | 8865 | 8871 | 8876 | 8882 | 8887 | 8893 | 8899 | 8904 | 8910 | 8915 |
| 78 | 8921 | 8927 | 8932 | 8938 | 8943 | 8949 | 8954 | 8960 | 8965 | 8971 |
| 79 | 8976 | 8982 | 8987 | 8993 | 8998 | 9004 | 9009 | 9015 | 9020 | 9025 |
| 80 | 9031 | 9036 | 9042 | 9047 | 9053 | 9058 | 9063 | 9069 | 9074 | 9079 |
| 81 | 9085 | 9090 | 9096 | 9101 | 9106 | 9112 | 9117 | 9122 | 9128 | 9133 |
| 82 | 9138 | 9143 | 9149 | 9154 | 9159 | 9165 | 9170 | 9175 | 9180 | 9186 |
| 83 | 9191 | 9196 | 9201 | 9206 | 9212 | 9217 | 9222 | 9227 | 9232 | 9238 |
| 84 | 9243 | 9248 | 9253 | 9258 | 9263 | 9269 | 9274 | 9279 | 9284 | 9289 |
| 85 | 9294 | 9299 | 9304 | 9309 | 9315 | 9320 | 9325 | 9330 | 9335 | 9340 |
| 86 | 9345 | 9350 | 9355 | 9360 | 9365 | 9370 | 9375 | 9380 | 9385 | 9390 |
| 87 | 9395 | 9400 | 9405 | 9410 | 9415 | 9420 | 9425 | 9430 | 9435 | 9440 |
| 88 | 9445 | 9450 | 9455 | 9460 | 9465 | 9469 | 9474 | 9479 | 9484 | 9489 |
| 89 | 9494 | 9499 | 9504 | 9509 | 9513 | 9518 | 9523 | 9528 | 9533 | 9538 |
| 90 | 9542 | 9547 | 9552 | 9557 | 9562 | 9566 | 9571 | 9576 | 9581 | 9586 |
| 91 | 9590 | 9595 | 9600 | 9605 | 9609 | 9614 | 9619 | 9624 | 9628 | 9633 |
| 92 | 9638 | 9643 | 9647 | 9652 | 9657 | 9661 | 9666 | 9671 | 9675 | 9680 |
| 93 | 9685 | 9689 | 9694 | 9699 | 9703 | 9708 | 9713 | 9717 | 9722 | 9727 |
| 94 | 9731 | 9736 | 9741 | 9745 | 9750 | 9754 | 9759 | 9763 | 9768 | 9773 |
| 95 | 9777 | 9782 | 9786 | 9791 | 9795 | 9800 | 9805 | 9809 | 9814 | 9818 |
| 96 | 9823 | 9827 | 9832 | 9836 | 9841 | 9845 | 9850 | 9854 | 9859 | 9863 |
| 97 | 9868 | 9872 | 9877 | 9881 | 9886 | 9890 | 9894 | 9899 | 9903 | 9908 |
| 98 | 9912 | 9917 | 9921 | 9926 | 9930 | 9934 | 9939 | 9943 | 9948 | 9952 |
| 99 | 9956 | 9961 | 9965 | 9969 | 9974 | 9978 | 9983 | 9987 | 9991 | 9996 |

## Values of Trigonometric Functions

| Angle | Sin | Cos | Tan | Cot | Sec | Csc | |
|---|---|---|---|---|---|---|---|
| 0°00′ | 0.0000 | 1.0000 | 0.0000 | — | 1.000 | — | 90°00′ |
| 10′ | 0.0029 | 1.0000 | 0.0029 | 343.8 | 1.000 | 343.8 | 50′ |
| 20′ | 0.0058 | 1.0000 | 0.0058 | 171.9 | 1.000 | 171.9 | 40′ |
| 30′ | 0.0087 | 1.0000 | 0.0087 | 114.6 | 1.000 | 114.6 | 30′ |
| 40′ | 0.0116 | 0.9999 | 0.0116 | 85.94 | 1.000 | 85.95 | 20′ |
| 50′ | 0.0145 | 0.9999 | 0.0145 | 68.75 | 1.000 | 68.76 | 10′ |
| 1°00′ | 0.0175 | 0.9998 | 0.0175 | 57.29 | 1.000 | 57.30 | 89°00′ |
| 10′ | 0.0204 | 0.9998 | 0.0204 | 49.10 | 1.000 | 49.11 | 50′ |
| 20′ | 0.0233 | 0.9997 | 0.0233 | 42.96 | 1.000 | 42.98 | 40′ |
| 30′ | 0.0262 | 0.9997 | 0.0262 | 38.19 | 1.000 | 38.20 | 30′ |
| 40′ | 0.0291 | 0.9996 | 0.0291 | 34.37 | 1.000 | 34.38 | 20′ |
| 50′ | 0.0320 | 0.9995 | 0.0320 | 31.24 | 1.001 | 31.26 | 10′ |
| 2°00′ | 0.0349 | 0.9994 | 0.0349 | 28.64 | 1.001 | 28.65 | 88°00′ |
| 10′ | 0.0378 | 0.9993 | 0.0378 | 26.43 | 1.001 | 26.45 | 50′ |
| 20′ | 0.0407 | 0.9992 | 0.0407 | 24.54 | 1.001 | 24.56 | 40′ |
| 30′ | 0.0436 | 0.9990 | 0.0437 | 22.90 | 1.001 | 22.93 | 30′ |
| 40′ | 0.0465 | 0.9989 | 0.0466 | 21.47 | 1.001 | 21.49 | 20′ |
| 50′ | 0.0494 | 0.9988 | 0.0495 | 20.21 | 1.001 | 20.23 | 10′ |
| 3°00′ | 0.0523 | 0.9986 | 0.0524 | 19.08 | 1.001 | 19.11 | 87°00′ |
| 10′ | 0.0552 | 0.9985 | 0.0553 | 18.07 | 1.002 | 18.10 | 50′ |
| 20′ | 0.0581 | 0.9983 | 0.0582 | 17.17 | 1.002 | 17.20 | 40′ |
| 30′ | 0.0610 | 0.9981 | 0.0612 | 16.35 | 1.002 | 16.38 | 30′ |
| 40′ | 0.0640 | 0.9980 | 0.0641 | 15.60 | 1.002 | 15.64 | 20′ |
| 50′ | 0.0669 | 0.9978 | 0.0670 | 14.92 | 1.002 | 14.96 | 10′ |
| 4°00′ | 0.0698 | 0.9976 | 0.0699 | 14.30 | 1.002 | 14.34 | 86°00′ |
| 10′ | 0.0727 | 0.9974 | 0.0729 | 13.73 | 1.003 | 13.76 | 50′ |
| 20′ | 0.0756 | 0.9971 | 0.0758 | 13.20 | 1.003 | 13.23 | 40′ |
| 30′ | 0.0785 | 0.9969 | 0.0787 | 12.71 | 1.003 | 12.75 | 30′ |
| 40′ | 0.0814 | 0.9967 | 0.0816 | 12.25 | 1.003 | 12.29 | 20′ |
| 50′ | 0.0843 | 0.9964 | 0.0846 | 11.83 | 1.004 | 11.87 | 10′ |
| 5°00′ | 0.0872 | 0.9962 | 0.0875 | 11.43 | 1.004 | 11.47 | 85°00′ |
| 10′ | 0.0901 | 0.9959 | 0.0904 | 11.06 | 1.004 | 11.10 | 50′ |
| 20′ | 0.0929 | 0.9957 | 0.0934 | 10.71 | 1.004 | 10.76 | 40′ |
| 30′ | 0.0958 | 0.9954 | 0.0963 | 10.39 | 1.005 | 10.43 | 30′ |
| 40′ | 0.0987 | 0.9951 | 0.0992 | 10.08 | 1.005 | 10.13 | 20′ |
| 50′ | 0.1016 | 0.9948 | 0.1022 | 9.788 | 1.005 | 9.839 | 10′ |
| 6°00′ | 0.1045 | 0.9945 | 0.1051 | 9.514 | 1.006 | 9.567 | 84°00′ |
| 10′ | 0.1074 | 0.9942 | 0.1080 | 9.255 | 1.006 | 9.309 | 50′ |
| 20′ | 0.1103 | 0.9939 | 0.1110 | 9.010 | 1.006 | 9.065 | 40′ |
| 30′ | 0.1132 | 0.9936 | 0.1139 | 8.777 | 1.006 | 8.834 | 30′ |
| 40′ | 0.1161 | 0.9932 | 0.1169 | 8.556 | 1.007 | 8.614 | 20′ |
| 50′ | 0.1190 | 0.9929 | 0.1198 | 8.345 | 1.007 | 8.405 | 10′ |
| 7°00′ | 0.1219 | 0.9925 | 0.1228 | 8.144 | 1.008 | 8.206 | 83°00′ |
| 10′ | 0.1248 | 0.9922 | 0.1257 | 7.953 | 1.008 | 8.016 | 50′ |
| 20′ | 0.1276 | 0.9918 | 0.1287 | 7.770 | 1.008 | 7.834 | 40′ |
| 30′ | 0.1305 | 0.9914 | 0.1317 | 7.596 | 1.009 | 7.661 | 30′ |
| 40′ | 0.1334 | 0.9911 | 0.1346 | 7.429 | 1.009 | 7.496 | 20′ |
| 50′ | 0.1363 | 0.9907 | 0.1376 | 7.269 | 1.009 | 7.337 | 10′ |
| 8°00′ | 0.1392 | 0.9903 | 0.1405 | 7.115 | 1.010 | 7.185 | 82°00′ |
| 10′ | 0.1421 | 0.9899 | 0.1435 | 6.968 | 1.010 | 7.040 | 50′ |
| 20′ | 0.1449 | 0.9894 | 0.1465 | 6.827 | 1.011 | 6.900 | 40′ |
| 30′ | 0.1478 | 0.9890 | 0.1495 | 6.691 | 1.011 | 6.765 | 30′ |
| 40′ | 0.1507 | 0.9886 | 0.1524 | 6.561 | 1.012 | 6.636 | 20′ |
| 50′ | 0.1536 | 0.9881 | 0.1554 | 6.435 | 1.012 | 6.512 | 10′ |
| 9°00′ | 0.1564 | 0.9877 | 0.1584 | 6.314 | 1.012 | 6.392 | 81°00′ |
| | Cos | Sin | Cot | Tan | Csc | Sec | Angle |

## Values of Trigonometric Functions

| Angle | Sin | Cos | Tan | Cot | Sec | Csc | |
|---|---|---|---|---|---|---|---|
| 9°00' | 0.1564 | 0.9877 | 0.1584 | 6.314 | 1.012 | 6.392 | 81°00' |
| 10' | 0.1593 | 0.9872 | 0.1614 | 6.197 | 1.013 | 6.277 | 50' |
| 20' | 0.1622 | 0.9868 | 0.1644 | 6.084 | 1.013 | 6.166 | 40' |
| 30' | 0.1650 | 0.9863 | 0.1673 | 5.976 | 1.014 | 6.059 | 30' |
| 40' | 0.1679 | 0.9858 | 0.1703 | 5.871 | 1.014 | 5.955 | 20' |
| 50' | 0.1708 | 0.9853 | 0.1733 | 5.769 | 1.015 | 5.855 | 10' |
| 10°00' | 0.1736 | 0.9848 | 0.1763 | 5.671 | 1.015 | 5.759 | 80°00' |
| 10' | 0.1765 | 0.9843 | 0.1793 | 5.576 | 1.016 | 5.665 | 50' |
| 20' | 0.1794 | 0.9838 | 0.1823 | 5.485 | 1.016 | 5.575 | 40' |
| 30' | 0.1822 | 0.9833 | 0.1853 | 5.396 | 1.017 | 5.487 | 30' |
| 40' | 0.1851 | 0.9827 | 0.1883 | 5.309 | 1.018 | 5.403 | 20' |
| 50' | 0.1880 | 0.9822 | 0.1914 | 5.226 | 1.018 | 5.320 | 10' |
| 11°00' | 0.1908 | 0.9816 | 0.1944 | 5.145 | 1.019 | 5.241 | 79°00' |
| 10' | 0.1937 | 0.9811 | 0.1974 | 5.066 | 1.019 | 5.164 | 50' |
| 20' | 0.1965 | 0.9805 | 0.2004 | 4.989 | 1.020 | 5.089 | 40' |
| 30' | 0.1994 | 0.9799 | 0.2035 | 4.915 | 1.020 | 5.016 | 30' |
| 40' | 0.2022 | 0.9793 | 0.2065 | 4.843 | 1.021 | 4.945 | 20' |
| 50' | 0.2051 | 0.9787 | 0.2095 | 4.773 | 1.022 | 4.876 | 10' |
| 12°00' | 0.2079 | 0.9781 | 0.2126 | 4.705 | 1.022 | 4.810 | 78°00' |
| 10' | 0.2108 | 0.9775 | 0.2156 | 4.638 | 1.023 | 4.745 | 50' |
| 20' | 0.2136 | 0.9769 | 0.2186 | 4.574 | 1.024 | 4.682 | 40' |
| 30' | 0.2164 | 0.9763 | 0.2217 | 4.511 | 1.024 | 4.620 | 30' |
| 40' | 0.2193 | 0.9757 | 0.2247 | 4.449 | 1.025 | 4.560 | 20' |
| 50' | 0.2221 | 0.9750 | 0.2278 | 4.390 | 1.026 | 4.502 | 10' |
| 13°00' | 0.2250 | 0.9744 | 0.2309 | 4.331 | 1.026 | 4.445 | 77°00' |
| 10' | 0.2278 | 0.9737 | 0.2339 | 4.275 | 1.027 | 4.390 | 50' |
| 20' | 0.2306 | 0.9730 | 0.2370 | 4.219 | 1.028 | 4.336 | 40' |
| 30' | 0.2334 | 0.9724 | 0.2401 | 4.165 | 1.028 | 4.284 | 30' |
| 40' | 0.2363 | 0.9717 | 0.2432 | 4.113 | 1.029 | 4.232 | 20' |
| 50' | 0.2391 | 0.9710 | 0.2462 | 4.061 | 1.030 | 4.182 | 10' |
| 14°00' | 0.2419 | 0.9703 | 0.2493 | 4.011 | 1.031 | 4.134 | 76°00' |
| 10' | 0.2447 | 0.9696 | 0.2524 | 3.962 | 1.031 | 4.086 | 50' |
| 20' | 0.2476 | 0.9689 | 0.2555 | 3.914 | 1.032 | 4.039 | 40' |
| 30' | 0.2504 | 0.9681 | 0.2586 | 3.867 | 1.033 | 3.994 | 30' |
| 40' | 0.2532 | 0.9674 | 0.2617 | 3.821 | 1.034 | 3.950 | 20' |
| 50' | 0.2560 | 0.9667 | 0.2648 | 3.776 | 1.034 | 3.906 | 10' |
| 15°00' | 0.2588 | 0.9659 | 0.2679 | 3.732 | 1.035 | 3.864 | 75°00' |
| 10' | 0.2616 | 0.9652 | 0.2711 | 3.689 | 1.036 | 3.822 | 50' |
| 20' | 0.2644 | 0.9644 | 0.2742 | 3.647 | 1.037 | 3.782 | 40' |
| 30' | 0.2672 | 0.9636 | 0.2773 | 3.606 | 1.038 | 3.742 | 30' |
| 40' | 0.2700 | 0.9628 | 0.2805 | 3.566 | 1.039 | 3.703 | 20' |
| 50' | 0.2728 | 0.9621 | 0.2836 | 3.526 | 1.039 | 3.665 | 10' |
| 16°00' | 0.2756 | 0.9613 | 0.2867 | 3.487 | 1.040 | 3.628 | 74°00' |
| 10' | 0.2784 | 0.9605 | 0.2899 | 3.450 | 1.041 | 3.592 | 50' |
| 20' | 0.2812 | 0.9596 | 0.2931 | 3.412 | 1.042 | 3.556 | 40' |
| 30' | 0.2840 | 0.9588 | 0.2962 | 3.376 | 1.043 | 3.521 | 30' |
| 40' | 0.2868 | 0.9580 | 0.2994 | 3.340 | 1.044 | 3.487 | 20' |
| 50' | 0.2896 | 0.9572 | 0.3026 | 3.305 | 1.045 | 3.453 | 10' |
| 17°00' | 0.2924 | 0.9563 | 0.3057 | 3.271 | 1.046 | 3.420 | 73°00' |
| 10' | 0.2952 | 0.9555 | 0.3089 | 3.237 | 1.047 | 3.388 | 50' |
| 20' | 0.2979 | 0.9546 | 0.3121 | 3.204 | 1.048 | 3.356 | 40' |
| 30' | 0.3007 | 0.9537 | 0.3153 | 3.172 | 1.049 | 3.326 | 30' |
| 40' | 0.3035 | 0.9528 | 0.3185 | 3.140 | 1.049 | 3.295 | 20' |
| 50' | 0.3062 | 0.9520 | 0.3217 | 3.108 | 1.050 | 3.265 | 10' |
| 18°00' | 0.3090 | 0.9511 | 0.3249 | 3.078 | 1.051 | 3.236 | 72°00' |
| | Cos | Sin | Cot | Tan | Csc | Sec | Angle |

## Values of Trigonometric Functions

| Angle | Sin | Cos | Tan | Cot | Sec | Csc | |
|---|---|---|---|---|---|---|---|
| 18°00′ | 0.3090 | 0.9511 | 0.3249 | 3.078 | 1.051 | 3.236 | 72°00′ |
| 10′ | 0.3118 | 0.9502 | 0.3281 | 3.047 | 1.052 | 3.207 | 50′ |
| 20′ | 0.3145 | 0.9492 | 0.3314 | 3.018 | 1.053 | 3.179 | 40′ |
| 30′ | 0.3173 | 0.9483 | 0.3346 | 2.989 | 1.054 | 3.152 | 30′ |
| 40′ | 0.3201 | 0.9474 | 0.3378 | 2.960 | 1.056 | 3.124 | 20′ |
| 50′ | 0.3228 | 0.9465 | 0.3411 | 2.932 | 1.057 | 3.098 | 10′ |
| 19°00′ | 0.3256 | 0.9455 | 0.3443 | 2.904 | 1.058 | 3.072 | 71°00′ |
| 10′ | 0.3283 | 0.9446 | 0.3476 | 2.877 | 1.059 | 3.046 | 50′ |
| 20′ | 0.3311 | 0.9436 | 0.3508 | 2.850 | 1.060 | 3.021 | 40′ |
| 30′ | 0.3338 | 0.9426 | 0.3541 | 2.824 | 1.061 | 2.996 | 30′ |
| 40′ | 0.3365 | 0.9417 | 0.3574 | 2.798 | 1.062 | 2.971 | 20′ |
| 50′ | 0.3393 | 0.9407 | 0.3607 | 2.773 | 1.063 | 2.947 | 10′ |
| 20°00′ | 0.3420 | 0.9397 | 0.3640 | 2.747 | 1.064 | 2.924 | 70°00′ |
| 10′ | 0.3448 | 0.9387 | 0.3673 | 2.723 | 1.065 | 2.901 | 50′ |
| 20′ | 0.3475 | 0.9377 | 0.3706 | 2.699 | 1.066 | 2.878 | 40′ |
| 30′ | 0.3502 | 0.9367 | 0.3739 | 2.675 | 1.068 | 2.855 | 30′ |
| 40′ | 0.3529 | 0.9356 | 0.3772 | 2.651 | 1.069 | 2.833 | 20′ |
| 50′ | 0.3557 | 0.9346 | 0.3805 | 2.628 | 1.070 | 2.812 | 10′ |
| 21°00′ | 0.3584 | 0.9336 | 0.3839 | 2.605 | 1.071 | 2.790 | 69°00′ |
| 10′ | 0.3611 | 0.9325 | 0.3872 | 2.583 | 1.072 | 2.769 | 50′ |
| 20′ | 0.3638 | 0.9315 | 0.3906 | 2.560 | 1.074 | 2.749 | 40′ |
| 30′ | 0.3665 | 0.9304 | 0.3939 | 2.539 | 1.075 | 2.729 | 30′ |
| 40′ | 0.3692 | 0.9293 | 0.3973 | 2.517 | 1.076 | 2.709 | 20′ |
| 50′ | 0.3719 | 0.9283 | 0.4006 | 2.496 | 1.077 | 2.689 | 10′ |
| 22°00′ | 0.3746 | 0.9272 | 0.4040 | 2.475 | 1.079 | 2.669 | 68°00′ |
| 10′ | 0.3773 | 0.9261 | 0.4074 | 2.455 | 1.080 | 2.650 | 50′ |
| 20′ | 0.3800 | 0.9250 | 0.4108 | 2.434 | 1.081 | 2.632 | 40′ |
| 30′ | 0.3827 | 0.9239 | 0.4142 | 2.414 | 1.082 | 2.613 | 30′ |
| 40′ | 0.3854 | 0.9228 | 0.4176 | 2.394 | 1.084 | 2.595 | 20′ |
| 50′ | 0.3881 | 0.9216 | 0.4210 | 2.375 | 1.085 | 2.577 | 10′ |
| 23°00′ | 0.3907 | 0.9205 | 0.4245 | 2.356 | 1.086 | 2.559 | 67°00′ |
| 10′ | 0.3934 | 0.9194 | 0.4279 | 2.337 | 1.088 | 2.542 | 50′ |
| 20′ | 0.3961 | 0.9182 | 0.4314 | 2.318 | 1.089 | 2.525 | 40′ |
| 30′ | 0.3987 | 0.9171 | 0.4348 | 2.300 | 1.090 | 2.508 | 30′ |
| 40′ | 0.4014 | 0.9159 | 0.4383 | 2.282 | 1.092 | 2.491 | 20′ |
| 50′ | 0.4041 | 0.9147 | 0.4417 | 2.264 | 1.093 | 2.475 | 10′ |
| 24°00′ | 0.4067 | 0.9135 | 0.4452 | 2.246 | 1.095 | 2.459 | 66°00′ |
| 10′ | 0.4094 | 0.9124 | 0.4487 | 2.229 | 1.096 | 2.443 | 50′ |
| 20′ | 0.4120 | 0.9112 | 0.4522 | 2.211 | 1.097 | 2.427 | 40′ |
| 30′ | 0.4147 | 0.9100 | 0.4557 | 2.194 | 1.099 | 2.411 | 30′ |
| 40′ | 0.4173 | 0.9088 | 0.4592 | 2.177 | 1.100 | 2.396 | 20′ |
| 50′ | 0.4200 | 0.9075 | 0.4628 | 2.161 | 1.102 | 2.381 | 10′ |
| 25°00′ | 0.4226 | 0.9063 | 0.4663 | 2.145 | 1.103 | 2.366 | 65°00′ |
| 10′ | 0.4253 | 0.9051 | 0.4699 | 2.128 | 1.105 | 2.352 | 50′ |
| 20′ | 0.4279 | 0.9038 | 0.4734 | 2.112 | 1.106 | 2.337 | 40′ |
| 30′ | 0.4305 | 0.9026 | 0.4770 | 2.097 | 1.108 | 2.323 | 30′ |
| 40′ | 0.4331 | 0.9013 | 0.4806 | 2.081 | 1.109 | 2.309 | 20′ |
| 50′ | 0.4358 | 0.9001 | 0.4841 | 2.066 | 1.111 | 2.295 | 10′ |
| 26°00′ | 0.4384 | 0.8988 | 0.4877 | 2.050 | 1.113 | 2.281 | 64°00′ |
| 10′ | 0.4410 | 0.8975 | 0.4913 | 2.035 | 1.114 | 2.268 | 50′ |
| 20′ | 0.4436 | 0.8962 | 0.4950 | 2.020 | 1.116 | 2.254 | 40′ |
| 30′ | 0.4462 | 0.8949 | 0.4986 | 2.006 | 1.117 | 2.241 | 30′ |
| 40′ | 0.4488 | 0.8936 | 0.5022 | 1.991 | 1.119 | 2.228 | 20′ |
| 50′ | 0.4514 | 0.8923 | 0.5059 | 1.977 | 1.121 | 2.215 | 10′ |
| 27°00′ | 0.4540 | 0.8910 | 0.5095 | 1.963 | 1.122 | 2.203 | 63°00′ |
| | Cos | Sin | Cot | Tan | Csc | Sec | Angle |

# Values of Trigonometric Functions

| Angle | Sin | Cos | Tan | Cot | Sec | Csc | |
|---|---|---|---|---|---|---|---|
| 27°00′ | 0.4540 | 0.8910 | 0.5095 | 1.963 | 1.122 | 2.203 | 63°00′ |
| 10′ | 0.4566 | 0.8897 | 0.5132 | 1.949 | 1.124 | 2.190 | 50′ |
| 20′ | 0.4592 | 0.8884 | 0.5169 | 1.935 | 1.126 | 2.178 | 40′ |
| 30′ | 0.4617 | 0.8870 | 0.5206 | 1.921 | 1.127 | 2.166 | 30′ |
| 40′ | 0.4643 | 0.8857 | 0.5243 | 1.907 | 1.129 | 2.154 | 20′ |
| 50′ | 0.4669 | 0.8843 | 0.5280 | 1.894 | 1.131 | 2.142 | 10′ |
| 28°00′ | 0.4695 | 0.8829 | 0.5317 | 1.881 | 1.133 | 2.130 | 62°00′ |
| 10′ | 0.4720 | 0.8816 | 0.5354 | 1.868 | 1.134 | 2.118 | 50′ |
| 20′ | 0.4746 | 0.8802 | 0.5392 | 1.855 | 1.136 | 2.107 | 40′ |
| 30′ | 0.4772 | 0.8788 | 0.5430 | 1.842 | 1.138 | 2.096 | 30′ |
| 40′ | 0.4797 | 0.8774 | 0.5467 | 1.829 | 1.140 | 2.085 | 20′ |
| 50′ | 0.4823 | 0.8760 | 0.5505 | 1.816 | 1.142 | 2.074 | 10′ |
| 29°00′ | 0.4848 | 0.8746 | 0.5543 | 1.804 | 1.143 | 2.063 | 61°00′ |
| 10′ | 0.4874 | 0.8732 | 0.5581 | 1.792 | 1.145 | 2.052 | 50′ |
| 20′ | 0.4899 | 0.8718 | 0.5619 | 1.780 | 1.147 | 2.041 | 40′ |
| 30′ | 0.4924 | 0.8704 | 0.5658 | 1.767 | 1.149 | 2.031 | 30′ |
| 40′ | 0.4950 | 0.8689 | 0.5696 | 1.756 | 1.151 | 2.020 | 20′ |
| 50′ | 0.4975 | 0.8675 | 0.5735 | 1.744 | 1.153 | 2.010 | 10′ |
| 30°00′ | 0.5000 | 0.8660 | 0.5774 | 1.732 | 1.155 | 2.000 | 60°00′ |
| 10′ | 0.5025 | 0.8646 | 0.5812 | 1.720 | 1.157 | 1.990 | 50′ |
| 20′ | 0.5050 | 0.8631 | 0.5851 | 1.709 | 1.159 | 1.980 | 40′ |
| 30′ | 0.5075 | 0.8616 | 0.5890 | 1.698 | 1.161 | 1.970 | 30′ |
| 40′ | 0.5100 | 0.8601 | 0.5930 | 1.686 | 1.163 | 1.961 | 20′ |
| 50′ | 0.5125 | 0.8587 | 0.5969 | 1.675 | 1.165 | 1.951 | 10′ |
| 31°00′ | 0.5150 | 0.8572 | 0.6009 | 1.664 | 1.167 | 1.942 | 59°00′ |
| 10′ | 0.5175 | 0.8557 | 0.6048 | 1.653 | 1.169 | 1.932 | 50′ |
| 20′ | 0.5200 | 0.8542 | 0.6088 | 1.643 | 1.171 | 1.923 | 40′ |
| 30′ | 0.5225 | 0.8526 | 0.6128 | 1.632 | 1.173 | 1.914 | 30′ |
| 40′ | 0.5250 | 0.8511 | 0.6168 | 1.621 | 1.175 | 1.905 | 20′ |
| 50′ | 0.5275 | 0.8496 | 0.6208 | 1.611 | 1.177 | 1.896 | 10′ |
| 32°00′ | 0.5299 | 0.8480 | 0.6249 | 1.600 | 1.179 | 1.887 | 58°00′ |
| 10′ | 0.5324 | 0.8465 | 0.6289 | 1.590 | 1.181 | 1.878 | 50′ |
| 20′ | 0.5348 | 0.8450 | 0.6330 | 1.580 | 1.184 | 1.870 | 40′ |
| 30′ | 0.5373 | 0.8434 | 0.6371 | 1.570 | 1.186 | 1.861 | 30′ |
| 40′ | 0.5398 | 0.8418 | 0.6412 | 1.560 | 1.188 | 1.853 | 20′ |
| 50′ | 0.5422 | 0.8403 | 0.6453 | 1.550 | 1.190 | 1.844 | 10′ |
| 33°00′ | 0.5446 | 0.8387 | 0.6494 | 1.540 | 1.192 | 1.836 | 57°00′ |
| 10′ | 0.5471 | 0.8371 | 0.6536 | 1.530 | 1.195 | 1.828 | 50′ |
| 20′ | 0.5495 | 0.8355 | 0.6577 | 1.520 | 1.197 | 1.820 | 40′ |
| 30′ | 0.5519 | 0.8339 | 0.6619 | 1.511 | 1.199 | 1.812 | 30′ |
| 40′ | 0.5544 | 0.8323 | 0.6661 | 1.501 | 1.202 | 1.804 | 20′ |
| 50′ | 0.5568 | 0.8307 | 0.6703 | 1.492 | 1.204 | 1.796 | 10′ |
| 34°00′ | 0.5592 | 0.8290 | 0.6745 | 1.483 | 1.206 | 1.788 | 56°00′ |
| 10′ | 0.5616 | 0.8274 | 0.6787 | 1.473 | 1.209 | 1.781 | 50′ |
| 20′ | 0.5640 | 0.8258 | 0.6830 | 1.464 | 1.211 | 1.773 | 40′ |
| 30′ | 0.5664 | 0.8241 | 0.6873 | 1.455 | 1.213 | 1.766 | 30′ |
| 40′ | 0.5688 | 0.8225 | 0.6916 | 1.446 | 1.216 | 1.758 | 20′ |
| 50′ | 0.5712 | 0.8208 | 0.6959 | 1.437 | 1.218 | 1.751 | 10′ |
| 35°00′ | 0.5736 | 0.8192 | 0.7002 | 1.428 | 1.221 | 1.743 | 55°00′ |
| 10′ | 0.5760 | 0.8175 | 0.7046 | 1.419 | 1.223 | 1.736 | 50′ |
| 20′ | 0.5783 | 0.8158 | 0.7089 | 1.411 | 1.226 | 1.729 | 40′ |
| 30′ | 0.5807 | 0.8141 | 0.7133 | 1.402 | 1.228 | 1.722 | 30′ |
| 40′ | 0.5831 | 0.8124 | 0.7177 | 1.393 | 1.231 | 1.715 | 20′ |
| 50′ | 0.5854 | 0.8107 | 0.7221 | 1.385 | 1.233 | 1.708 | 10′ |
| 36°00′ | 0.5878 | 0.8090 | 0.7265 | 1.376 | 1.236 | 1.701 | 54°00′ |
| | Cos | Sin | Cot | Tan | Csc | Sec | Angle |

## Values of Trigonometric Functions

| Angle | Sin | Cos | Tan | Cot | Sec | Csc | |
|---|---|---|---|---|---|---|---|
| 36°00′ | 0.5878 | 0.8090 | 0.7265 | 1.376 | 1.236 | 1.701 | 54°00′ |
| 10′ | 0.5901 | 0.8073 | 0.7310 | 1.368 | 1.239 | 1.695 | 50′ |
| 20′ | 0.5925 | 0.8056 | 0.7355 | 1.360 | 1.241 | 1.688 | 40′ |
| 30′ | 0.5948 | 0.8039 | 0.7400 | 1.351 | 1.244 | 1.681 | 30′ |
| 40′ | 0.5972 | 0.8021 | 0.7445 | 1.343 | 1.247 | 1.675 | 20′ |
| 50′ | 0.5995 | 0.8004 | 0.7490 | 1.335 | 1.249 | 1.668 | 10′ |
| 37°00′ | 0.6018 | 0.7986 | 0.7536 | 1.327 | 1.252 | 1.662 | 53°00′ |
| 10′ | 0.6041 | 0.7969 | 0.7581 | 1.319 | 1.255 | 1.655 | 50′ |
| 20′ | 0.6065 | 0.7951 | 0.7627 | 1.311 | 1.258 | 1.649 | 40′ |
| 30′ | 0.6088 | 0.7934 | 0.7673 | 1.303 | 1.260 | 1.643 | 30′ |
| 40′ | 0.6111 | 0.7916 | 0.7720 | 1.295 | 1.263 | 1.636 | 20′ |
| 50′ | 0.6134 | 0.7898 | 0.7766 | 1.288 | 1.266 | 1.630 | 10′ |
| 38°00′ | 0.6157 | 0.7880 | 0.7813 | 1.280 | 1.269 | 1.624 | 52°00′ |
| 10′ | 0.6180 | 0.7862 | 0.7860 | 1.272 | 1.272 | 1.618 | 50′ |
| 20′ | 0.6202 | 0.7844 | 0.7907 | 1.265 | 1.275 | 1.612 | 40′ |
| 30′ | 0.6225 | 0.7826 | 0.7954 | 1.257 | 1.278 | 1.606 | 30′ |
| 40′ | 0.6248 | 0.7808 | 0.8002 | 1.250 | 1.281 | 1.601 | 20′ |
| 50′ | 0.6271 | 0.7790 | 0.8050 | 1.242 | 1.284 | 1.595 | 10′ |
| 39°00′ | 0.6293 | 0.7771 | 0.8098 | 1.235 | 1.287 | 1.589 | 51°00′ |
| 10′ | 0.6316 | 0.7753 | 0.8146 | 1.228 | 1.290 | 1.583 | 50′ |
| 20′ | 0.6338 | 0.7735 | 0.8195 | 1.220 | 1.293 | 1.578 | 40′ |
| 30′ | 0.6361 | 0.7716 | 0.8243 | 1.213 | 1.296 | 1.572 | 30′ |
| 40′ | 0.6383 | 0.7698 | 0.8292 | 1.206 | 1.299 | 1.567 | 20′ |
| 50′ | 0.6406 | 0.7679 | 0.8342 | 1.199 | 1.302 | 1.561 | 10′ |
| 40°00′ | 0.6428 | 0.7660 | 0.8391 | 1.192 | 1.305 | 1.556 | 50°00′ |
| 10′ | 0.6450 | 0.7642 | 0.8441 | 1.185 | 1.309 | 1.550 | 50′ |
| 20′ | 0.6472 | 0.7623 | 0.8491 | 1.178 | 1.312 | 1.545 | 40′ |
| 30′ | 0.6494 | 0.7604 | 0.8541 | 1.171 | 1.315 | 1.540 | 30′ |
| 40′ | 0.6517 | 0.7585 | 0.8591 | 1.164 | 1.318 | 1.535 | 20′ |
| 50′ | 0.6539 | 0.7566 | 0.8642 | 1.157 | 1.322 | 1.529 | 10′ |
| 41°00′ | 0.6561 | 0.7547 | 0.8693 | 1.150 | 1.325 | 1.524 | 49°00′ |
| 10′ | 0.6583 | 0.7528 | 0.8744 | 1.144 | 1.328 | 1.519 | 50′ |
| 20′ | 0.6604 | 0.7509 | 0.8796 | 1.137 | 1.332 | 1.514 | 40′ |
| 30′ | 0.6626 | 0.7490 | 0.8847 | 1.130 | 1.335 | 1.509 | 30′ |
| 40′ | 0.6648 | 0.7470 | 0.8899 | 1.124 | 1.339 | 1.504 | 20′ |
| 50′ | 0.6670 | 0.7451 | 0.8952 | 1.117 | 1.342 | 1.499 | 10′ |
| 42°00′ | 0.6691 | 0.7431 | 0.9004 | 1.111 | 1.346 | 1.494 | 48°00′ |
| 10′ | 0.6713 | 0.7412 | 0.9057 | 1.104 | 1.349 | 1.490 | 50′ |
| 20′ | 0.6734 | 0.7392 | 0.9110 | 1.098 | 1.353 | 1.485 | 40′ |
| 30′ | 0.6756 | 0.7373 | 0.9163 | 1.091 | 1.356 | 1.480 | 30′ |
| 40′ | 0.6777 | 0.7353 | 0.9217 | 1.085 | 1.360 | 1.476 | 20′ |
| 50′ | 0.6799 | 0.7333 | 0.9271 | 1.079 | 1.364 | 1.471 | 10′ |
| 43°00′ | 0.6820 | 0.7314 | 0.9325 | 1.072 | 1.367 | 1.466 | 47°00′ |
| 10′ | 0.6841 | 0.7294 | 0.9380 | 1.066 | 1.371 | 1.462 | 50′ |
| 20′ | 0.6862 | 0.7274 | 0.9435 | 1.060 | 1.375 | 1.457 | 40′ |
| 30′ | 0.6884 | 0.7254 | 0.9490 | 1.054 | 1.379 | 1.453 | 30′ |
| 40′ | 0.6905 | 0.7234 | 0.9545 | 1.048 | 1.382 | 1.448 | 20′ |
| 50′ | 0.6926 | 0.7214 | 0.9601 | 1.042 | 1.386 | 1.444 | 10′ |
| 44°00′ | 0.6947 | 0.7193 | 0.9657 | 1.036 | 1.390 | 1.440 | 46°00′ |
| 10′ | 0.6967 | 0.7173 | 0.9713 | 1.030 | 1.394 | 1.435 | 50′ |
| 20′ | 0.6988 | 0.7153 | 0.9770 | 1.024 | 1.398 | 1.431 | 40′ |
| 30′ | 0.7009 | 0.7133 | 0.9827 | 1.018 | 1.402 | 1.427 | 30′ |
| 40′ | 0.7030 | 0.7112 | 0.9884 | 1.012 | 1.406 | 1.423 | 20′ |
| 50′ | 0.7050 | 0.7092 | 0.9942 | 1.006 | 1.410 | 1.418 | 10′ |
| 45°00′ | 0.7071 | 0.7071 | 1.000 | 1.000 | 1.414 | 1.414 | 45°00′ |
| | Cos | Sin | Cot | Tan | Csc | Sec | Angle |

# GLOSSARY

**ABS** (217)   The ABS function is a function in which ABS(X) gives the absolute value of X. If X < Ø, then ABS(X) = −X. If X >= Ø, then ABS(X) = X.

**algorithm** (192)   A general rule or process used to solve a problem is called an algorithm.

**alphanumeric data** (173)   Alphanumeric data are data that contain both numbers and strings.

**analog computer** (4)   Analog computers operate using smooth, continuous changes in electrical signals.

**AND** (112)   AND is a keyword used to join conditions in an IF-THEN statement when all conditions must be true to cause the branch.

**arithmetic and logic unit** (4)   The arithmetic and logic unit is part of the CPU and performs operations such as addition, subtraction, and comparing numbers.

**arithmetic operators** (225)   The symbols +, −, *, and / are called arithmetic operators because they are used for arithmetic operations.

**array** (182)   A set of data stored in memory locations named by a variable is called an array.

**ASC** (231)   The ASC function is a function in which ASC(X$) gives the ASCII code for any string character X$.

**ASCII** (231)   ASCII stands for American Standard Code for Information Interchange and includes code numbers for characters and controlling I/O devices.

**ATN** (242)   The ATN function is a function in which ATN(X) gives the measure in radians of the angle whose tangent is X.

**BASIC** (19)   BASIC stands for Beginners All-purpose Symbolic Instruction Code and is one of the most widely used languages for microcomputers and time-sharing systems.

**bit** (15)   One electrical signal in a digital computer is called a bit.

**branch** (107) A branch is used to transfer control of a program from the line containing the branch statement to another line.

**BREAK** (9) Pressing the BREAK key stops whatever the computer is doing.

**bubble sort** (192) A bubble sort is an algorithm that can be used to sort data.

**bug** (60) An error in a program is called a bug.

**byte** (15) A byte usually consists of eight bits.

**cathode-ray tube** (5) A cathode-ray tube (CRT) is an electronic tube with a screen upon which output is displayed.

**central processing unit** (4) The central processing unit (CPU) is the heart of a computer and contains an arithmetic and logic unit and a control unit.

**CHR$** (231) The CHR$ function is a function in which CHR$(N) gives the character that has ASCII code N.

**command** (41) An instruction that is carried out as soon as it is entered is called a command.

**computer** (3) A computer is a programmable electronic device that can store, retrieve, and process data.

**computer graphics** (253) Computer graphics is the process of displaying output in the form of graphs, diagrams, or pictures.

**conditional branch** (110) A conditional branch is a branch that is taken only when the condition is true.

**CONTROL** (9) When the CONTROL key is held down, it changes what happens when some of the other keys are pressed.

**control unit** (4) The control unit is part of the CPU and is a master set of programs which interprets the user's program and supervises the overall operation of the computer.

**COS** (242) The COS function is a trigonometric function in which COS(X) gives the cosine of X.

**cursor** (8) A cursor is an indicator that is usually displayed on the monitor to show where the next input will be printed.

**data** (4) Data are facts or information.

**debug** (60) To debug means to correct errors in a program.

**DEF** (236) A DEF statement is used to define functions not already programmed into the computer. The format of this statement is DEF FN A(X) (or DEF A(X)), where A is any letter and X is the variable in the function.

**digital computer** (4) Digitial computers use electrical signals that switch on and off. It is the most common meaning of the word computer.

**DIM** (187) A DIM statement is used to increase the number of subscripts allowed for an array. The format of the statement is DIM X(index).

**disk** (83) A device on which programs and data are stored is called a disk.

**disk drive** (83) A device that is used to copy programs from read-write memory onto a disk is called a disk drive.

**dummy data** (115) Data added after the last usable data are called dummy data.

**edit** (10) To edit means to move, change, or erase characters and words after they are typed.

**E-form** (36) E-form (exponential form) is a form of scientific notation which consists of a sign (+ or −), a number equal to or greater than 1 but less than 10 (the number of digits vary from computer to computer), an "E" representing the base (which is ten), a sign for the exponent, and the exponent (which must be an integer).

**electronic device** (3) An electronic device is operated by electricity and does its work using electricity.

**END** (42) An END statement tells the computer that no statements follow.

**ENTER** (9) Pressing the ENTER key results in all characters typed after it was last pressed being entered into the computer as input.

**erase** (11) Clearing the entire screen or just the part of a line to the right of the cursor is called erasing.

**ESCAPE** (9) When the ESCAPE key is pressed first, it may change what happens when some of the other keys are pressed.

**EXP** (240) The EXP function is a function in which EXP(X) gives the value of $e^x$.

**external storage** (14) Programs and data are stored outside of the computer in external storage.

**final value** (125) The number, variable, or expression following the keyword TO in a FOR statement is called the final value.

**fixed memory** (13) See read-only memory.

**flowchart** (94) A flowchart is used to show the logical flow of a program.

**FOR/NEXT** (124) FOR/NEXT statements are the beginning and ending statements of a loop.

**GOSUB** (132) A GOSUB statement sends control to a subroutine. The format of the statement is GOSUB line number.

**GOTO** (107) An unconditional branch starts with a GOTO statement. The format of the statement is GOTO *n* where *n* is the number of the line to be executed next.

**hardware** (4) Hardware is the computer itself.

**IF-THEN** (110) The IF-THEN statement is used in a conditional branch. The format of the statement is IF condition THEN line number.

**IF-THEN-ELSE** (222) An IF-THEN-ELSE statement is used to combine conditional branches and statements. The format of the statement is IF condition THEN line number or statement ELSE line number or statement.

**increment** (125) The number, variable, or expression following the keyword STEP in a FOR statement is called the increment.

**index** (125, 187) 1. The variable on the left-hand side of the equals sign in a FOR statement is called the index. 2. In a DIM statement, the positive integer or, in some BASICs, a variable or expression whose value is a positive integer that is the largest subscript allowed for the array named.

**initialize** (120) To initialize a variable means to assign a starting value to the variable.

**initial value** (125) The initial value is the number, variable, or expression following the equals sign and preceding the keyword TO in a FOR statement.

**input** (5) Programs and data entered into a computer are called input.

**INPUT** (78) An INPUT statement is used to enter data during program execution.

**INT** (116) The INT function is a function in which INT(X) is the greatest integer that is not greater than X.

**I/O devices** (5)   Input and output devices together are called I/O devices.

**keyboard** (5)   A keyboard is a common input device.

**LEN** (232)   The LEN function is a function in which LEN(X$) gives the number of characters in X$.

**LET** (48)   A LET statement is used to assign a value to a variable.

**LIST** (59) A command that causes all program lines stored in read-write memory to scroll onto the screen in numerical order.

**LOAD** (84)   The LOAD command is used to copy a program from tape or disk into read-write memory.

**LOG** (241)   The LOG function is a function in which LOG(A) gives the natural logarithm of A.

**logical operators** (225)   The keywords AND, OR, and NOT are called logical operators because they are used for logical operations.

**logical value** (224)   True (1 or −1) and false (0) are the logical values used by a computer.

**loop** (124)   A loop occurs when program control returns to lines that have already been executed. The word usually refers to a group of lines controlled by FOR/NEXT statements.

**machine language** (17)   Machine language programs tell the computer exactly which bits are to be switched on and which are to be switched off. Machine language is a low-level language.

**mass-storage** (14)   See external storage.

**matrix** (196)   A matrix is a two-dimensional array.

**memory** (4)   The memory of a computer is where programs and data are stored.

**menu** (220)   A list of choices given in a program is called a menu.

**microcomputer** (5)   A microcomputer is a small computer with a CPU and I/O devices all in one case or in several closely attached cases.

**monitor** (5)   A CRT with its controls is called a monitor.

**nested loops** (128)   Loops used inside other loops are called nested loops.

**NEW** (44) The NEW command clears read-write memory.

**NOT** (225) The keyword NOT is used for logical operations and is called a logical operator.

**ON-GOSUB** (221) An ON-GOSUB statement is used to combine many GOSUB statements. The format of the statement is ON variable name GOSUB line numbers.

**ON-GOTO** (220) An ON-GOTO statement is used to combine many branches. The format of the statement is ON variable name GOTO line number.

**OR** (112) OR is a keyword used to join conditions in an IF-THEN statement when only one of the conditions must be true to cause the branch.

**output** (5) The result of processing data is called output.

**Pascal** (19) *Pascal* is a computer programming language that somewhat resembles BASIC.

**personal computer** (5) A personal computer is a microcomputer.

**PRINT** (33) A PRINT command or statement tells the computer to print the strings, the values of the variables, or the values of the expressions that follow the keyword PRINT.

**printer** (5) A printer produces a printout or hard copy of computer output.

**PRINT USING** (233) PRINT USING statements are used to align output.

**process** (4) To process means to calculate, compare, arrange, or otherwise act upon.

**program** (3, 54) A sequence of instructions to a computer for solving a problem is called a program.

**programmable device** (3) A programmable device is able to receive, store, and carry out a set of instructions.

**RANDOM** (194) The keyword RANDOM (or RANDOMIZE) can be used to seed some random number generators.

**READ/DATA** (73) READ/DATA statements are used to enter data into a computer.

**read-only memory** (13) The computer can read (retrieve) the instructions, but it cannot write (store) anything more in read-only memory.

**read-write memory** (13) The computer can read (retrieve) and write (store) in read-write memory.

**REM** (91) REM statements are used for documentation within a program and are not executed.

**reserved words** (62) Reserved words are words that are not allowed in variables because they have special uses for which they are reserved.

**RESET** (9) See BREAK.

**RESTORE** (218) A RESTORE statement tells the computer to go back to the beginning of the data.

**retrieve** (3) To retrieve means to get and bring back. When done by a computer, retrieving is also called reading.

**RETURN** (9, 132) 1. See ENTER. 2. A RETURN statement sends control back to the line following the GOSUB statement.

**RND** (193) The RND function generates a random number greater than 0 and less than 1.

**RUN** (42) A RUN command tells the computer to execute the statements.

**SAVE** (83) The SAVE command is used to store a program on tape or disk.

**SGN** (216) The SGN function is a function in which SGN(X) indicates the sign (+ or −) of X. If $X<0$, then $SGN(X) = -1$. If $X = 0$, then $SGN(X) = 0$. If $X > 0$, then $SGN(X) = 1$.

**SIN** (242) The SIN function is a trigonometric function in which SIN(X) gives the sine of X.

**software** (4) Software consists of computer programs.

**SQR** (147) The SQR function is a function in which SQR(X) is the principal square root of X, where X is a nonnegative number.

**statement** (42) A numbered instruction line that is executed after the RUN command is entered is called a statement.

**STEP** (124) STEP is a keyword that precedes the increment in a FOR statement.

**store** (3) To store means to put somewhere for safekeeping or later use. When done by a computer, storing is also called writing.

**STR$** (232) The STR$ function is a function in which STR$(X) changes the number represented by X to a string.

**string** (41) A string is an expression in quotation marks that will be printed in output.

**string variable** (173) A string variable is a letter followed by a dollar sign ($) that is used to name a memory location in which a string is stored.

**subroutine** (132) A line or a group of lines that can be used more than once in a program is called a subroutine.

**subscripted variable** (180) A subscripted variable is any valid variable followed by a nonnegative integer, or a variable or expression whose value is a nonnegative integer, enclosed in parentheses.

**syntax** (18) The pattern of a language is called syntax.

**TAB** (87) The TAB function can be used in PRINT statements to control the spacing of output.

**TAN** (242) The TAN function is a trigonometric function in which TAN(X) gives the tangent of X.

**tape** (83) A device on which programs and data are stored is called a tape.

**tape recorder** (83) A device that is used to copy programs from read-write memory onto a tape is called a tape recorder.

**time-sharing system** (6) In a time-sharing system a computer is used by more than one person at the same time.

**unconditional branch** (107) An unconditional branch is a branch that is taken every time it is read by the computer.

**VAL** (231) The VAL function is a function in which VAL(X$) changes the string X$ to a number.

**variable** (48) A variable is a single letter, and sometimes several letters and numbers, that is assigned to a location in the memory of a computer where a value can be stored.

# SELECTED ANSWERS

## CHAPTER 1   INTRODUCTION TO COMPUTERS

**Exercises   Page 7   2.** It can receive, store, and carry out a set of instructions.   **4.** a device operated by electricity; It does its work using electricity, works much faster, and wears out much more slowly.   **8.** central processing unit, memory, input devices, output devices   **10.** to store programs and data   **16.** a system in which more than one person uses the same computer

**Exercises   Page 11   1.** character keys, shift key, space bar   **2.** to print the characters marked on them   **9.** the computer carries out the command immediately   **10.** the input is stored in memory and the cursor is sent to the beginning of the next line   **11.** to avoid damaging programs and data   **16.** It scrolls off the top of the screen.

**Exercises   Pages 15-16   1.** It can retrieve information stored in it.   **2.** It can store information   **3.** read-only memory   **8.** 1; 0   **10.** $1,000; 1,024 bytes

**Exercises   Page 20   1.** machine language   **6.** yes   **7.** yes; yes   **9.** 4

*Pascal* **Exercises   Page 22   1.** invalid; embedded blank   **3.** valid   **5.** valid   **7.** valid   **9.** valid   **11.** valid   **13.** invalid; special character ($\uparrow$)   **15.** valid

## CHAPTER 2   INTRODUCTION TO BASIC

**Exercises   Page 34   1.** $5+4-1$   **3.** $27-9$   **5.** $4*3-2*1+7$   **7.** $6-4\uparrow 3$   **9.** $3*(5+4)$   **11.** $(5+10+15)/5$   **13.** $3+((6*7-2)/(3+8*6))$   **15.** $4*(3+5)/2*7\uparrow 3-8$   **17.** $(12*(3-1))/(2\uparrow 2*(5+6))$   **19.** $10-3+5$   **21.** $7-2\times 3$   **23.** $36\div 9+2$   **25.** $2((4+8)\div 2)^5$   **27.** $2^5-6(8\div 4)$   **29.** $3(2^3-6)\div(4\times 7+2)4^2$   **31.** $(2*3)+1$   **33.** $(4+((2*3)/6))-1$   **35.** $(-2-(12\uparrow 2))-((4*6)/3$   **37.** $((3\uparrow 2)-((5*6)/3))-2$   **39.** $((2\uparrow 4)-5)+((6*(3\uparrow 2))/12)$   **41.** 18   **43.** 4   **45.** 4   **47.** 13   **49.** 64   **51.** 27

**Laboratory Activities   Page 35   5.** 1603.6   **7.** 393.5   **9.** 1635.12   **11.** 113.42   **13.** $-681.275$   **15.** 8.445   **17.** $4\uparrow 2*586*3-15486;12642$   **19.** $15.8\uparrow 2/10\uparrow 3-65; -.40036$   **21.** $-15.6*(-12.3)-8.4/4.2-2\uparrow 5+4.8; 162.68$

**Exercises   Pages 38-39   1.** .0156   **3.** 1.24E+02   **5.** 6.78E−03   **7.** −.003   **9.** 5.34231E−03   **11.** $1.27548\times 10^2$; 1.27548E+02   **13.** $1.54326\times 10^{-1}$;1.54326E−01 **15.** $6.6874005048\times 10^6$; 6.874005048E+06

**17.** $2.3 \times 10^{-7}$; 2.3E−07   **19.** 12,400,000; 1.24E+07   **21.** 0.0007281; 7.281E−04   **23.** 0.0081819; 8.1819E−03   **25.** 514,210,000; 5.1427E+08   **27.** 320; 3.2E+02   **29.** 4.031E+06   **31.** 4.028E+13   **33.** 7.69E−06   **35.** 3.1045E+01

**Laboratory Activities   Pages 39-41   13.** 15000   **15.** 4   **25.** .00498 ↑ 5; 3.062998E−12   **27.** 2 ↑ 50; 1.12589991E+15   **29.** (4.05E−05)*10 ↑ 7; 405   **31.** (.00144/.00012) ↑ 2/4 ↑ 2/3 ↑ 2; 1   **33.** (1.04E+08)*(2.01E+04); −.0462646484   **37.** 2.3 billion barrels   **39.** $4,986   **41.** $1,277   **43.** 5.446%

**Exercises   Page 44   1.** string   **6.** PRINT   **7.** PRINT "⩜⩜⩜FIVE"   **8.** PRINT "⩜⩜⩜⩜⩜⩜⩜⩜⩜⩜X"   **13.** misspelling a.keyword, incorrect punctuation, improper use of parentheses   **14.** It is easy to make errors.

**Laboratory Activities   Pages 45-47   31.** SYNTAX ERROR; 80 PRINT 4*5/(2*(4+7))   **33.** SYNTAX ERROR; 100 PRINT "EDNA, TEXAS"   **35.** SYNTAX ERROR; 20 PRINT (5+1)/6   **37.** SYNTAX ERROR; 60 PRINT "2*3=6"

**Exercises   Pages 50-51   1.** valid   **3.** invalid; first character (2)   **5.** valid   **7.** invalid; special character (+)   **9.** invalid; first character (5)   **11.** invalid; special character (!)   **13.** valid   **15.** valid   **17.** invalid; special character (+)   **19.** invalid; special character (−)   **21.** 10 LET A = 1/2*B*H   **23.** 10 LET A = S ↑ 2   **25.** 10 LET R = (F*(P+1))/(N*(N+1))   **27.** 10 LET T = B/(H*W)   **29.** 10 LET F = 2.338*(1E−09*X ↑ 2+1.579*1E−05*X+.999)   **31.** 2*X is not a valid variable; 10 LET A = 2*X   **33.** 2*L+2*W is not a valid variable; 30 LET P = 2*L+2*W   **35.** 1B is not a valid variable; 50 LET B1 = A/C   **37.** 36   **39.** 0   **41.** 5   **43.** −3   **45.** −4   **48.** 8

**Laboratory Activities   Pages 51-52   3.** 11, 12   **5.** 12   **7.** 9

*Pascal* **Exercises   Page 53   1.** invalid; no digit precedes decimal point   **3.** valid   **5.** invalid; scientific notation   **7.** invalid; no digit precedes decimal point   **9.** invalid; no digit precedes decimal point   **11.** invalid; comma

**Exercises   Pages 56-57   1.** to erase the program from the screen before output is printed   **4.** 25   **6.** to tell the computer no more lines follow   **8.** 3.63   **19.** 6   **21.** 2   **23.** 18

**Exercises   Pages 62-63   1.** LIST   **3.** numerical order   **7.** LIST *m, n* or LIST *m − n*   **8.** retype the entire line or edit the line   **10.** use test values for which the correct result is known   **13.** a, b, d, e, f

**Laboratory Activities   Pages 63-64   5.** DIVISION BY ZERO; In line 20, M*2−2*M = 0.   **7.** OVERFLOW ERROR; In line 20, 10 ↑ D has a great value.

## CHAPTER 3   PUTTING THE COMPUTER TO WORK

**Exercises   Pages 75-76   3.** DATA misspelled in line 10; 10 DATA 6.5,3.4,7.3   **5.** 4 variables, 3 data; 20 DATA 5,10,15,20

**7.** comma after READ in line 10; 10 READ M,N,P,Q,R   **9.** dollar signs ($) in DATA statement in line 10; 10 DATA 1,2,3   **11.** no line numbers;
10 READ M,N
20 DATA 7.2,9.8
**13.** The READ statement, line 30, should come before line 10. 5 READ X,Y (Delete line 30.)

**15.** 10 READ A,B
   20 DATA 3,4
   (Lines 30-60 are
   not changed.)
**19.** 0   **21.** AVERAGE IS
   4

**17.** 10 READ M
   15 DATA 16
   (Lines 20-60 are
   not changed.)

**Exercises  Pages 79-80  1.** It stops executing the program, prints a question mark (?), and waits for data.   **4.** No statements in the program need to be changed.   **5.** using PRINT statements to print instruction   **7.** 10 INPUT X1,X2,X3,X4; data: 1000,.08,.5,10   **9.** 10 INPUT P,R; data: 1.3E−04, 3.14E+10   **11.** 10 INPUT X1,Y1,Z1; data: −50,50,0   **13.** 10 INPUT A,BA; data: 1E+06, 3.33333E−12   **15.** commas between variables missing; 10 INPUT X1,X2,X3   **17.** & between B and C; 10 INPUT A,B,C   **19.** comma after INPUT; 10 INPUT X,Y,Z   **21.** invalid variable names; 10 INPUT A1,B1

**23.** 10 INPUT T1,T2,T3
   (Delete lines 20 and 30.)
   (Lines 40-60 are not changed.)

**25.** 10 INPUT M      10 INPUT M,N
   30 INPUT N   or  (Delete line 30.)
   (Lines 20 and 40-70
   are not changed.)

*Pascal* Exercises  **Page 82  1.** AREA := 3.14*RADIUS*RADIUS;   **3.** AREA := LENGTH*WIDTH;   **5.** VOLUME := LENGTH*WIDTH*HEIGHT;   **7.** AREA := 0.5*BASE*HEIGHT;   **9.** INTEREST := PRINCIPAL*RATE*TIME;   **11.** VOLUME := 1/3*LENGTH*WIDTH*HEIGHT;   **13.** CELCIUS := 5/9*(FAHRENHEIT−32);   **15.** SALES TAX := RATE*COST;   **17.** CENTIMETERS := MILLIMETERS/10;   **19.** KILOMETERS := METERS/1000;   **21.** FEET := INCHES/12;   **23.** LITERS := MILLILITERS/1000;

**Exercises  Page 84  1.** because switching off the computer clears its read-write memory   **2.** to clear read-write memory for a new program   **5.** list or run the program

**Exercises  Pages 88-89  1.** a whole number   **4.** It is ignored.   **6.** strings; variables for which values are to be printed

**Exercises  Page 93  1.** to give the name, author, and purpose of the program, as well as other information about the program   **5.** Line 20 should be a REM statement.   **7.** Since the name of this program is PRODUCT PROGRAM, line 50 should contain a product.

**Exercises  Pages 96-97  1.** to plan the steps for a task and to show how they are related   **2.** no

**5.** 10 REM PROGRAM: BATTING AVERAGE
15 REM AB = TIMES AT BAT, H = NUMBER OF HITS
20 REM AV = BATTING AVERAGE
30 READ AB,H
40 DATA . . .
50 LET AV = H/AB
60 PRINT "AT BAT","HITS","AVERAGE"
70 PRINT AB,H,AV
80 END

**7.** 10 REM PROGRAM: GAS MILEAGE
15 REM D = DISTANCE IN MILES, GA = GALLONS OF GAS
20 REM GM = GAS MILEAGE
30 READ D,GA
40 DATA . . .
50 LET GM = D/GA
60 PRINT "GAS MILEAGE IS"
70 PRINT GM
80 END

**9.** 10 REM PROGRAM: BUDGET
15 REM MI = MONTHLY INCOME, PH = PERCENT SPENT ON HOUSING
20 REM PF = PERCENT SPENT ON FOOD, H = AMOUNT SPENT ON HOUSING
25 REM F = AMOUNT SPENT ON FOOD
30 PRINT "ENTER MONTHLY INCOME, PERCENT (IN DECIMAL FORM)"
35 PRINT "SPENT ON HOUSING, AND PERCENT (IN DECIMAL FORM)"
40 PRINT "SPENT ON FOOD, SEPARATED BY COMMAS"
50 INPUT MI,PH,PF
60 LET H = MI*PH
70 LET F = MI*PF
80 PRINT "AMOUNT SPENT ON HOUSING IS "; H
90 PRINT "AMOUNT SPENT ON FOOD IS "; F
100 END

## CHAPTER 4   BRANCHES AND LOOPS

**Exercises   Page 109   2.** unconditional   **4.** An error message is printed. **6.** b

**Exercises   Pages 112-113   1.** IF-THEN   **4.** a diamond shape   **9.** yes **11.** no   **13.** no   **15.** yes   **17.** no   **19.** yes   **21.** yes   **23.** no

**Exercises   Page 117   1.** the order in which they are listed   **3.** data added at the end of usable data; to cause a conditional branch to be taken   **4.** data appearing in the usable data; branch might be taken before all usable data are used   **6.** to give the person using the program a choice between rerunning the program and quitting   **8.** only the headings and the last line of output shown will be printed   **9.** 19   **11.** 0   **13.** −5

**Exercises   Page 121   1.** a counter and a conditional branch   **4.** C will be initialized to 0 each time and will not function as a counter.

**5.** 15 PRINT "COUNTS FROM 2 TO 13"
20 LET C = 1
50 IF C < 13 THEN 30

**7.** 15 PRINT "COUNTS FROM 25 TO 10"
20 LET C = 26
30 LET C = C − 1
50 IF C > 10 THEN 30

**9.** 15 PRINT "COUNTS FROM 10 TO 0 BY TWOS"
20 LET C = 12
30 LET C = C − 2
50 IF C > 0 THEN 30

**11.** 15 PRINT "COUNTS FROM 0 TO 15 BY THREES"
20 LET C = −3
30 LET C = C + 3
50 IF C < 15 THEN 30

**13.** the same as the output in Example 1   **15.** 58 IF E = 1 THEN 10

*Pascal* **Exercises   Page 123**
**1.** FIRST IS ∧ −3.7 ∧ SECOND IS ∧ 12.86 ∧ THIRD IS ∧ 0.58
**3.** ∧∧∧∧∧∧∧∧A∧∧∧∧∧∧∧∧B
∧∧∧∧∧−3.7∧∧∧∧∧12.86

**Exercises    Pages 126-127   1.** FOR;NEXT    **2.** change the increment
**5.** until the correct input is entered the loop should not be executed **7.** 40 NEXT
C   **9.** NEXT statement missing; 25 NEXT C   **11.** NEXT statement missing; 40
NEXT D

**13.** 10 FOR C = 2 TO 10 STEP 2    **15.** 10 FOR X = −10 TO 10 STEP 5
20    PRINT C                        20    PRINT X
30 NEXT C                            30 NEXT X
40 END                               40 END

| 17. | | | 19. | | |
|---|---|---|---|---|---|
| 1 | .015 | | | 0 | 5 |
| 2 | .03 | | | 5 | 5 |
| 3 | .045 | | | 0 | 15 |
| 4 | .06 | | | 15 | 15 |
| 5 | .075 | | | 0 | 25 |
| 6 | .09 | | | 25 | 25 |
| 7 | .105 | | | 0 | 35 |
| 8 | .12 | | | 35 | 35 |
| 9 | .135 | | | | |
| 10 | .15 | | | | |

**Exercises   Page 130   2.** inner loop   **4.** No, but at some point the computer will run out of memory.

**Exercises Pages 134-136 1.** a, b, c, d **5.** yes **6.** no

**11.** 12.5    5    62.5

      12.5    3    37.5

## CHAPTER 5   PROBLEM SOLVING WITH COMPUTERS

**Exercises Pages 147-149 1.** to understand what will happen when a program is run **5.** 4 **7.** error message **9.** −6 **11.** 1.41421

**Exercises Pages 153-154 1.** human tasks and computer tasks **3.** no **5.** no

**Exercises Pages 157-158 1.** yes; the program will probably need less debugging **3.** yes; the variables remind you of their meanings **6.** It must be analyzed further. **9.** no, as long as the same units are used throughout

***Pascal* Exercises   Page 159**

**1.** PROGRAM SIMPLEINTEREST;
   VAR INTEREST,PRINCIPAL,RATE,TIME,TOTALCOST : REAL;
   BEGIN
      PRINCIPAL := 1864.0;
      RATE := 0.05;
      TIME := 2.0;
      INTEREST := PRINCIPAL*RATE*TIME;
      TOTALCOST := PRINCIPAL+INTEREST;
      WRITELN (INTEREST,TOTALCOST)
   END.

**3.** PROGRAM COMPUTATION;
   VAR A,B,C : REAL;
   BEGIN
      A := 15.0;
      B := 3.0;
      C := (A+B)/(B*B);
      WRITELN (C)
   END.

**5.** PROGRAM AREA;
   VAR LENGTH,WIDTH,AREA : REAL;
   BEGIN
      LENGTH := 17.0;
      WIDTH := 12.0;
      AREA := LENGTH*WIDTH;
      WRITELN (LENGTH,WIDTH,AREA)
   END.

**Exercises Pages 161-162 3.** PRINT **7.** You do not know in what line OT will be computed. OT would retain its old value if OP = 0. **9.** 10 LET NC = (INT(N∗10↑2 + .5))/10↑2

## CHAPTER 6  VARIABLES, ARRAYS, AND MATRICES

**Exercises Pages 175-176 1.** alphanumeric **3.** when they are enclosed in quotation marks **5.** when the strings represented by A$ and B$ have exactly the same characters, including spaces **6.** never **8.** invalid; incorrect order **10.** valid **16.** invalid; special character (?) **17.** 20 READ N$,S$ **19.** 20 READ N$,N **23.** Z$ should be listed first in the READ statement. 10 READ Z$,X,Y **25.** A$ should not be in quotation marks. 10 IF A$ = "AIM" THEN 100 **27.** true **29.** false **31.** false

### *Pascal* Exercises  Page 179

**1.** PROGRAM SQUARES;
```
    VAR X, SQUARE: REAL;
    BEGIN
        WRITELN ('ENTER A NUMBER');
        READLN (X);
        SQUARE := X∗X;
        WRITELN (X,SQUARE)
    END.
```

**3.** PROGRAM COSTOFCOFFEE;
```
    VAR COSTFOR9LB,POUNDS,COSTPERPOUND,COSTPEROUNCE : REAL;
    BEGIN
        WRITELN ('ENTER COST FOR 9 POUNDS AND NUMBER OF
        POUNDS');
        WRITELN ('LEAVE SPACES BETWEEN THE NUMBERS');
        READLN (COSTFOR9LB,POUNDS);
        COSTPERPOUND := COSTFOR9LB/POUNDS;
        COSTPEROUNCE := COSTPERPOUND/16.0;
        WRITELN (COSTFOR9LB,POUNDS);
        WRITELN (COSTPERPOUND);
        WRITELN (COSTPEROUNCE)
    END.
```

**5.** PROGRAM CUBE;
```
    VAR NUMBER,CUBE : REAL;
    BEGIN
        WRITELN ('ENTER ANY NUMBER');
        READLN (NUMBER);
        CUBE := NUMBER∗NUMBER∗NUMBER;
        WRITELN (CUBE)
    END.
```

**7.** PROGRAM CIRCUMFERENCE;
VAR DIAMETER,CIRCUMFERENCE : REAL;
BEGIN
    WRITELN ('ENTER THE DIAMETER');
    READLN (DIAMETER);
    CIRCUMFERENCE := 3.14*DIAMETER;
    WRITELN (CIRCUMFERENCE)
END.

**Exercises Pages 183-185 1.** use different subscripts with the variable **3.** the set of data in array A and the memory locations for array A **13.** invalid; negative subscript **22.** invalid; special character (#) as subscript **27.** A(2) **29.** B(I+J) **31.** X(0) **33.** 3 **35.** 3.56 **38.** −1 1 0 **43.** N(6) = 6, N(5) = 5, N(4) = 4, N(3) = 3, N(2) = 2, N(1) = 1 **45.** LISTIC

**Exercises Pages 188-189 1.** DIM **3.** before any of the subscripted variables in the array are used in the program **11.** 10 DIM A(36) **13.** 30 DIM N(15),S(15) **15.** 20 DIM R(20)

**Exercises Pages 194-195 1.** consecutive **3.** to keep track of whether any exchanges are made **6.** algorithm **7.** false **9.** false **11.** false **13.** true **15.** random events

**Exercises Pages 198-199 2.** two **5.** 8 rows, 7 columns **7.** 1 row, 12 columns **9.** row 8, column 8 **11.** row 6, column 1

**16.**

| I | J | A(I,J) |
|---|---|--------|
| 1 | 1 | 20 |
| 1 | 2 | 40 |
| 1 | 3 | 50 |
| 2 | 1 | 80 |
| 2 | 2 | 10 |
| 2 | 3 | 25 |
| 3 | 1 | 45 |
| 3 | 2 | 15 |
| 3 | 3 | 35 |

**Exercises Page 205 1.** They must have the same number of rows and columns. **4.** 6; 6 **6.** W2(3, 4); W1(2, 6) **9.** 7 rows, 4 columns **10.** a constant by which a matrix is multiplied **12.** 5 rows, 8 columns

## CHAPTER 7 EXTENDING BASIC

**Exercises Pages 218-219 1.** documentation within the program **5.** 1 **7.** −1 **9.** 1 **11.** 48 **13.** 2 **15.** 6 **16.** 0,1 **17.** 1

**Exercises Pages 222-223 2.** to combine many branches **3.** to combine many GOSUB statements into one statement **5.** as many as there are values for the variable or expression after ON **6.** to combine branching statements **8.** 10 IF A < 0 THEN X = 5

**Exercises Page 228 1.** true and false **4.** an arithmetic operator is used for arithmetic operations and a logical operator is used for logical operations **5.** true **7.** true **9.** false **11.** true **13.** false **15.** true **17.** false **19.** true **20.** PRINT statement

**22.** 20 IF N THEN 26
    22 LET V = 2
    24 GOTO 30
    26 LET V = 6+2

**25.** 1 or −1; 0 **27.** NOT (N <= 15) **29.** no **31.** yes

*Pascal* **Exercises Page 230**
**1.** PROGRAM COUNT1;
    VAR COUNTER : REAL;
    BEGIN
        COUNTER := 0.0;
        REPEAT
            COUNTER := COUNTER+2;
            WRITELN (COUNTER)
        UNTIL COUNTER = 10.0
    END.
**3.** PROGRAM COUNT3;
    VAR X : REAL;
    BEGIN
        X := −15.0;
        REPEAT
            X: = X+5;
            WRITELN (X)
        UNTIL X = 10.0
    END.
**5.** PROGRAM CIRCUMFERENCE;
    VAR CIRCUMFERENCE,DIAMETER : REAL;
    BEGIN
        REPEAT
            READLN (DIAMETER);
            CIRCUMFERENCE := 3.14*DIAMETER;
            WRITELN (CIRCUMFERENCE)
        UNTIL DIAMETER = 0.0
    END.

**Exercises Page 233 1.** ASCII **3.** ASC("C") **5.** CHR$(80) **7.** VAL (A$) **9.** no

**Exercises Page 238 1.** It can make short work of even the most difficult computations. **2.** It is between −10 and −8.

**Exercises Page 242 3.** the natural logarithm of d **4.** LOG(4)/LOG(10) **5.** radians **8.** find the arctangent (ATN) of the angle; radians

## APPENDIX  COMPUTER GRAPHICS

**Exercises Pages 259-260  2.** the second loop with index C  **4.** the loop with index G  **6.** increase the final value in line 80; decrease the final value in line 80  **8.** to print 16 blank lines and move the crawler up the screen

**Exercises  Pages  265-266  1.** the size of the page or screen  **4.** when the bars will be too long for the screen or page  **5.** number of lines or columns for longest bar/greatest datum  **7.** .25

**Exercises  Page 271  1.** along the far left-hand side of the screen; along the bottom of the screen  **5.** (17, 12)  **7.** (29, 19)  **9.** (27, 10)

# INDEX